PROGRESS AND REGRESS
IN PHILOSOPHY

LEONARD NELSON

PROGRESS AND REGRESS
IN PHILOSOPHY

FROM HUME AND KANT TO
HEGEL AND FRIES

Edited by
JULIUS KRAFT
Translated by
HUMPHREY PALMER

VOLUME II

OXFORD
BASIL BLACKWELL
1971

ISBN 0 631 13850 1

This work was originally published in one volume in German
as *Fortschritte und Rückschritte der Philosophie*, © 1962 by
Verlag Öffentliches Leben, Frankfurt am Main. The
translation is published by arrangement.

Printed in Great Britain by
Alden & Mowbray Ltd at the Alden Press, Oxford
and bound at the Kemp Hall Bindery

ACKNOWLEDGEMENTS

The Society for the Furtherance of the Critical Philosophy, which has helped to make the publication of this English edition of Nelson's work possible, wishes to make the following acknowledgements: to the translator, Dr. N. H. Palmer, who has also prepared the Index; to Verlag Öffentliches Leben, Frankfurt am Main, for granting copyrights; to the Leonard Nelson Foundation (Scarsdale, N.Y.) for its donation; and to Professor Stephan Körner for his advice at all stages in the preparation of the book.

TRANSLATOR'S NOTE

The following equivalences and distinctions have been used in translating:

Ahndung...intimation

allgemein...general, universal

Anschauung...intuition, sense-perception
anschaulich...intuitive, perceptual, sensible
Intuition...Intuition
rein anschaulich...pure-intuitive

Annahme...supposition, hypothesis
Voraussetzung...assumption, presupposition
Vorurteil...prejudice, preconception (see p. 24, note)

Antrieb...motive
Trieb...impulse, drive
Triebfeder...motive
Lust-Unlust...pleasure, displeasure
Begehren...desire

Bestimmung...description, determination

Bewusstsein überhaupt...universal consciousness

Bezeichnung...reference

Ding an sich...thing-as-it-really-is
Gegenstand...object, *thing*
Objekt...object

dialektisch...dialectical, logical

Erkenntnisse...items of knowledge, information
Urteil...judgment
Vergleichsformel...formula of comparison

Erkenntnisgrund...epistemic ground
Fundament...basis

Grund...basis, foundation, ground
Begründung...justification
Evidenz...self-evidence

figürlich...figurative

Fundament...basis
Grund...basis, reason, ground
Erkenntnisgrund...epistemic ground
begründen...justify, base on
Begründung...backing, justification
zurückführen...trace back to, derive from

Gegenstände der möglichen Erfahrung...things we could experience
Lebensäusserung...expression of life
Lebenstätigkeit...living activity
Selbsttätigkeit...autonomous activity

Lehre...theory, doctrine

Leitfaden...guideline

Mannigfaltige...Variety
mannigfaltig...manifold

Naturform...nature-form
Naturbegriff...concept of nature

Politik...politics, political philosophy

Prinzip...principle
Gesetz...law
Grundsatz...basic proposition, law, principle
Unterordnung...subsumption

Realität...reality
wirklich...actual
das an sich Wirkliche...the really real

Verstand...intellect, understanding, mind
verständig...intellectual, intelligent
Verständigkeit...intelligence
aus blossem Verstand...from reason alone, purely intellectual
intellektuell...intellectual
Vernunft...reason, mind

vernünftig...rational
rein-vernünftig...purely rational
Geist...mind, spirit

Vorstellung...idea, representation, notion
Begriff...concept
Idee...Idea

Wille...will
Wollen...willing
Willkür...arbitrary choice
willkürlich...arbitrarily, at will
Vorsatz...resolve
Entschluss...decision

*

A few references have been added in this translation. Titles of foreign books (englished in the text) are given in the Bibliographical Note at the end. There is also a note on Fries.

*

The translator acknowledges his debts to dictionaries and translators; and wishes again to thank several patient and understanding friends for their help in this work.

CONTENTS

II. JAKOB FRIEDRICH FRIES

TABLES AND DIAGRAMS

CONTENTS

Note: Diagrams I, III and XII are formally similar to Diagrams III, XV and XVI of Volume I, though the wording varies and some items are positioned differently.

LEONARD NELSON
PROGRESS AND REGRESS IN PHILOSOPHY
VOLUME II

I

Regress after Kant

1

The Point of Studying the Regress in Philosophy after Kant

Goethe says somewhere (in *Conversations with Eckermann*):

Once Right has been found, I wish people would not obscure it again and turn it upside down. Man needs something positive to hand on from one generation to another. If only that positive tradition were also Right, and True! But people can't keep quiet; and all of a sudden confusion gets on top again.

Goethe's knowledge of human nature was profound; and the cultural history of Europe is full of tragic examples confirming the truth of his remark. Yet nowhere is it so monstrously, not to say uncannily, confirmed as by the reaction in philosophy after Kant. As Goethe's remark shows, this is a topic of universal interest.

At the end of his *Critique of Pure Reason* (published in 1781) Kant expressed the confident hope that the path he had discovered, by which philosophy was to become a solid science, would be a regular highway by the end of the century; in a space, that is, of less than twenty years. Never have hopes been so bitterly disappointed! Kant himself lived to see ambitious successors ruining his life's work and confusion getting on top again, the worst confusion for centuries in the history of philosophy.

The title 'Regress in Philosophy' sounds discouraging—as though human knowledge would hardly be enriched by studying the subject. But regress, and mistakes in general, have a special position in the history of philosophy. In an area where definite and recognized science is in such short supply, even the study of errors is significant; all the more so when the errors in question are typical, i.e. such as lie always near at hand, and can indeed cast their spell time and again over an entire age. The errors we shall be dealing with are of this character. Indeed the historians of philosophy are still engaged, almost to a man, in extolling these errors as the greatest intellectual achievements of mankind.

Nor is the study of such errors of historical value alone. Even from a purely philosophical point of view the erroneous systems may be of considerable importance—though not indeed for the reason commonly given that they enlarge the range of available opinions. Science has no

B   3

concern for that! It is not the business of science to increase the variety of opinions on a topic but rather to decrease it as far as possible. The scientifically ideal state will be reached when this profusion is reduced to a minimum, to a single opinion, i.e. the right one. But we may be helped on our way to the right answer by studying the mistaken systems in the history of philosophy. That is what gives those systems their significance.

I have referred to mistaken *systems* of philosophy. In a system, the full content of its fundamental principles is revealed, and so to speak X-rayed piece by piece, by setting out the various consequences which flow from those principles. The systematic exposition of a mistaken principle is thus of great value in philosophy, as it enables people to see, perhaps for the first time, the full significance of the mistake. Consider, for example, how Leibniz' system contributed to the great advance made in philosophy by Kant. Leibniz provided Logical Dogmatism with a complete and rigorous structure. But for this, Kant could hardly have discovered the fundamental mistake in Logical Dogmatism and so at last got free of it.

Hume's development of empiricist philosophy was equally important for Kant. The logical consequences of Empiricism were first worked out by Hume. This put Kant in a position to rid himself, once for all, of the fundamental mistake of Empiricism.

The erroneous post-Kantian systems, which dazzled the world under the arrogant name of 'German Idealism' and still dazzle it, have a similar importance for the history of philosophy. I shall have much more to say about this later, but one thing can be said now. I have already indicated (in Vol. I) the mistakes which still remained in Kant's philosophy. It is not easy to make them out at first sight, and it is even more difficult to separate them off while preserving unharmed the positive and valuable contributions made by his theory. But things become easier if we examine those mistakes through a sort of magnifying glass. This we can do by studying them in the form in which they recur in Kant's successors, who went to extremes in working out their consequences. Consideration of these consequences brings out the true significance of Kant's mistakes. It helps us to reach a final position on these matters.

There is yet a further and important reason for studying the regress in philosophy after Kant. That study acquired a special and profound importance at the time of the First World War. What we lived through in those years, and are still living through, must give any thoughtful person the idea that there is something wrong with our culture, some still undiscovered flaw in the foundations on which we have so far built. For we cannot assume that external history goes on its way quite independently of the intellectual life of mankind, of the development of the thoughts which men frame about the course of events and of the ideas by which they try to make sense of it. Why, after all, was reason given to man? Presumably not just to make him a suffering spectator of the business of life, which passes him by without his being able to do anything to guide it on another course. The events of the present time,* then, provide us with a motive for enquiring into our own spiritual past, where false ideas may have driven us off the true path. We have had a disastrous experience which—to put it mildly—the ruling ideas were unable to prevent. That may make it easier for us to swallow our pride and admit that ideas we were so proud of have led us astray, to disaster. We must therefore make enquiry, and see *which* ideas led us astray. Study of the post-Kantian regress in philosophy can help us to do this.

* About 1920.

2

Possible Lines of Further Development of Kant's Theory

I

Before describing and discussing the actual developments which the Kantian philosophy underwent, I want to give separate consideration to its *possible* developments. The material before us in this particular stage of the history of philosophy is extremely complicated and obscure, and some preparation is essential before we make a start on it, if we are to achieve a clear and synoptic view. We need to bring some guideline with us by which to make our way through the material and to find our bearings in it. We should set up some sort of axes of reference first, so as to assign intellectual co-ordinates to each phenomenon in the chaos which confronts us.

I shall therefore begin by sketching an outline plan of these developments (see Diagrams I–IV, summarized in *V*). In this I can then locate the various historical phenomena. The plan is based on my critique of Kant's philosophy (Vol. I, pp. 93 ff.)

It is a special mark of Kant's greatness as a discoverer that his various fundamental discoveries stand alongside one another in comparative independence. The connections between them, in his system, are fairly loose. He did not let any short-sighted mania for system prejudice the wealth of discoveries that he had made. That shows his genius as a philosopher. As we emphasized before, a great discoverer in philosophy will not give decisive weight to considerations of consistency. He will allow himself to be led by his feeling-for-truth and will set one discovery alongside another regardless of the unity of the system. His successors may then take exception to the inconsistencies which appear when they review his teaching as a whole. But if a philosopher is from the outset concerned solely with the consistency of his system, he will not make any great discoveries. Like other men, the philosopher is a child of his age and shares in its most basic philosophical presuppositions, without realizing what they are, and precisely because he does not realize what they are. If he concentrates only on consistency, he will never be able to rise above those presuppositions, but will remain completely bound by them. He can overcome them only by devoting himself without reserve to new discoveries, without enquiring into their logical relationship to other theories already taken as established, and by following up the new discoveries until he reaches a clear contradiction between them and the old presuppositions in which he also shares.

Philosophers can be divided into two basic types. There are those who are mainly discoverers, and those whose main contribution lies in system-building. Very few philosophers, only those of the very first rank, belong to both types fully and equally. Those of the former type are marked out by a strong and imperturbable feeling-for-truth. Real contributions to the substance of science are due to them. Those of the latter type, having special logical gifts or at least an interest in logical form, are impelled to build a system from the material already discovered by the others. The content of their philosophy is thus provided for them by their predecessors' discoveries.

For all his greatness as a system-builder, Kant's epoch-making importance in philosophy is entirely due to his work as a discoverer. Not so his first successors. They were bound to notice the lack of systematic unity in his teaching and to take exception to it. Contradictions became evident between the different parts of his theory. Kant's philosophical successors naturally set themselves to remove these contradictions. The ensuing philosophical debate was therefore concerned with the systematic unity of Kant's theory as a whole.

As this question of systematic unity is the main point at issue here, we shall be well advised, in attempting a methodical survey of the various post-Kantian theories, to consider our material from three distinct points of view. Kant's theory left three great puzzles unresolved; puzzles which his successors stumbled on, and tried to solve. Corresponding to these are the three fundamental mistakes from which, as we showed, all the defects in Kant's theory flowed. The first of these concerns Kant's method; the second relates to his procedure in what he called the Subjective Deduction; and the third to that in the Objective Deduction. The first mistake is logical in character, the second psychological, while the third is directly concerned with metaphysics. The point at issue in the first is Kant's theory about the justification of judgments, i.e. the critical method for establishing the basic principles of metaphysics. The second mistake concerns the psychological theory in the Critique of Reason about the sources of knowledge. The third concerns his proof for Transcendental Idealism and for the Theory of Ideas.

Let us first of all consider the puzzle about method. The Critique of Reason was supposed to be a preliminary enquiry, essential to all future attempts at erecting a system of metaphysics. This preliminary enquiry was essential, in Kant's view, in order to discover and establish the principles of the system, as these are not self-evident. But to what sort of science does this critical investigation itself belong? Kant himself never went into this question, but his successors could hardly avoid coming up against it. It is, however, a very deep and puzzling point. What, after all, could this 'critical propaedeutic to every metaphysical system' be supposed to be? Some sort of metaphysical knowledge? That seems absurd when one reflects that its job is to decide whether or not any metaphysic is possible at all. If one tries to settle *this* question by some metaphysical means, then clearly everything is lost, and the new method turns out to be no better than the old dogmatism. Should the Critique of Reason then belong to formal logic? That also seems impossible. It was Kant himself who propounded, against his logicist predecessors, the thesis that metaphysics cannot be constructed from logic and logic alone. The remaining alternative is for the Critique of Reason to be an empirical science. But this also seems unacceptable. Certainly Kant himself expressly rejected such an assumption. It seems unacceptable because the principles whose foundation is to be provided belong to knowledge of a rational, not an empirical, variety. How could the foundation of rational principles be empirical? Rational principles are those which hold good independently of all experience, whose foundation, therefore, is not to be found within experience.

A further consideration is relevant at this point. One of Kant's basic discoveries, by which he undermined Empiricism, was precisely this: that experience is not possible at all, except in reliance on certain presuppositions which are not derived from experience. There are, as he showed, metaphysical principles for the possibility of experience. So if the Critique of Reason were a science of experience, it would involve metaphysical presuppositions. It thus seems as though any attempt at providing empirical foundations for metaphysical principles is bound to lead to circular argument. This really is a peculiar and very profound problem, which must be solved before any sound and satisfactory further development of the Critique of Reason can be even contemplated. This point remained obscure in Kant's own work, and he himself offers us no way out of the difficulty, owing to an error of method which he committed and which I will recall quite briefly at this point. It derived from a wrong idea of what the Critique of Reason was meant to do, an idea which we earlier referred to as 'the transcendental preconception';* the idea, namely,

* Vol. I, p. 186f.

that the Critique of Reason is intended to prove the basic propositions of metaphysics. This would imply that the critique provided knowledge of the same type as the system of metaphysics and so itself belonged to some mode of *a priori* knowledge.

Before investigating the further implications of this mistake let us consider the second problem left by Kant's Critique of Reason, which concerns what he called the Subjective Deduction. This problem is psychological in character and relates to the theory of the sources of knowledge. A considerable advance was made in this theory with Kant's proof that our knowledge is not, as his predecessors had all assumed, restricted to purely empirical knowledge on the one side and purely logical on the other. This contribution to science was due to Kant's discovery of synthetic *a priori* judgments, which although independent of experience do carry our knowledge beyond the mere concept of their object. Kant made this discovery in connection with the profound enquiry undertaken by Hume. Assuming—what to him still seemed self-evident—that sense and reason are the only possible sources of knowledge for us, Hume drew the conclusion—which on that assumption is really unavoidable—that all attempts at constructing a metaphysic are and always will be futile, as none such can be developed from either logic or experience. For metaphysics consists, in Kant's phrase, entirely of synthetic *a priori* judgments; but on the assumption just mentioned the only possible types of judgment are analytic judgments on the one hand and on the other synthetic judgments *a posteriori*, i.e. synthetic judgments based on experience. Hume's sceptical conclusion was thus due to that psychological assumption; an assumption which we can trace back through the history of philosophy as far as Aristotle, who first set it up almost as an axiom. This hoary philosophical mistake was eliminated by Kant's demonstration that some *a priori* knowledge is synthetic and so must derive from a source other than either logic or experience. This proof invalidated Hume's sceptical inference.

It will be helpful to remind ourselves at this point how Kant came to his discovery. He realized that Hume's conclusion—which indisputably followed from his premises—would if correct apply to geometry just as much as to metaphysics. Kant showed that geometrical judgments are synthetic and so could not have their origin in logic. Yet they could not be of empirical origin either, for, as Hume saw, that would contradict their apodeictic character.

Kant thus reached his refutation of Hume simply by transferring the problem Hume had posed from metaphysics to geometry. This transference is illustrated in Diagram I (cp. Diagram III, p. 19).

(I) Geometrical Knowledge is Possible

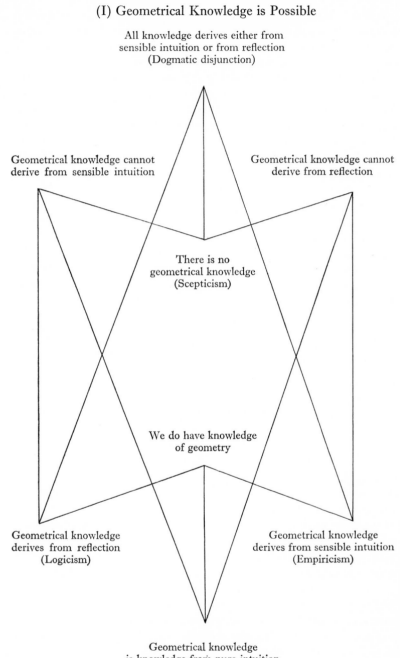

All knowledge derives either from
sensible intuition or from reflection
(Dogmatic disjunction)

Geometrical knowledge cannot
derive from sensible intuition

Geometrical knowledge cannot
derive from reflection

There is no
geometrical knowledge
(Scepticism)

We do have knowledge
of geometry

Geometrical knowledge
derives from reflection
(Logicism)

Geometrical knowledge
derives from sensible intuition
(Empiricism)

Geometrical knowledge
is knowledge from pure intuition
(Criticism)

If the conclusion which Hume drew about metaphysics were unavoidable, we should have to draw an analogous conclusion from the same premises: that as our knowledge of geometry can derive neither from sensible intuition nor from reflection, and as there can be no third source of knowledge in addition to these two, geometrical knowledge must be impossible. This consideration showed Kant that there must be some mistake in Hume's theory of the sources of knowledge. As there is no mistake in his inference, it must lie in his assumptions. As Kant showed, the mistake lies in the assumption that reflection and sensible intuition are the only sources of knowledge. This mistake was shown up by Kant's demonstration of pure intuition as the source of geometrical knowledge.

Kant was less fortunate with metaphysics than with geometry. As he showed, metaphysical like geometrical judgments are synthetic *a priori*, but they are judgments from concepts alone, not from pure intuition. The question thus remains, how can such judgments be made, synthetic *a priori* judgments deriving not from pure intuition but from pure concepts? This question is far more difficult and obscure than the one about geometry. As a source of knowledge, intuition fails us completely at this point. For this very reason, the source of knowledge underlying these judgments is totally obscure. Kant's efforts did nothing to dispel that obscurity. Indeed, one could say that his theory not only failed to explain the epistemological basis of metaphysical judgments, but did not even show them to be logically possible. The concept of a judgment which is supposed to be synthetic and yet is a judgment from concepts alone seems to involve an insoluble paradox. Being synthetic, the judgment must extend our knowledge of the object further than the concept of it; but precisely this would seem to be denied to it, as a judgment from concepts alone.

How can there be synthetic *a priori* judgments from concepts alone? This puzzle is unsolved. The problem is partly that the concept of such a judgment is logically paradoxical; partly, also, that it cannot be reconciled with the assumption about the possible sources of knowledge, even if following Kant's discovery we extend these to include pure intuition. For the old division of sources of knowledge into sensible intuition and reflection is then replaced by a division into intuition (in general) and reflection. But even pure intuition, being intuition, cannot be responsible for the knowledge expressed in metaphysical judgments, for these are supposed to derive from concepts alone, independently of any and every intuition. We do not have metaphysical intuition: as Kant puts it, our intuition is not intellectual. We do indeed have a pure as well as a merely sensible intuition. But this pure intuition refers only to the form of possible objects of sensible intuition. By its means we come to know that objects are combined in space and time but not that they are connected. Now combination merely is a contingent relationship, whereas connection is a necessary one. It is this necessary connection knowledge of which is expressed in metaphysical judgments. One would need an intellectual intuition, an intuition of the connection and not merely of the combination of objects, in order on Kant's extended classification of the possible sources of knowledge to find a source for metaphysical knowledge. Kant's assumption that intuition and reflection are the only possible sources of knowledge rules out metaphysical judgments as impossible, just as did Hume's assumption that reflection and merely sensible intuition are the only possible sources of knowledge. Thus, the basic psychological assumption of Kant's Critique of Reason excludes the possibility of synthetic judgments from concepts alone. This is the psychological puzzle which Kant's Critique of Reason left unsolved.

This discussion has made it clear where Kant's error lay. He was led astray by a preconception˙to which I gave the title 'dogmatic disjunction of sources of knowledge': by the assertion that every item of knowledge must derive either from reflection or from intuition. This preconception prevented him from discovering the source of metaphysical judgments in an immediate metaphysical knowledge which is neither reflective nor intuitive.

Lastly there is the third puzzle, which concerns metaphysics itself. Kant's presentation of metaphysics is based on his great theory of Transcendental Idealism, the theory that we cannot get to know things as they really are, but only as they appear to us, i.e. in spatial and temporal forms. The final justification for this theory, in Kant, lies in his Formal Idealism, and in particular in its implication that pure intuition, as synthetic *a priori* knowledge, cannot apply to things-as-they-really-are.

Now the odd thing is that this justification conflicts with the very theory it is supposed to justify, namely with Kant's Theory of Ideas, and especially with its centrepiece, the thesis that freedom is possible.

Ideas are concepts which our reason necessarily has, of objects which lie beyond all possible experience. Our concepts of things-as-they-really-are must be of this sort for, according to Transcendental Idealism, our experience is restricted to appearances. Transcendental Idealism was supposed to make room for the world of Ideas, for the world of things as they exist apart from the nature-form to which our knowledge of them is confined: apart from space, from time, and from laws of nature. In brief, it was Transcendental Idealism that enabled Kant to limit the naturalism of science, and to make room next to it, or over it, for Ideas, for a world of freedom.

But what is the ultimate justification for this line of thought? According to Formal Idealism, synthetic *a priori* principles cannot hold for things-as-they-really-are. From this it follows that Ideas also cannot relate to things-as-they-really-are. Indeed, the very assertion of things-as-they-really-are contradicts Formal Idealism. For we cannot form a concept of a thing-as-it really-is except by means of the Categories and of the Ideas which derive from them, i.e. of synthetic *a priori* principles, which according to Formal Idealism cannot hold for things-as-they-really-are.

This is the third fundamental mistake in Kant's version of the Critique of Reason. It lies in his theory of Formal Idealism and in its consequences for the Theory of Ideas, which compelled Kant to deny objective reality to the speculative Ideas and to assign them a regulative use in natural science.

These three fundamental mistakes were allowed to stand uncorrected in Kant's theorizing. As we showed, all the other defects in his theory can be traced back to them.

These three mistakes are not, however, independent of each other. There is a remarkably profound and close connection between them.

The basic reason for all these mistakes lies in Kant's psychological preconception,* viz. that intuition and reflection form an exhaustive division of the sources of knowledge. Kant was prevented from recognizing this as a preconception by his exclusion of empirical psychological enquiries from the programme of his Critique of Reason. Yet this psychological preconception led inevitably to that methodological mistake. For if one starts from the position that there can be no third source of knowledge besides intuition and reflection, then it follows unavoidably that as the source of the knowledge contained in metaphysical judgments cannot lie in intuition, it must lie in reflection. Such judgments can therefore be justified only by deriving them from other judgments, that is by a proof. From this it would follow that the Critique of Reason is logically prior to the system of metaphysics. For the Critique would have to contain the grounds of proof for the principles of the system of metaphysics. And that brings us unavoidably to Kant's transcendental preconception, to his conclusion that the justification given for

* See p. 24, note.

metaphysical judgments in the Critique of Reason should be *a priori* in character.

Moreover, if one allows only intuition and reflection as possible sources of knowledge, and if in consequence one will not admit any immediate knowledge as a basis for metaphysical judgments, one is at once driven to Formal Idealism. For in the absence of any immediate metaphysical knowledge the principles in question cannot be justified by means of a subjective deduction. Kant was thus driven at this point to leave aside the subjective method of the Critique of Reason and to turn it into an objective deduction instead, which one could call epistemological rather than critical, as it leads to a comparison of one item of knowledge not with another such item, but with its object. Kant therefore felt compelled to work out a theory about the relation of knowledge to its object in order to justify the principles of metaphysics. Now it is not the case for metaphysical knowledge, as it is for empirical, i.e. for knowledge from sensible intuition, that the object is the basis for the knowledge in question. So for Kant only the reverse possibility remained: to make the knowledge itself the basis on which the object is possible, and to ground its truth on this relationship.

This epistemological theory is really the same as Formal Idealism, which says that synthetic *a priori* principles cannot hold good for things-as-they-really-are. For in any knowledge of things-as-they-really-are the object, as gound of the knowledge, would have to precede it, and not the other way about—as Kant supposes in the case of synthetic *a priori* principles, where the knowledge is taken as ground of the object. So we, like Kant, would have to infer from the *a priori* nature of the synthetic judgments of metaphysics to their ideal character, and to deny the reality of the speculative Ideas as a transcendental illusion.

This shows that the mistakes of Kant which we have analysed are not isolated and brought together only by coincidence. They are the necessary result of the basic assumptions which Kant shared with his predecessors and especially with Hume.

2

Which of the possible developments of Kant's theory deserve our consideration, having in mind its principal defects? Our main interest here is in developments intended to provide the systematic unity which Kant's theory lacks, by furnishing a satisfactory logical connection between those parts of his theory which Kant left unconnected or even in contradiction to each other. How were these contradictions to be overcome? There are in fact several different ways of doing this.

Let us first of all raise this question from the point of view of method. Kant's error of method was due, as I showed, to supposing that the Critique of Reason should not only show on what subjective basis metaphysical principles are known, but should itself provide a foundation for proof of their objective validity. Such a foundation could be found only in some ultimate premises from which the basic propositions of metaphysics followed logically. On this epistemological re-interpretation the Critique of Reason would stand logically prior to the system of metaphysics. From this it would follow that the Critique of Reason must be knowledge of a similar type to that of the system of metaphysics. For the logical ground of any item of knowledge must be similar in type to the knowledge which is grounded upon it.

Various different and indeed contrary conclusions can be drawn from this. These are presented synoptically in Diagram II.

From the assumption that critique and system, since they are related logically as ground and consequence, are of the same type, two contrary conclusions can be drawn. One can either infer the type of knowledge found in the critique from that of the system: or, *vice versa*, that found in the system from that of the critique.

On one side we have the assumption that as metaphysical principles are independent of experience their logical ground cannot lie in experience. From this it would follow that the critique cannot be a science of experience. On the other side we have the assumption that as the critique is a science concerned with knowledge (namely with the basis for the knowledge expressed in metaphysical judgments) it must be a science of inner experience. On the former inference it would follow that the critique is no science of experience, which contradicts this latter assumption; from the latter it follows that the principles for which proof is required are based on inner experience, which contradicts the assumption made in the former inference. We gave the name 'transcendental preconception' to the view that the Critique of Reason, as it contains the basis on which metaphysical principles are to be proved, cannot be a science of experience and so cannot contain any psychological knowledge. The contrary view is that as the justification provided for metaphysical principles by the Critique of Reason is psychological in type, they must themselves be based on psychology. This could be called the psychologistic preconception.

It is immediately obvious that this does not exhaust all possible

(II) Critique and System: Possible Relationships

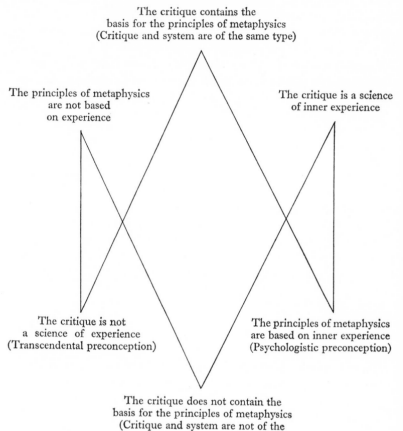

The critique contains the
basis for the principles of metaphysics
(Critique and system are of the same type)

The principles of metaphysics
are not based
on experience

The critique is a science
of inner experience

The critique is not
a science of experience
(Transcendental preconception)

The principles of metaphysics
are based on inner experience
(Psychologistic preconception)

The critique does not contain the
basis for the principles of metaphysics
(Critique and system are not of the
same type)

positions on the matter. One could also combine the two assumptions
which have so far been opposed and drop the third assumption which
those two inferences had in common. This is just what is done in the
third and remaining mode of inference. If the Critique of Reason is a
science of inner experience, and if the metaphysical principles whose
bases are sought are not to be based on experience, it follows that the
Critique of Reason, though providing justification for metaphysical
principles, does not itself contain their logical ground; and further
that the critique need not after all be knowledge of the same type as

the system of metaphysics. For if the critique does not contain the ground of metaphysical principles, the rule that a piece of knowledge must be of the same type as its logical ground will not apply at all to the relationship between system and critique.

We shall later discuss each of these positions in detail. Our present business is simply to make out which positions could be held. We have shown that the problem of method in Kant's Critique of Reason can in principle be tackled in three different ways. We shall have to decide in favour of one of them, if we wish to achieve a consistent and methodical view of the relationship between the Critique of Reason and the system of metaphysics it was meant to justify.

The second point for our enquiry is this: how can the psychological defects in Kant's deduction be eliminated? Is his theory of the sources of knowledge open to consistent further development?

I have shown that we can find in Kant all the premisses required for proving the existence of a metaphysical knowledge which is neither intuitive nor reflective but immediate. This form of the subjective deduction rests on three fundamental propositions, which suffice to prove the point, and which were already recognized as true in Kant's *Critique of Pure Reason*. All we need do is to pick them out and put them together in the right way. They run like this:

P_1 We do make metaphysical judgments or, as Kant says, synthetic judgments from concepts alone, as against synthetic judgments from intuition, whether of a sensible or a non-sensible variety. Kant has established the fact that we do make metaphysical judgments. Whatever their basis may be, whether they have one or not, whether they are objectively valid or not, such judgments do in fact occur.

P_2 Our intuition is not intellectual in character. Even pure intuition is not an intellectual intuition. It is concerned only with the form of objects of sensible intuition. And there is a further restriction. As Kant puts it, pure intuition is concerned with the figurative synthesis of appearances, not with their intellectual synthesis; with the contingent combination of things in space and time, not with their necessary connection.

P_3 Reflection is empty. That is, from reflection only analytic judgments can be derived. All it does is to recapitulate knowledge obtained from some other source. One could say that reflective knowledge is always mediate.

These three propositions suffice to demonstrate the existence of a knowledge non-intuitive and yet immediate, and so not reflective either, as the source of metaphysical judgments. For if, as the first premiss states, we do in fact make metaphysical judgments, and if the source of the knowledge these judgments contain cannot lie in intuition (second premiss), and if it cannot lie in reflection either (third premiss), then it must lie in a form of knowledge belonging neither to intuition nor to reflection: in short, in knowledge which is immediate and non-intuitive.

Kant did not draw this conclusion. For on his assumptions it must have seemed intolerably paradoxical to conceive of knowledge which was neither reflective nor intuitive. He took it for granted that there could be no third type of knowledge in addition to judgment and intuition, not noticing that the three propositions which he did acknowledge led to a contradictory conclusion. So alongside the three factual premisses mentioned there stands in his work, like an axiom, a fourth and dogmatic premiss,

P_4 Every item of knowledge is either a judgment or an intuition.

If we want to make the theory of the sources of knowledge consistent, we must either drop one of the three propositions mentioned first or else discard the fourth, the assumption that the sources of knowledge divide exhaustively into intuition and reflection. We are thus required to abandon the assumption that we do possess metaphysical judgments, or the proposition that intuition is not intellectual in character, or the proposition that reflection is empty, or, finally, the dogmatic disjunction of the sources of knowledge. Each one of these propositions is incompatible with the conclusion to which the others lead. This is really Hume's problem all over again, for that was basically concerned with the origin of metaphysical judgments. In Kant's attempted solution of this problem one point remains obscure. Four ways are open to us for removing that obscurity. Let us see what conclusions could follow, on each of these:

C_1 Dropping the proposition that we do in fact possess metaphysical judgments means reverting to the sceptical conclusion of Empiricism in metaphysics, to the theory that metaphysical knowledge is impossible.

C_2 Dropping the proposition that intuition is not intellectual in character means reverting to Mysticism in metaphysics, to the claim to possess an intellectual intuition as source of our metaphysical knowledge.

C_3 Dropping the proposition that reflection is empty means reverting to Logicism in metaphysics, and making reflection the source of metaphysical knowledge.

(III) Origin of Metaphysical Knowledge

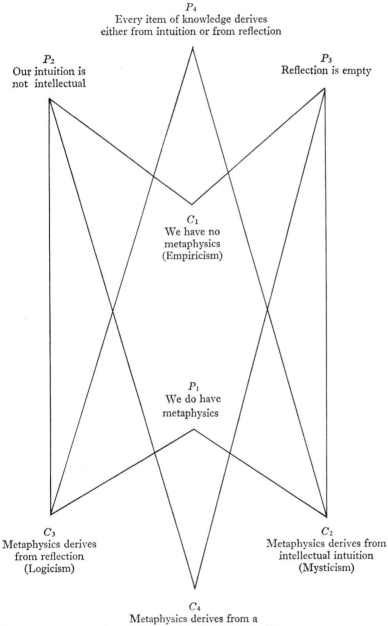

P_4
Every item of knowledge derives
either from intuition or from reflection

P_2
Our intuition is
not intellectual

P_3
Reflection is empty

C_1
We have no
metaphysics
(Empiricism)

P_1
We do have
metaphysics

C_3
Metaphysics derives
from reflection
(Logicism)

C_2
Metaphysics derives from
intellectual intuition
(Mysticism)

C_4
Metaphysics derives from a
knowledge non-intuitive yet immediate
(Criticism)

C

C_4 Lastly, we can drop the dogmatic disjunction of sources of knowledge and combine the three factual premisses to yield the conclusion that there is a third source of knowledge in addition to intuition and reflection. This leads us to claim an immediate knowledge, neither intuitive nor reflective, as the source of metaphysical judgments. This view could be called metaphysical Criticism, for short, as it rests only on the factual premisses established by Kant and discards the dogmatic assumption on which the other views depend.

The logical relationship between these various possible modes of inference may be set out as in Diagram III.

It is easy to see that this diagram is formally similar to the one I used to describe Hume's problem.* In the present instance, combining any three of the four premisses yields a conclusion. Four possible conclusions thus result. In each case the fourth and remaining premiss contradicts the conclusion derived from the other three.

What, finally, are the possible lines of development of Kant's philosophy with regard to the third problem we mentioned, the problem of metaphysics? As we saw, Kant's Formal Idealism, the theory that synthetic *a priori* knowledge cannot hold for things-as-they-really-are, is in conflict with our even supposing such things-as-they-really-are. For if one holds to Kant's theory that in order for our judgments to relate to objects they must all presuppose synthetic *a priori* principles, without which they could not be made at all, then this will also apply to our judgments about things-as-they-really-are and so to the general judgment that there are any things-as-they-really-are—quite apart from whether such things could be known. As soon as we say anything about things-as-they-really-are, we use metaphysical principles in the judgment which we make. For a metaphysical presupposition is already involved in our using the concepts 'thing' and 'exist'.

Kant's theory thus contains three propositions which cannot be combined without contradiction. One is Formal Idealism. The second is the proposition that judgments which have some content (as distinct from judgments of logic) are conditioned by synthetic *a priori* principles. The third is the supposition of things-as-they-really-are. Each pair of these three propositions leads to a conclusion which contradicts the third.

One way to remove this contradiction is to take as premisses Formal Idealism plus the proposition that all non-empty judgments have *a priori* principles as their conditions. This inference leads us to

* Vol. I, pp. 84 and 229.

reject the supposition of things-as-they-really-are. For if synthetic *a priori* principles do not hold for things-as-they-really-are, and yet all our judgements including those about things-as-they-really-are require synthetic *a priori* principles, then the supposition of things-as they-really-are is not admissible.

Another way would be to base our inference on the supposition of things-as-they-really-are, together with Formal Idealism. This would compel us to abandon the proposition that all judgements are conditioned by *a priori* principles. For Formal Idealism can be combined with the assertion of things-as-they-really-are only on the assumption that we have knowledge of things-as-they-really-are, a knowledge not conditioned by *a priori* principles.

The third and last alternative is to combine the proposition that all judgements are conditioned by *a priori* principles with the other proposition about there being things-as-they-really-are. This would compel us to give up Formal Idealism.

These logical connections are presented in Diagram IV.

(IV) Is Formal Idealism Tenable?

Formal Idealism

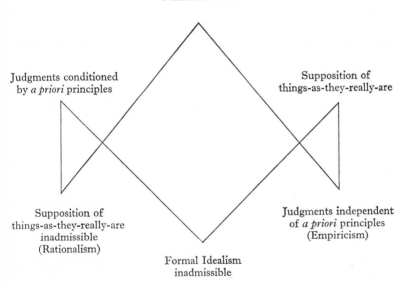

Judgments conditioned
by *a priori* principles

Supposition of
things-as-they-really-are

Supposition of
things-as-they-really-are
inadmissible
(Rationalism)

Judgments independent
of *a priori* principles
(Empiricism)

Formal Idealism
inadmissible

In this connection we must also consider the epistemological significance of Formal Idealism. Kant Regards as *a posteriori* any knowledge based on the giveness of the object and as *a priori* any knowledge which contains that on which the possibility of the object is based. Kant here explains the distinction between *a priori* and *a posteriori* knowledge by means of a different, epistemological relationship, the causal relationship between knowledge and object.

This epistemological interpretation has an important implication. If one abandons the supposition of things-as-they-really-are, one would also have to deny that there can be any knowledge *a posteriori*. For *a posteriori* knowledge presupposes things-as-they-really-are, without which it would be impossible. This drives us to the rationalist conclusion that all knowledge must be *a priori*. If, however, in order to keep the supposition of things-as-they-really-are, we infer that our judgments do not depend on *a priori* principles, we arrive at an empiricist conclusion.

The implications of Formal Idealism thus lead to a renewal of the old dispute between Rationalism and Empiricism. And it is only by rejecting Formal Idealism that we can hold both rational and empirical knowledge to be possible. This last position corresponds to the critical conclusion.

This comment shows the connection between Diagrams II, III and IV, portraying in outline the possible developments of Kant's philosophy. The connection of Diagram II, concerning method, with Diagram IV, about metaphysics, is obvious. The transcendental preconception corresponds to the rationalist conclusion, and the psychologistic preconception corresponds to the empiricist conclusion. The separation of critique from system corresponds to the critical conclusion, the abandonment of Formal Idealism.

What about Diagram III? Here also we find a contrast between an empiricist and a rationalist conclusion. In this case the rationalist conclusion has only two possible interpretations, Logicism and Mysticism, corresponding to the two possible types of *a priori* knowledge from which metaphysics could derive. For if we want to profess Rationalism in metaphysics, there are only two alternatives: either the source of metaphysical knowledge must be sought in reflection, or it must be transferred to an intellectual intuition. One alternative leads us to metaphysical Logicism, the other to metaphysical Mysticism.

We now have what we were looking for, a system by which to find our bearings in the development of philosophy after Kant. I do not mean to assert that all the philosophers who have appeared on the scene since Kant do us the favour of fitting easily into this system, so that we can at once assign each one a definite place in it while still preserving the analogy between our three diagrams. What I do say is something rather different: that if a philosopher cannot be fitted into our system in that way, that is simply due to a lack of logical consistency in his thought.

We may finally combine the various diagrams into a single one (Diagram V), which can serve as a sort of pedigree for the development of philosophy after Kant, as it shows the mutual interdependence of the various philosophical theses.

(V) Possible Lines of Further Development of Kant's philosophy

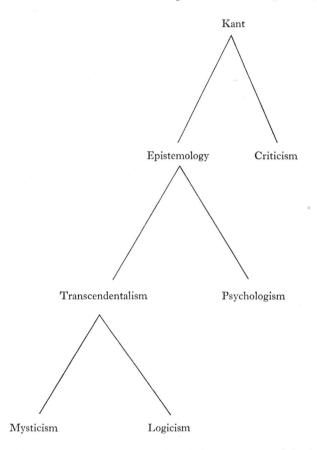

Kant

Epistemology   Criticism

Transcendentalism   Psychologism

Mysticism   Logicism

The theses we shall consider have their common origin in the philosophy of Kant. As our discussion showed, there are two fundamentally different versions of the Kantian Critique of Reason. One of these appeared in the diagrams under the name of 'Criticism'. This version remains faithful to the special feature of the new method which Kant called the Critique of Reason. The other version involves

a reinterpretation of the critical method, what we could call the 'epistemological re-interpretation', to bring out the element common to the
various theories referred to and also to contrast them with those under
the heading of 'criticism'. For it comes down in the end to this: in
place of the critical (and so, subjective) justification of knowledge by
deriving mediate knowledge from some immediate knowledge, it
substitutes an objective relationship, that of knowledge to its object.
The epistemological interpretation then divides, as Diagram II
shows, into Transcendentalism and Psychologism, according as one
develops the Critique of Reason, taken as epistemology, by means of
the transcendental or the psychologistic preconception (as seen in
Diagram IV: towards the rationalist conclusion or the empiricist).
Within Transcendentalism two further alternatives appear, which we
distinguish as metaphysical Logicism and metaphysical Mysticism.

As we shall see, these various alternative versions all had actual
representatives. Indeed, they were historically embodied in a surprisingly pure form.

Translator's note: The distinctions made in this chapter are taken up in
chapters 4–6. The following note may be found helpful.

Nelson holds three 'preconceptions' or prejudicial assumptions responsible
for the regress in philosophy after Kant (see Diagram II):

(i) *the epistemological or methodological preconception* (pp. 13–14, 38–54) that
the system of metaphysical truths is to be justified or validated by the
Critique of Reason, so that Critique and system must both consist of knowledge of the same mode or type;

(ii) *the transcendental preconception* (pp. 8, 13, 55–144) that both are rational
in character, the Critique providing the principles of metaphysics with a
proof;

(iii) *the psychologistic or psychological preconception* (pp. 15, 145–153) that as
the propositions of the Critique are drawn from inner experience, the metaphysics they support must also be empirical and psychological in character.

(On p. 13 the dogmatic disjunction of sources of knowledge, i.e. that every
bit of our knowledge must come either from perception or from reflection,
was also called a 'psychological preconception'.)

Nelson himself follows Fries in discarding all three preconceptions and
denying that dogmatic disjunction, holding instead the 'critical' view that
the Critique, itself empirical and psychological, does not so much justify as
bear witness to a non-perceptual and non-reflective immediate knowledge
of metaphysical truths (pp. 164–196).

Kant's Early Critics

Before considering the various systematic transformations which Kant's philosophy underwent I want to spend a short time on his immediate contemporaries and pupils. Here we may distinguish two different attitudes to the Critique of Pure Reason. Some concentrated on studying the new theory. They tried to explain it, to render what was new and difficult in it comprehensible, and to defend it against misunderstandings and attacks. The others sought to develop it further and so appear from the start as critics of Kant.

JOHANN SCHULTZ, KARL CHRISTIAN ERHARD SCHMID, GEORG SAMUEL ALBERT MELLIN

Of the first group, the friends who rallied to Kant's philosophy as soon as it appeared, three seem to me particularly worth mentioning: Johann Schultz, Karl Christian Erhard Schmid and Georg Samuel Albert Mellin.

Johann Schultz was a personal friend of Kant's and a mathematical colleague of his at the University of Königsberg. He wrote two books which are relevant here: *Explanation of Professor Kant's Critique of Pure Reason* (1784) and *Investigation of the Kantian Critique of Pure Reason* (1789 and 1792). Even today, it would be difficult to find a better introduction to Kant's philosophy than these books by Johann Schultz.

Schmid was Professor of Philosophy at Jena and worked there as one of the earliest and keenest disciples and evangelists of Kantian philosophy. He wrote a number of books, the titles of which are closely similar to those of Kant's own works.

Mellin compiled the big six-volume *Encyclopaedic Dictionary of the Critical Philosophy* (1797). This again is one of the most reliable aids available for the study of Kant's philosophy.

These men usually receive scant attention in works on the history of philosophy. They did not, admittedly, carry philosophy on beyond Kant's position; they had no ambition to do so. That in no way reduces their contribution—a lasting one—to philosophy. For these men, reverence for truth was indissolubly linked with reverence for their teacher's superior genius. It was not feeble parroting which led them to trust his leadership and to stand by his teaching, but rather the consciousness that metaphysics, as Kant put it, is not everybody's job, and that for all the defects which Kant's theory may contain, one is on the whole likely to be nearer the truth by following him than by trying to set up a new system all on one's own. They knew well enough that it is not difficult to expose some defect here or there in a theory as comprehensive and ramified as Kant's. But they also knew that it was beyond any ordinary person's powers to eliminate those defects with such a sure touch, and to develop the system so consistently as to preserve unobscured the decisive basic ideas of the new theory. The main thing really was to get these fundamental ideas into the general consciousness of thinkers, to win citizenship for them in the republic of science. This was all the more difficult, as people were not yet in a position to decide which were the essential and permanent fundamental ideas in Kant's theory, and which were more in the nature of contingent and erroneous accessories. There was considerable danger of the foundations which Kant had laboriously laid being lost under over-hasty attempts at developing his theories.

These men were conscious of all this, though they could not of course foresee precisely the fate which lay in store for Kant's philosophy. The modest limits which they set to their work appear all the wiser when comparison is made (as we can make it now) with the achievement of those who strove to transform Kant's philosophy at once. *They* brought more confusion than clarification into philosophy. In place of the science established for all time, which their common teacher had laboured to bring in, they left behind only a heap of ruins, a chaos worse than any known to history as far back as our records reach. If people had spent longer on the quiet and cautious work of explanation and clarification undertaken by the former group of men, the development of philosophy and so the whole cultural history of Europe in the last century would have taken a happier turn. It is quite wrong to measure a philosopher's contribution by the revolutions he has brought about in the world of literature.

FRIEDRICH HEINRICH JACOBI

Of Kant's earliest critics I shall briefly mention three who pointed out the three weak points in his theory: his method in the transcendental proof, his unsatisfactory version of the Subjective Deduction, and his Formal Idealism. These three basic defects in the Critique of Reason were noticed very early on.

To begin with, however, critics understandably concentrated less on the method and the difficult enquiries connected with the deduction than on the results of Kant's system. A new and startling world-view had appeared in Kant's philosophy. It was natural that his contemporaries should be mainly interested in this view of the world.

Here Friedrich Heinrich Jacobi was the first to oppose Kant, pointing out the mistake in his proof of Transcendental Idealism. The book of Jacobi's which is particularly relevant here appeared in 1787, six years after the *Critique of Pure Reason*. It is called *David Hume on Belief, or Realism and Idealism*. Our concern is only with the appendix, which has the title 'On Transcendental Idealism'.

Jacobi shows in this treatise that the epistemological presupposition on which Kant bases his theory of Transcendental Idealism in the Transcendental Aesthetic and the Analytic conflicts with the result which it is supposed to prove. This presupposition comes out in certain assumptions about the causal relationship between the knowing subject and the things-as-they-really-are which that knowledge concerns. The assumption that the knowing subject is causally related to the thing-as-it-really-is conflicts with the results of Kant's theory, for on that theory the Categories, including our concept of causality, must not be applied to things-as-they-really-are, but only to appearances. The result of this theory of Kant's thus contradicts the grounds on which it is supposed to be based. In Jacobi's pregnant phrase, one cannot get into Kant's system *without* assuming that things-as-they-really-are affect us causally, and one cannot stay in the system *with* that assumption. In drawing the conclusion of Formal Idealism one is compelled to drop the assumption that things-as-they-really-are have a causal effect on the mind which knows them. This drives one, as Jacobi said, to affirm the most extreme Idealism that has ever been taught: to construct epistemology without positing things-as-they-really-are. On Jacobi's interpretation this conclusion is true to the spirit of Kant's system. It is against that spirit, according to Jacobi, to posit things-as-they-really-are.

Is this approach acceptable? According to Jacobi, the true spirit of Kant's system is to be found in a single result of his Critique of Reason, in the theory of Transcendental Idealism, and more particularly in the form which Kant gave to that theory in Formal Idealism. But the true spirit of a philosophy is not to be found in any one result, however important, but rather in the methodological idea which guided its creator. This is the creative and living principle of his whole system. It is by this that the value of the system must be reckoned, not by some isolated consequence. Now Kant's basic methodological idea was the critical method, which he discovered. This critical method does not depend at all on the theory of Transcendental Idealism. It is more or less accidental, as far as the method is concerned, that its application should give rise to a system which has that as consequence.

There is a further and special reason why Jacobi drew this mistaken conclusion from the supposed spirit of Kant's philosophy. Nor was Jacobi the only one to be thus misled. This mistake soon spread so far abroad, and settled in so firmly, that the misinterpretation of Kant's philosophy to which it led is still put forward even today.

The point is this. It is a peculiarity of Kant's critical method that it is limited to a subjective consideration of items of knowledge, in the sense that it has these very items of knowledge as its object and makes comparisons only between them. To this extent the method could well be called 'idealistic' in approach. This 'Idealism', this restriction to a subjective comparison of items of knowledge with each other, without considering the relation of the knowledge in question to its object, i.e. without ever judging the object in itself, but always only by the knowledge that we have of it: this methodological idea is the true spirit of Kant's philosophy.

This point can easily be misinterpreted. Unless one takes the subjective approach of the Critique of Reason in a strictly methodological sense, one may confuse it with the idealist theory that there are no things-as-they-really-are corresponding to our knowledge, so that our knowledge is knowledge only of appearances. It is easy to fall into this confusion, with the result that one comes to think of Kant's Transcendental Idealism not, as I said, as a more or less accidental result of applying the critical method, but as a postulate already included in that method and so requiring no further justification. This mistake sometimes takes the form of replacing the methodological principle of the Critique of Reason by the metaphysical assertion of Transcendental Idealism, and sometimes the converse form of turning that metaphysical assertion into a merely methodological principle.

One can of course describe the approach taken by the critical method by saying that it comes down to treating our knowledge as though the object had to conform to the knowledge, and not the other way about. For if that were the position, an item of knowledge would be judged not by comparison with its object, but only by its relation to other items of knowledge. This, however, is not the meaning of Kant's theory of Transcendental Idealism, as is clearly shown by Kant's application of that theory, by the consequences which he draws from it, and by his theory of the Antinomies, in particular by his solution of the problem how freedom is possible. One cannot, therefore, take his Transcendental Idealism simply as a postulate of method, requiring one to treat knowledge as if it did not refer to things-as-they-really-are. Everything here depends on the proposition that our knowledge really refers only to appearances and not to things-as-they-really-are. This theory that the object of our knowledge is ideal cannot be put forward simply on the basis of the methodological principle of the Critique of Reason. It is really an accidental result of the theory, as far as that principle is concerned. The Idealism of Kant's method—if we like to describe it so—has nothing to do with the Idealism of Kant's world-view.

We must therefore distinguish sharply between Kant's method, Criticism, and his world-view, Idealism. Jacobi confused these two and consequently mistook the whole spirit of Kant's philosophy, thinking to find it in what is really an accidental by-product of that philosophy. Jacobi proposed, in effect, to drop Kant's justification for his idealistic world-view, and instead to set that idealistic world-view up at the head of the system like an axiom, without the justification, as expressing the true spirit of his philosophy. This, on Jacobi's claim, would be a consistent development of Kant's philosophy.

This claim, however, is diametrically opposed to what the critical method really requires, if applied consistently. For Jacobi's claim is in effect the proclamation of a new dogmatism.

Although Jacobi did notice the contradiction in which Kant had become involved at this point, he did not realize the underlying basis of Kant's mistake. He thought the mistake lay in the particular way in which Kant conceived the causal relationship between knowledge and its object, which was supposed to help decide whether knowledge had any objective validity. The mistake however was not in Kant's particular way of expounding this theory. It lay much deeper, in the incorrect posing of the problem which Kant intended his theory of knowledge to solve. In this Kant really was unfaithful to the true spirit of his own philosophy. He deserted the critical method when he tried to set up a theory of the relationship of knowledge to its object. It was this error of method which led him to his Formal Idealism.

Once the basis of Kant's mistake is recognized, Jacobi's postulate of Dogmatic Idealism becomes unnecessary.

It should, however, be pointed out that Jacobi did not himself mean to adopt this idealistic approach. He was an opponent of Idealism. His intention, in bringing out the unavoidable implications of Kant's Idealism, was really to show that this theory led to absurdity. But Jacobi's personal position on the matter is not relevant here. The point he did establish is this: Kant's Formal Idealism implies Absolute Idealism. This demonstration had considerable influence in later philosophy.

SALOMON MAIMON

The second critic of Kant deserving notice here is Salomon Maimon, a Polish Jew who migrated to Germany at an early age without means or education and made his way in spite of great privations, impelled by a passion to investigate at its source the philosophy of Kant, which was just becoming known at that time.

Maimon's criticism was philosophically more profound than Jacobi's. He fastened at once on the weak point in Kant's method, the transcendental proof.

The most important works of Maimon's are his *Transcendental-philosophy* (1790), his *Attempt at a new Logic or Theory of Thought* (1794), and his *Critical Enquiries into the Human Mind* (1797).

Maimon shows with extraordinary clarity and skill that the transcendental proof offered by Kant for the basic propositions of metaphysics and derived from the so-called principle of the possibility of experience is circular, that it involves a *petitio principii*.

The basic propositions of metaphysics are supposed to be justified, in Kant, by being shown to be conditions for the possibility of experience.

Now Maimon asks: How, on this method, can we infer the validity of these basic propositions? Such an inference would be justified only if we could first take the validity of experience for granted. For only then could we begin to reason back to the validity of the conditions on which experience is possible. But how can we assert that experience is valid? The validity of any assertion depends on the validity of the premises from which that assertion follows. So the validity of experience depends on the validity of the basic propositions, which was what we originally set out to prove. The procedure adopted in the transcendental proof is thus shown to be circular.

On Kant's concept of experience, on which the proof is based, we cannot even decide whether we have experience or not. For according to the concept of it which is here presupposed experience consists simply in applying those same basic propositions whose validity is under discussion. So in order to establish that experience is possible we should first have to assume the point which was up for proof. As Maimon shows, what Kant proves is the hypothetical proposition that if those basic propositions of metaphysics do not hold good, then empirical propositions cannot be valid either; and conversely, if experience is valid then those basic propositions of metaphysics are valid too. But whether any experience is valid is not decided by his proof. His mode of argument does not touch this point at all.

Kant's attempted proof, then, does not point out any grounds for knowledge of the basic propositions of metaphysics; which is what must be done if they are really to be justified. Kant's attempted refutation of Hume's metaphysical scepticism was thus less successful in the end than his solution of the other problem which concerned the possibility of mathematics. Kant really did point out a basis for the knowledge expressed in the synthetic *a priori* judgments of mathematics: pure intuition. Hume's problem, however, was about metaphysical judgments, and here the position is quite different. Kant could find no grounds for such knowledge. So the question can still be raised, as before, whether metaphysical judgments are possible. Kant banished scepticism from the realm of mathematics, but not from that of metaphysics; which was precisely where Hume had raised his doubts. So while Maimon recognized Kant's demonstration as convincing and compelling in respect of mathematics, he maintained the sceptical position of Hume towards metaphysics.

Sigismund Beck

The third critic of Kant's deserving consideration in this context is Sigismund Beck. Beck was Kant's own student, and a personal friend of his. He compiled an *Explanatory Abstract* from Kant's works which although rather brief is very readable. The third volume is the most relevant here, entitled *The only possible Standpoint for judging the Critical Philosophy* (1796).

Beck here tackles the problem of the Subjective Deduction of the Categories, and he really does get to the heart of it. His aim is to illuminate Kant's concept of original synthesis, to which the Categories are supposed to be traced back in the Subjective Deduction. The Categories are concepts of necessary connection: so any knowledge expressed in a judgment is to that extent dependent on them. So the Categories, if they have any epistemic ground at all, must be based on some original synthesis. This, however, is possible only if there is some representation, independent of concepts, of objective synthetic unity. Beck points out that a correct view of this relationship makes all the difference to our understanding of the deduction of the Categories. And indeed it is here, if anywhere, that one can repair the gaps discovered by Maimon in Kant's justification of metaphysics, gaps which led that acute thinker to return to Hume's Metaphysical Scepticism. This was what Beck really tried to do; to find a solution to the problem of metaphysics corresponding to that which Kant had achieved for mathematics.

The position taken up in the original synthesis is what Beck calls the transcendental standpoint, or the standpoint of original representation. He distinguishes between 'logical understanding', the ability to represent by means of concepts, and 'transcendental understanding', the original ability to represent objective synthetic unity. One must, he says, put oneself in this transcendental standpoint in order to recognize the validity of the Categories.

This is a very profound insight, for it involves a clear recognition of the fact that reflective knowledge is mediate, and also of the existence of immediate metaphysical knowledge, which cannot be any sort of knowledge by concepts. This fact, profoundly and clearly grasped, is of considerable importance; it enabled Beck to bring light into the darkness of Kant's Deduction at an important point.

Beck did not, however, stop there. He went on, indeed he was driven on by the very nature of the problem to define more precisely the character of that original representation. As first premiss of the Deduction he puts forward what he calls the postulate of original representation. For him this is really the basic proposition of the Critique. It does not express a fact, but involves a request: that one should represent originally, i.e. take up the transcendental standpoint. Compliance with this request provides the justification of the Categories.

What Beck entirely overlooks is that transcendental synthesis is originally quite obscure. He makes it out to be such a simple matter, as if by an arbitrary decision one could take up the standpoint of original representation and thereby come to perceive without more ado the validity of the Categories. Now this description of the situation would clearly be correct only if original representation were originally clear, and so intuitive; as is the case, for example, in the mode of representation on which geometry is based. In other words, this description would be correct only if we were here dealing with some self-evident knowledge. For that is what we call an instance of knowledge whose validity can be perceived simply by our deciding to attend to its object. Beck, then, is here arguing, quite naturally, from the non-conceptual character of the original synthesis to its being intuitive. This inference is admittedly quite comprehensible, granted the preconception on which Kant's Critique of Pure Reason also rests: that items of knowledge divide exhaustively into those based on concepts and those based on intuition. Beck thus concludes his enquiries just where the most profound and difficult task of the Critique of Pure Reason begins. He does not realize that original representation could only be pointed out indirectly, by reference to its content. He does not see that the whole history of philosophy is one long and overwhelming experimental disproof of the self-evidence he assumes for original representation; so that requests that we take up the standpoint of original representation, though well meant, cannot help us to make philosophical truth self-evident at last.

The real weaknesses of Kant's philosophy were thus recognized in a remarkably short time, in spite of the difficulties in understanding the new theory. Nothing like a remedy, however, was found for these mistakes. All the same, the contributions of these men do show the very high standard of training in logical thinking which must have obtained in Germany at that time. And it can hardly have been an accident that most of these men were trained in mathematics. I mentioned earlier that Schultz was a Professor of Mathematics. Jacobi had a command of mathematics, having studied under the French mathematician Le Sage. Maimon's early studies were all mathematical. Beck, again, was a Professor of Mathematics. This is in remarkable contrast to another group of philosophers with whom we shall deal later on, philosophers who achieved far greater fame, were certainly much more original, and had incomparably greater influence on the course of history. These philosophers had no grounding in mathematics or in natural science, but were originally students of theology.

FRIEDRICH VON SCHILLER

There is another point that we ought to consider before turning to this group of philosophers. Our discussion has so far been concerned only with Kant's speculative philosophy. Let us therefore take one more look at the practical side of his philosophy and at an important attempt at further development in this direction.

To improve a theoretical system such as Kant's is in a way even more difficult in the field of practical philosophy, for this requires a synoptic understanding of the entire system, of its results and also of its dialectical principles.

If we look round among Kant's contemporaries we find only one man who was equal to the task of carrying critical ethics on beyond the stage to which Kant had developed it. This man's contribution to philosophy is still far from receiving the attention it deserves, although he is quite well known in other ways, and although Kant himself paid tribute to his mastery in this very field. His name is Friedrich Schiller. Schiller himself never meant to be more than a pupil of Kant's. As the usually received accounts give a totally false and misleading impression of Schiller's philosophical importance, and as I have never yet found his basic ideas correctly assessed, I will make an attempt to bring out the essence of them here.

It is usually said that Schiller's contribution to ethics was to mitigate the rigorism of Kant. The precise contrary is the truth. One way to summarize Schiller's contribution to the development of ethics would be to say that he was the first to free moral rigorism from that association with moralism which had previously been the rule in ethics—thereby making it possible, as it had not really been before, to establish the validity of moral rigorism in its true significance.

The rigorism of Kant's ethic is a logical consequence of the very concept of an ethic and so is inseparable from this. Its real meaning is that the moral law is strictly valid, without any exceptions. To mitigate moral rigorism, then, would really be to take away the moral law.

Moral rigorism is, however, quite different from the moralism of Kantian ethics, i.e. its peculiarity of admitting no other principle of evaluation, for judging an action, than the law of morality. Only by eliminating this moralism could moral rigorism acquire its full purity and strength, which it did not achieve even in Kant's own work. As long as it was confused with moralism it was bound to seem harsh and one-sided, appearing to imply the exclusion from ethics of any aesthetic ideal of life. Any ethic which confuses rigorism with moralism is bound to seem harsh and one-sided, and all the more so the more consistently it tries to establish moral rigorism.

Kant began his ethics by enquiring into the concept of a moral action. Schiller accepted unreservedly Kant's analysis of this concept: that an action is moral if it is done from a consciousness of duty. But he added that a man's being moral is a question quite distinct from the quantity of moral actions he performs. How often he acts morally is a contingent matter as far as his moral character is concerned, for it depends on external circumstances how often, if ever, he is in a position to act morally, i.e. to be able to fulfil his duty only by overcoming inclination. Whether one's inclination coincides with one's duty depends, in fact, on the circumstances. Only when duty and inclination happen not to be in contingent agreement does the fulfilment of duty require a moral action. For while if inclination and duty coincide the action will always be in accordance with duty, when duty conflicts with inclination an action can accord with duty only if it is done from a sense of duty. So one must not confuse a man's morality with particular moral actions of his, though these are admittedly its only sign. The morality of character consists only in being prepared to fulfil one's duty. Such preparedness cannot, of course, result from an inclination alone. For no inclination, however benign it may appear, will continually and reliably coincide with duty. Moral character cannot, then, depend simply on goodness of temperament, i.e. on a contingent coincidence of inclination with duty, but must consist of preparedness to act against inclination, i.e. from a sense of duty, *if* the occasion should arise.

Schiller eliminated the error in Kant's moralism by removing the duty to act morally, thus making room for some other evaluation of action. He went further and actually introduced this other form of evaluation, defining its special character in contrast to moral evaluation; for alongside the moral requirements of duty he set the ideal of humanity, as a principle for the positive evaluation of actions. In between the motives of sense and of morality he thus inserted a third, the aesthetic, whose aim is beauty of spirit. The ideal of spiritual beauty is however subject to the limitation of coinciding with duty, as is clear from the fact that in a conflict (which is always possible) between the requirements of humanity and those of duty the latter would take precedence. In such a conflict beauty of spirit must become sublimity of spirit, and gracefulness must give place to worthiness of conduct.

Schiller was not so misguided as to abandon Kant's moral rigorism. Far from it. With a clarity and rigour which no previous philosopher had achieved he refuted the arrogant claim made by inclination, and indeed by love, that regard for some positive value of our action could release us from the strict requirements of duty.

The significance attributed by Schiller to aesthetic evaluation explains why he could not feel satisfied with Kant's aesthetics, for he was bound to feel its lack of an objective principle of taste. Not only did he see that there is a problem here, but in his various attempts at mastering it he came near to giving the right solution, as can be seen from his definition 'Beauty is freedom in appearance'. The profundity of this remark could not, however, be properly grasped at this stage, for the basic mistake in Kant's speculative theory of Ideas—

D

which was the main logical obstacle in the way of a critical solution to the problem Schiller faced—had yet to be removed. That theory was still a theory of Transcendental Illusion: a fault which the methods and techniques provided by Kant's Critique of Reason would hardly suffice to cure. So Schiller himself abandoned the problem, as he could not achieve complete clarity on it. Some attempts of his in that direction may be found in some letters to Körner, which are among the best things we have in the literature of aesthetics.

The principal weakness in Schiller's aesthetics is closely connected with this resignation. He did improve Kant's theory of the disinterestedness of aesthetic evaluation by introducing an aesthetic motive in addition to those of sense and of morality. Yet in other respects he held to the position that aesthetic satisfaction is disinterested, without explaining or even noticing the contradiction to which he was thereby committed. Indeed, his final version of this theory of the disinterested character of aesthetic satisfaction is much starker and more definite than Kant's. This is Schiller's well-known theory of aesthetic illusion.

In this he follows up the fundamentally sound idea that aesthetic evaluation does not involve reference to any end or aim determined either by a moral or a sensible interest. So while for an object which is real in a physical sense one can always ask about its suitability (for some end), for a beautiful illusion no such requirement holds good; for this object, a purely aesthetic evaluation does not require that we first abstract from all reference to its suitability. It is however wrong to infer from this that the existence of the object makes no difference to aesthetic evaluation. Schiller asserts that a living feminine beauty does not afford us more aesthetic pleasure than one equally beautiful but only painted. This is correct to this extent that the latter would not otherwise be 'equally beautiful'. But if the amount of aesthetic value in an object depends on its beauty, still the reality of that value depends on the object being real. To a beautiful illusion value is attributed only hypothetically, as the possible form of an actual object. This merely hypothetical evaluation in a judgment of taste must not be confused with categorical aesthetic evaluation.

This mistake goes back to Kant. My reason for mentioning it here is that the misleading theory of the beautiful illusion, to which it gave rise, has won general acceptance in aesthetics. This has helped to obscure the new insights which Schiller won for us and to promote a romanticizing tendency of mind and taste, hostile to reality. Nothing could be more foreign to this tendency than the clear, strong and manly spirit of Schiller's ethic; an ethic which is really just the conceptual expression of that same spirit to which the *Ode to Joy* testifies and to which the hero of Schiller's *Don Carlos* pays homage. It is no accident that as Schiller the poet has gone down in the general estimation, so also has Schiller the philosopher come to be despised. It is no part of my present task to pass judgment on Schiller the poet. But I may be allowed to quote a remark of a more qualified judge, Carl Spitteler, who once said this about Schiller's fall from esteem:

'If all the present poets of every nation were to come together, they could not jointly achieve a single stanza as good as one of Schiller's, nor seven iambic verses resounding with Schiller's greatness of style.'

'From the degree of admiration with which someone mentions Schiller's name you can tell he himself is any good or not.'

'Anyone who refers to Schiller by name without the greatest respect and admiration is incapable of achieving anything himself.'

People may think what they like about this judgment on Schiller the poet, but it certainly fits Schiller the philosopher. So let me add that if all the philosophers of every nation came together, they could not jointly produce even the tiniest treatise as full, profound and clear in thought and as perfect in form as Schiller's philosophical treatises.

4

Systematization of the Epistemological Preconception and Reversion of the Critical Philosophy to Cartesianism

KARL LEONHARD REINHOLD

In order to find our bearings we have been looking into the possible developments of Kant's theory without reference to historical reality. We have also made the acquaintance of Kant's first critics. We shall now go on to discuss the first stage of the development, as indicated by our sketch plan (see Diagram V). In this stage what I called the epistemological preconception was made systematic, and the Critique reverted in consequence to Cartesianism.

The philosopher most central to our enquiry on this point is Karl Leonhard Reinhold. He gained literary fame by his *Letters about the Kantian Philosophy*, in which he came forward as a supporter of Kant. Then in 1789 he published his *Theory of the Representative Faculty*, treating the *Critique of Pure Reason* as epistemology. I may also mention his *Contributions to the Correction of previous Misunderstandings by Philosophers*, which came out in 1790, in two volumes; and more especially the work published in 1791, *On the Basis of Philosophical Science* (not to be confused with volume one of the *Contributions*, which has a similar title). This small book, concisely written in summary form and in a clear and unpretentious style, is his most important work, for it is here that Reinhold formulates in the clearest and most comprehensible way his basic idea of the task and method of philosophy. One could say—though this judgment can be justified only in the course of our whole exposition—that this is the most important work in the whole history of epistemological philosophy after Kant. It contains the basic idea of method on which this whole line of development is based. Anyone claiming to pass judgment on the history of philosophy after Kant requires an exact knowledge of this work.

As we know, Kant's theory contains parts which are mutually incompatible. For philosophy to progress beyond Kant, his theory as a whole had to be made self-consistent. Where two sections of theory are in discord, one or the other must be put aside. Whether it is error that is thereby excluded or truth is another question, and quite an important one. But it is still progress of a sort, or at least a contribution to progress, for an error to be followed out in all its consequences. As I have remarked before, this is in some cases the only way by which an error can be recognized as such. It is in this sense that Reinhold's book must be reckoned an outstanding contribution to progress in the history of philosophy. That is what makes it so important for our purposes. The methodological preconception which Kant, though founder of the Critique of Reason, never overcame and which in consequence limited his application of the critical method, is taken up by Reinhold, established firmly and made systematic. Those parts of Kant's theory which conflict with it are put aside. As a result, the Critique reverts to Dogmatism at this point.

The Critique as set out by Kant was bound to seem unsatisfactory, judged by the principles of Logical Dogmatism, unless and until its whole content could be systematically derived from first principles. On this view, the Critique of Reason itself had to acquire the form of a system. To set out the Critique adequately and systematically the individual items of knowledge of which it is made up had to be logically derived from first principles.

Kant had himself suggested one such principle from which the Critique of Reason could derive the basic statements of metaphysics: the principle of the possibility of experience. This can be stated somewhat as follows: The conditions on which experience is possible hold good, for that very reason, for all objects which could possibly be experienced. Now Reinhold remarks that this basic proposition of Kant's Critique clearly cannot be an absolutely basic, general and ultimate proposition, but must itself be derived from some still higher principle, if the requirements of a rigorously logical method are to be satisfied. The disputes which had broken out over Kant's Critique could on Reinhold's view be settled only by finding some higher principle from which to derive the statements which in Kant's Critique are taken for granted without proof. Reinhold therefore set himself the task of finding some highest principle of philosophy, from which to demonstrate rigorously the objective validity not only of experience, but of knowledge quite in general. To the science based on this fundamental principle and deducing from it the propositions which appear in Kant as basic principles, Reinhold gave the very appropriate and pregnant name of Basic Philosophy

(*Elementarphilosophie*). Basic Philosophy, he says, has to lay the foundation for the whole of philosophy. This foundation must be the ultimate principle of all philosophy. As the highest and only principle for the whole of philosophy, it must be the basis for both logic and metaphysics, and must supply the common principle for both speculative and practical philosophy. The lack of such a principle, in Reinhold's view, was the reason why dispute was raging in philosophy.

The special character of this transition from Kant's Critique to Reinhold's Basic Philosophy can be brought out in another way. In Kant the Critique has the task of reducing metaphysical judgments logically to their principles, and also the further task of the Subjective Deduction, i.e. of tracing these principles back to the subjective ground which makes them possible. Now if the method adopted in the Critique of Reason is taken, as Reinhold takes it, as intended to produce a system of philosophy, the Subjective Deduction will inevitably appear as a further attempt at logical reduction, going even beyond the principles of metaphysics. The logical regress to the basic propositions of metaphysics is quite different from the Subjective Deduction of those basic propositions. To Reinhold, however, this was bound to appear simply as a difference in the degree of generality of the grounds of proof reached in the logical regress. That is why the Subjective Deduction seemed to him the supreme logical task of all philosophy, the business of Basic Philosophy.

The concept of *a thing* had in all previous philosophy been reckoned the most general, as people had taken it as covering anything at all that could be thought of. This concept could no longer be regarded as the most general. One even more general had now to be sought, to which even this could be reduced. Reinhold argues as follows:* Thing means anything thinkable. Now thinking is just a particular form of representing. So the concept of *representation* is that more general concept he was looking for. It is the most general concept that philosophy can reach. So it must be with representation that the highest principle of philosophy is concerned. Basic Philosophy is therefore a theory of the representative faculty.

The highest principle of Basic Philosophy must directly concern representation. Reinhold thus arrives at the so-called Law of Consciousness as the highest principle of philosophy. He puts it like this: 'In consciousness the representation is distinct from both subject and object, and refers to both.' This law is supposed to hold good quite universally, without presupposing any experience as its basis; otherwise it would not be a philosophical principle. To perceive its

* *Über das Fundament*, p. 92 f.

truth, one has only to realize the meanings of the words which occur in it. All philosophical disputes would become baseless, Reinhold thought, once this law was asserted, for it could neither be doubted nor misunderstood.

From this law Reinhold derives the theorems of his Basic Philosophy, following the method of a strictly dogmatic science. He continues this logical chain down to the basic propositions of logic and metaphysics. That is as far as Basic Philosophy is supposed to go.

Reinhold's line of thought at this point could be summarized as follows. Every representation includes two dissimilar elements, form and matter. The form of the representation is that in it which concerns the subject; the matter is that in it which concerns the object. The subject provides the form of the representation and the object provides its matter. So both subject and object are essential in order for a representation to occur. The object, so far as it provides the matter of the representation, is the thing-as-it-really-is. The thing-as-it-really-is, as such, is unknowable; it cannot be represented at all. For it to be represented, there would have to be a representation involving only matter and no form, which is impossible. For every representation must, as a representation, contain both form and matter. So it follows from the concept of *a representation* that there can be no representation of a *thing-as-it-really-is*.

As we can see, the main aim of Reinhold's undertaking is to prove the epistemological theory of Idealism from the principle of Formal Idealism.

Reinhold's Basic Philosophy thus offers us a new version of Kant's Critique, modelled on the pre-Kantian dogmatic method. Descartes described this exactly when he said that the best way to present philosophy would be to derive the whole of philosophical knowledge by the mathematical method from a single highest principle. This theoretical pyramid, the ideal of Logical Dogmatism, was re-built by Reinhold. Though erected by the method of Logical Dogmatism, what it contains is a theory of epistemology, i.e. one concerned with the problem of the objective validity of knowledge. Reinhold thus met another demand that Descartes had made on philosophy, the demand for what we now call an epistemological basis for philosophy. Reinhold's Basic Philosophy thus fulfils both the fundamental requirements laid down by Descartes. It is an epistemology built up by the method of mathematics.

Here, once again, the spirit of Descartes breaks forth in overwhelming power. It had compelled all modern philosophy to follow his road. Kant's attack had not broken it, but only shaken its sway for a time. Reinhold's Basic Philosophy is the triumph of the counter-revolution against the revolution in thought introduced by Kant's Critique.

I turn now to criticism of Reinhold's idea of Basic Philosophy.
1. How does Reinhold come to his 'highest principle of philosophy'? Why does he hope that its discovery will settle all philosophical disputes?

Reinhold's aim is to point out the ultimate logical grounds of philosophical knowledge, so that its correctness may become evident. He supposes that if the correctness of the propositions on which Kant's philosophy is based is not yet universally apparent, this must be because the more basic grounds from which those propositions follow have yet to be pointed out. So all one need do is to point out these basic grounds, and the truth of those propositions will become evident to everyone.

This reasoning clearly assumes a necessary connection between a proposition being more general and its being more self-evident. For the lack of self-evidence in Kant's propositions is supposed to be due to the fact that the disputed propositions are not yet general enough. A single glance at the facts is sufficient to show that this assumption is a mere prejudice. The actual position is just the reverse. Philosophical disputes become more confused the more general are the propositions in dispute. If one is content to apply principles to particular given facts of experience, no dispute arises at all. But the more abstract one gets, and the more general the assumptions to which one ascends, the more violent the resulting dispute. It was observation of this very fact that led Kant to introduce the critical method into philosophy, i.e. to propose that instead of first establishing the most general principle so as to proceed thence to particular truths, one should work in the reverse direction, starting from particular self-evident propositions and ascending by an analytic procedure to the most general principles. Reinhold has not even grasped this fundamental idea of Kant's critical method.

2. Reinhold asserts that there could only be a single such universal principle. This is of course the thesis of Logical Dogmatism. But it is based on a dogma, and one which can easily be shown to be erroneous. No science at all can be worked out from a single principle, for no theorem could ever be derived from it. Every inference requires two premises. So with a single principle one could not even take the first step in Basic Philosophy. The notion of a single principle for

this science, or for the whole of philosophy, is essentially self-contradictory.

3. Leaving this point aside, let us ask whether there could be a common principle basic to both logic and metaphysics, as Reinhold assumes. Such a principle would have to be either an analytic or a synthetic judgment. Assuming it to be analytic, it would follow that only analytic theorems could be deduced from it. For a synthetic conclusion can never follow from analytic premises. Now the principles of metaphysics are synthetic propositions. So the proposition we seek cannot be analytic in character.

Let us then take it to be synthetic. Then all the theorems which follow from it will be synthetic too. For any conclusion whose premisses include even one synthetic proposition must itself be synthetic in character. Now the principles of logic are analytic propositions. So the propositions we seek cannot be synthetic either. It follows that there cannot be a principle common to both logic and metaphysics.

4. Let us, however, enquire if the principles of metaphysics might all the same be traced back some way at least, as Reinhold suggests, to some higher principles. This possibility is not ruled out by what has been said so far. It is still conceivable that the principles of metaphysics could be deduced from some logically higher principles; though in that case these cannot themselves be metaphysical principles, but must belong to some other science. Is that possible, or not?

These higher principles would have to be either analytic or synthetic. We have seen that they cannot be analytic. From analytic propositions synthetic ones never follow, so the principles of metaphysics do not follow either.

So they would have to be synthetic propositions. And these would be either synthetic *a priori* judgments or synthetic *a posteriori*. They cannot be synthetic *a priori* judgments, as the principles in question are already the most general in this field and so cannot be deduced from any higher synthetic *a priori* judgments. But they cannot by synthetic *a posteriori* judgments either, for from *a posteriori* judgments there follow only further *a posteriori* judgments and never *a priori* judgments. *A priori* judgments are those whose basis is independent of all experience. The principles of metaphysics, however, are *a priori* judgments.

The supposedly higher principles which we sought can therefore be neither synthetic *a priori* judgments, nor synthetic *a posteriori*. So they are quite impossible. The basic statements of metaphysics cannot be traced back to any principles logically superior to themselves.

5. What did Reinhold mean by the 'basis of philosophical science',

which his Basic Philosophy is supposed to contain? The phrase 'basis of a science' can mean very different things, and Reinhold confuses these different meanings disastrously. There are two concepts of a *basis of a science* which particularly need distinguishing. One could call them the logical and the constitutive basis. The logical basis of a science is the whole body of basic propositions from which the science can be derived logically. The constitutive basis of a science, on the other hand, is that on which our knowledge of these basic propositions themselves is based. So the constitutive basis of a science does not consist of the basic propositions of that science, and certainly not of any judgments belonging to it. If it consists of judgments at all, they must belong to some other science. But the constitutive basis of metaphysics cannot consist of judgments of any science, for as we saw there is no way of tracing the basic statements of metaphysics back to logically higher principles.

The logical basis of metaphysics, however, consists of the basic statements of metaphysics itself, and not, therefore, of Basic Philosophy as a science logically superior to metaphysics. Yet the constitutive basis of metaphysics cannot be found in Basic Philosophy either; for, as I showed, it is not to be found in any science at all. It must therefore consist of some immediate knowledge on which the basic judgments of metaphysics are based. Basic Philosophy, then, can be neither the logical nor the constitutive basis of metaphysics. There is no higher science containing the basis—logical or constitutive—of metaphysics. The sort of science that Reinhold's Basic Philosophy was meant to be is in fact impossible. The Critique of Pure Reason, which Reinhold wanted to develop from his Basic Philosophy, certainly has the task of justifying the basic statements of metaphysics. But although it contains the justification of the basic statements of metaphysics, it does not, for that very reason, contain their ground, but only points it out. This ground, the constitutive basis of metaphysics, is the object of the Critique of Reason, but not its content. It is found in a form of immediate knowledge and so not in any science, not even in the Critique.

6. Reinhold's failure to recognize this point was his most fundamental mistake and led him into serious errors. As he sought the constitutive basis of metaphysics in logical premises from which the basic judgments of metaphysics could be deduced, and not in an immediate knowledge on which those judgments are based, his Basic Philosophy became a science logically superior to metaphysics. Instead of making the constitutive basis of metaphysics the object of enquiry in the Critique and demonstrating the fact of its existence, he set Basic

Philosophy the task of working out a logical basis for the principles of metaphysics. In his transition to Basic Philosophy he thus confuses the object of the Critique with its content, the ground for the judgments which the Critique has to justify with that justification itself.

7. This mistake also led Reinhold to overlook the fact that the Critique belongs to a mode of knowledge different in kind from that of the system of metaphysics.

The knowledge which forms the object of the Critique is supposed to contain the ground for the propositions of the system of metaphysics. It must therefore be a rational knowledge. Critical knowledge itself, however, which has metaphysical knowledge as its object, is psychological and to that extent empirical. Now if the knowledge which is the object of the Critique is confused with that which makes up its content (which really belongs to inner experience), the illusion arises that this psychological knowledge contains the ground for metaphysical judgments. The consequence is that psychological knowledge, though empirical in character, is treated in the manner of rational knowledge; that one tries, as Reinhold does, to work it out progressively from general principles. For empirical knowledge, this procedure is quite inappropriate. For experience yields us only particular facts, not general laws which could be worked out in the form of a system. Particular facts of experience can be co-ordinated, but not subordinated to one another theoretically. There are, indeed, universal empirical propositions. But these are never principles, but are only inferred by induction from particular observations. So they must never be asserted dogmatically. They are not self-evident basic truths which could be set up *a priori* at the head of one's system.

8. Universal statements based on inner experience can therefore be justified only by means of induction. But every induction already presupposes the principles of metaphysics, being impossible without them. For metaphysical knowledge to be derived in the first place from general psychological statements would inevitably be circular. Thus Reinhold, for example, quite happily applies the law of causality when he ascribes to the subject a capacity for producing the form for representations, and by assuming that the subject is affected by the thing-as-it-really-is, which thus causes the matter of the representation. He does not realize that in this he is presupposing a metaphysical knowledge whose derivation ought really to be given first.

9. Underlying all this there runs a μετάβασις εἰς ἄλλο γένος,*

---

* Shift to a different class (cp. Aristotle *On the Heavens* a.i.), one term standing for concepts belonging to two different fields.

namely the alleged logical transition from psychology to metaphysics. This results from the failure to recognize that critique and system belong to dissimilar modes of knowledge. Reinhold provides a clear instance of this when he says: The concept of a thing is not the most general of all concepts, for being the concept of anything thinkable it presupposes the concept of thought, which in turn is only a particular sort of representation. The most general concept of all, then, is not that of a thing, but that of a representation (p. 92). So one is to ascend from the concept of *a thing* to that of *thought* simply by moving from particular to general. Here the transition from the field of philosophy to psychology is very clear. Reinhold does not notice it, because of the ambiguity of the word *representation* (*Vorstellung*). This word can refer objectively to that which is represented, the object of the representation; but it can also be used subjectively for the activity of representing. If these two meanings are not kept distinct, the general objective concept of *an object* or *thing* as anything representable gets confused with the concept of *representation* in the subjective sense of the word. In moving from the concept of *thing* to that of *representation* one is not, as Reinhold thinks, moving from a particular concept to one more general. On the contrary, the transition here is from a more general concept to a particular one. For representing is just one particular activity, among others, of the subject who represents. This concept is pyschological and therefore empirical; it is not a philosophical concept logically superior to that of *a thing*. A representation, moreover, is just one particular form of the thinkable, so it is just one thing among others.

Reinhold thus confuses the object of representation with its content and so arrives at his false abstraction. There is no regress here from particular to general, but rather the reverse, restriction of the generality of the concept to a narrow part of its field, transition from a general and philosophical concept to one that is empirical and particular.

10. The fundamental epistemological mistake in Reinhold's Basic Philosophy, once again, becomes quite obvious. Reinhold himself demonstrates that knowledge cannot possibly be proved objectively valid, if by objective validity one means agreement with things-as-they-really-are. For such a proof could proceed only by comparing our knowledge with the thing-as-it-really-is, whereas we are able only to compare our items of knowledge with each other.

Reinhold does not, however, conclude from this that it is a mistake to attempt an epistemological justification, i.e. a justification of our knowledge as objectively valid, but infers that it is impossible for knowledge to be objectively valid, in the sense defined. He does not conclude that it is quite impossible to solve the problem of epistemology, but solves that problem negatively. From the impossibility of proving objective validity he concludes that there is no objective validity; i.e. he sees this as a disproof of objective validity.

This conclusion assumes that one has no right to assert the objective validity of knowledge without proving it. For only then would the impossibility of proving it make objective validity itself impossible.

If, however, the falsity of a proposition really followed from its unprovability, the same considerations would also hold for the objective invalidity of knowledge. In that case one could equally well argue the other way, that as the objective invalidity of knowledge cannot be proved it is itself impossible. And this would prove the objective validity of the knowledge.

Thus the proof from the fact that the contrary is unprovable proves too much, for it would also be a proof of the contrary.

This mode of proof obviously rests on the epistemological axiom that every truth must be open to proof; an axiom that is certainly false, since if it were true its contrary would follow from its own unprovability.

This axiom led Reinhold to set up his own theory of knowledge, an idealistic one, as he argues from the fact that the objective validity of knowledge cannot be proved to its objective invalidity.

In the end, however, he wants in his Basic Philosophy to give a positive proof of the objective validity of knowledge, which can be done only by adopting a different concept of objective validity. This shift of terminology does not alter the facts, as already described. Reinhold's proof of objective validity depends on a re-definition of this term, such as we came across earlier in Kant.

This shows how Reinhold's Basic Philosophy follows logically once the fundamental mistake has been made. Reinhold was the first to work out these consequences and so to bring out a mistake which in Kant is still deeply concealed. That is why Reinhold is important in the history of philosophy; and his importance particularly deserves recognition by those who accept the fundamental idea of his Basic Philosophy, as taken up and developed by his successors. As we shall soon see, the philosophy of Fichte, Schelling and Hegel is based on a further development of Reinhold's idea of Basic Philosophy. So anyone who sees the theories of these men as a step forward in philosophy beyond Kant, or indeed as the summit of the history of philosophy—a view still common even today—must recognize the decisive contribution of Reinhold to philosophy after Kant.

We should also note that although Reinhold consistently interpreted the Critique as epistemology, and because of this consistency set aside the really critical content of Kant's theory, the type of Dogmatism to which he reverted was by no means unambiguous and definite. The Critique is completely displaced by Dogmatism, but this Dogmatism in its turn admits of various interpretations. As we saw, Reinhold did not realize that the Critique of Reason is modally dissimilar from the system of metaphysics, and sought to distinguish these two sciences simply by the degree of generality of the propositions they contain. But he did not put forward any positive theory as to the type of knowledge to which Basic Philosophy should belong. He never posed this question in a definite form.

This question has to be asked if one is to be clear about the nature of Basic Philosophy. How is one to conceive the modality of this science which is supposed to be logically superior to metaphysics, this mysterious science of Basic Philosophy which is to contain the foundation for metaphysics?

Various answers to this question are possible. One could argue back from the rational character of the metaphysical propositions whose ground is sought to the rational character of Basic Philosophy. But one could also argue the other way; that Basic Philosophy, as a theory of the faculty of representation, is knowledge of a psychological type, and that metaphysics must therefore be based on psychology, and so on experience.

A full exposition of Reinhold's Basic Philosophy would thus lead one either to Transcendentalism or to Psychologism. Reinhold never came to a decision either way. It was therefore inevitable that his successors should divide into two schools, some constructing systems upon the transcendental preconception, others upon a preconceived Psychologism.

This inevitably led to renewed conflict between a rationalist and an empiricist conception of metaphysics. The old dispute between Rationalism and Empiricism was bound to come to life again. And so it did among Reinhold's successors.

Transcendentalism, in turn, can be taken in two distinct ways. The transcendental knowledge contained in Basic Philosophy, being rational knowledge, can have its source either in an intuition or in concepts alone. Transcendentalism thus leads us back either to a metaphysic of intellectual intuition, that is to Neo-platonic Mysticism, or to a new version of a metaphysic from concepts alone, that is to Scholastic Logicism.

It is, however, important to note that these various developments of Basic Philosophy have something in common. They share an assumption which underlies Reinhold's whole approach to Basic Philosophy. This is the idea of a science whose content would be the constitutive basis of metaphysics. Reinhold's importance in the history of philosophy after Kant lies in his definite formulation of the idea of such a science.

In the more general historical context Reinhold's Basic Philosophy represents a regress from Kant to Descartes, for it is really a thorough-going attempt to fulfil the two fundamental requirements laid down by Descartes as the ideal of philosophy. One of these concerns the form, and the other the content of philosophy.

The first requirement, concerning the form, expresses the ideal of Logical Dogmatism: that metaphysics should be constructed strictly and systematically, on the model of the so-called mathematical method. Hence the need to put the most general principle at the head and to derive all the particular items of knowledge from it by means of logical inference.

Such an idea would hardly have struck such deep roots and been successfully asserted for so long, had it not contained a kernel of truth. And so it does. In itself, this requirement of Descartes as the ideal for philosophy is entirely correct. It really is the case that the only method suitable for a perfect and definitive exposition of philosophy is that which was long ago accepted in mathematics. Kant never doubted this, but he emphasized it explicitly. However, the mode of systematic construction of philosophy in its final form is one question; managing to obtain the first principles for such a construction is quite another. The latter question must be answered first, before there is any point in undertaking the ideal construction. Philosophy is here in a more difficult position than mathematics, which has its principles given to it, since they are evident; so that previous question does not really arise at all for mathematics. Philosophy is here faced with the profound problem of producing such evidence first, as its first principles are not equipped with it at the outset. The plain fact is that the principles of philosophy are hidden. They have to be sought out first. And even when they have been found, they require some justification to exclude all doubt of their certainty. Where Logical Dogmatism goes wrong is in con-fusing the postulate of method, which requires philosophy to be constructed systematically, with the question of whether the princi-ples of such a construction are evident. It is essential that this question be answered first, by the Critique of Reason, before syste-matic construction is undertaken.

Now on Reinhold's view the Critique, as a science of the faculty of representation, has representations for its object, yet is supposed at the same time to contain an objective basis for the proof of philosophical truths. It thus becomes a theory of knowledge, that is, it achieves the transition from its subjective starting-point to its objective goal by means of a theory of the relationship of knowledge to its object.

This epistemological application of the Critique involves a reversion to the other fundamental requirement which Descartes had set before philosophy and which here determines the content of Basic Philosophy.

It is no accident that this requirement about the content of Basic Philosophy should be linked with the other concerning its form. There is an inner connection here; the postulate which determines the epistemological content of Basic Philosophy necessarily involves the other postulate about its form. In fact, anyone who starts by posing the problem epistemologically, i.e. by proposing to investigate the objective validity of knowledge, will be led simply by the logic of the argument to the formal postulate of Logical Dogmatism. For if, as is assumed when the problem is posed epistemologically, every item of knowledge requires justification, this really means that any item of knowledge can be certain only by means of something else, and never by itself. No item of knowledge carries with it the certainty of its objective validity, but can obtain this only from some other item, derivation from which justifies it. Every item of knowledge, then, must have the form of a judgment, i.e. it has to start life as a problematic representation, to which assertion is then added from elsewhere, an assertion which in its turn requires some further justification. But if every item of knowledge has the form of a judgment, then epistemological justification can only take the form of a proof; for a proof is, simply, derivation from other and logically superior judgments. The justification, however, must also contain the grounds of proof for the judgments being justified; for a proof always contains the highest premises from which the proposition being justified can be inferred. So one comes to the notion of a closed system, combining in itself the very first grounds of proof and the ultimate conclusions. Here a purely logical transition can be made from the first epistemological principles to the propositions of the system which are justified by their means. This means that the postulate of systematic unity must apply to the relationship between the Critique, taken as theory of knowledge, and the system of metaphysics; for the Critique, as it contains the grounds of proof for the principles of metaphysics, will be logically superior to metaphysics. That is to say, the Critique, as theory of knowledge, will itself appear at the head of the system.

This shows the close connection between the epistemological approach, which determines the content of Basic Philosophy, and the ideal for the logical form of this science, i.e. that it should be modelled on the method of mathematics.

The postulate of systematic unity, in its turn, leads unavoidably to the postulate of modal similarity. For if Critique and metaphysics make up a single logical system, in which Critique is distinguished from metaphysics only by the higher degree of generality of its propositions, then it follows at once that the propositions of metaphysics, being inferences drawn from the Critique, must be of a similar mode of knowledge. Either both contain rational knowledge, or else both contain empirical knowledge. So once the postulate of systematic unity is found to apply to the relationship between Critique and metaphysics, consistency requires that we either rationalize the Critique or else make metaphysics empirical. The first alternative leads to Transcendentalism, the second to Psychologism. So a renewal of the dispute between Rationalism and Empiricism was an unavoidable consequence of the epistemological preconception.

It should now be clear how far Reinhold's Basic Philosophy is, as I said, a reversion to Cartesianism. For the special character of Cartesianism is due to the combination of the very same two postulates that make up the essentials of Reinhold's Basic Philosophy. This may be confirmed by glancing at the form in which Descartes himself tried to embody these ideas or, rather, at his preliminary sketch of this embodiment. He also set himself to provide philosophy with a strictly systematic exposition, in which the content of the principle at the head of the system would be an epistemological criterion; which meant, for him, that it should be a proposition in which the greatest objective certainty was combined with the greatest subjective self-evidence. In his sketch, this greatest certainty applies to *Cogitatio* (thought).* So Descartes also is seeking the basis of metaphysics in a proposition whose object is an item of knowledge, and which therefore must itself derive from inner experience; for *Cogitatio** itself is just an object of inner experience. It is on this circumstance alone that Descartes bases his claim that the proposition is self-evident. But for this very reason this self-evidence is in fact only psychological—a limitation which results in any case from the

---

* This might mean 'the *Cogito* (I think)' [trs.].

E

strict consistency of Descartes' theory of knowledge, on which inner perception is the only genuine form of immediate knowledge.   ·

The *Cogito* (I think) of Descartes, taken strictly, thus lands us in the same predicament as Reinhold's 'Law of Consciousness'. For how could the most general metaphysical certainty possibly be derived from a psychological certainty?

We are familiar with the circular argument by which Descartes achieved his illusory solution of this problem, when in contradiction to his first proposal he introduced the idea of God as the ultimate basis for truth and at the same time as an epistemological criterion. This, however, is a very significant contradiction. For we could say that it brings a third postulate to bear, which was fundamental to the further development of Cartesianism: the assumption that the ultimate basis of existence, in the metaphysical sense, would be bound to coincide with the ultimate basis of the truth of our knowledge, logically considered, so that the systematically ultimate principle of philosophy would have to refer directly to the ultimate basis of the being of things—a notion developed further with clarity and consistency by Spinoza in his theory that the ordering of ground and consequent in the system of philosophical science must correspond precisely to the ordering of ground and consequent in the beings of things. This idea also, which in effect claims a positive knowledge of the divine essence, became immensely influential once again, as Cartesianism was progressively revived among the successors of Reinhold.

GOTTLOB ERNST SCHULZE

When a dogmatic theory makes its appearance in philosophy, it cannot last long without a sceptical theory appearing in opposition to it. This is just what happened to the new Dogmatism of Reinhold. In 1792, one year after the publication of Reinhold's work *On the Basis of Philosophical Science*, Gottlob Ernst Schulze brought out an anonymous work with the title *Aenesidemus, or concerning the Foundation for the Basic Philosophy produced by Professor Reinhold in Jena, together with a Defence of Scepticism against the Pretensions of the Critique of Reason*. This *Aenesidemus* is the sceptical counterpart of Reinhold's dogmatics. As the title shows, his attacks are directed against Kant as well. And this is fair, to some extent, for the ideas of Reinhold were not taken up at random, but developed from definite tendencies in Kant's Critique of Reason, so that Schulze's fire at Reinhold hits Kant too. Yet the writer of *Aenesidemus* shares his opponent's epistemological preconception; indeed this receives a more definite and precise expression at his hands. The only difference between their points of view is that he draws a sceptical conclusion from the epistemological way of posing the problem. He does not himself try to solve this problem, but questions whether there can be any solution. In contrast to both Reinhold and Kant he retains the original concept of the objective validity of knowledge. By this he means the agreement of knowledge with its object; and he shows very convincingly that neither Kant nor Reinhold had proved them to agree, and that the whole frame of their enquiry makes such a proof impossible.

In this dispute, Scepticism has the last word. The Critique, like Basic Philosophy, has as its object ideas. Ideas can of course be compared with each other; and one can decide whether they agree with each other or not. But one cannot merely by comparing ideas reach any conclusion about the relationship of ideas to anything other than an idea, and which lies beyond all ideas; one cannot decide how ideas are related to things-as-they-really-are. As Schulze rightly remarks, we cannot draw a negative conclusion either about this relationship, as Kant and Reinhold wanted to. From a consideration of ideas alone we cannot draw the idealist conclusion that ideas do not agree with things-as-they-really-are. The question about the objective validity of our ideas must therefore be left open.

Kant had inferred from certain ideas being *a priori* that their object was ideal. Such an inference is impossible. But Schulze did not clearly distinguish being *a priori* from being ideal, any more than Reinhold had, so two concepts coalesce for him. So while attacking the proof that certain items of knowledge are ideal (such as pure intuition and the Categories), he also came to dispute Kant's assertion that they are *a priori*, thus reverting to a standpoint similar to that of Hume. He denied that the Critique had demonstrated the existence of synthetic *a priori* judgments. So in the end he also remained bound by the preconception of Formal Idealism.

Schulze also uses, both against Reinhold's Basic Philosophy and against the Critique of Pure Reason, the argument which Kant had used against the rational psychology of his predecessors. On Schulze's view, both Critique and Basic Philosophy are just new versions of rational psychology. He had good reasons for this view. For if the Critique, as Reinhold for one certainly assumed, is to contain the basis for metaphysical science, it must contain rational knowledge. But it has as its object ideas, what Reinhold calls facts of consciousness. So it must be a rational science of ideas, i.e. rational psychology. Kant had shown such a science to be impossible. Schulze therefore appeals to Kant's own argument to show that both Critique of Pure Reason and Basic Philosophy are impossible. Taken as theory of knowledge, the Critique is a new form of pre-Kantian transcendent metaphysics, which Kant himself had shown to be impossible.

The *Aenesidemus* thus deepens the objection, raised against Kant earlier by Jacobi, that an internal contradiction is involved in the Critique.

5

Systematization of the Transcendental Preconception and Reversion of the Critical Philosophy to Neo-Platonism and Scholasticism

We must now justify our earlier statement that the theories made famous by Fichte, Schelling and Hegel, theories which even today, or should I say again today, are considered the flower and crown of the whole history of philosophy, can all be traced back to Reinhold's fundamental idea of method. As these theories are held in high regard nowadays I shall discuss them in more detail than the scheme of this work would otherwise require; far enough to show that they do not after all mark a step forward in philosophy beyond Kant. They are really a reversion to certain errors which Kant had exposed. Not that they can claim originality even for this regressive step. All the credit for that (if credit is due) belongs to Reinhold. If, as I claim, these theories are just a further development of Reinhold's Basic Philosophy, then all I need do is to demonstrate that this claim is historically correct, for the theories themselves in essentials have been refuted already. We are not interested in the literary success or political influence of philosophical theories, but only in their scientific truth and justification. I shall not, therefore, recapitulate my criticism of the fundamental idea which derives from Reinhold. In what follows it will be taken for granted that this idea is untenable. In criticizing his successors one has only to show that they all pursue the mirage of Reinhold's Basic Philosophy.

JOHANN GOTTLIEB FICHTE

Reinhold confused Critique with system, and postulated an ultimate principle of philosophy. Both points, as I showed, are really due to a single fundamental error, to the epistemological preconception that the task of the Critique is to set up a general criterion of truth and to deduce a system of philosophical knowledge from that criterion. If this is the job of the Critique, then the Critique must itself stand at the head of the system of philosophy.

This mistake was taken over by the first of Reinhold's successors to become famous in the history of philosophy: Johann Gottlieb Fichte.* He took it up blindly and enthusiastically. He praised Reinhold for the 'immortal contribution' of introducing into philosophy the demand for an ultimate principle. Fichte combines this mistake of Reinhold's with Jacobi's misunderstanding of Kant and also with the views of the *Aenesidemus*, which were directed against the implications of Reinhold's idea.

The adoption of Jacobi's misconception of the Kantian Critique led Fichte to the dogmatic proclamation of Idealism. It thus became axiomatic for him to reject the assumption of things-as-they-really-are and so to set himself to solve the problem of epistemology in a purely idealistic way. Fichte thus follows Jacobi's view of the spirit of Critical philosophy. For him, this is to be found in an idealist theory of knowledge. This comes out very clearly in his direct contrasting of Idealism with Dogmatism. By Dogmatism he no longer means, as Kant did, a particular method of philosophizing, but a certain result of a philosophical theory which ascribes the validity of our knowledge to our being affected by things-as-they-really-are. With this assertion he contrasts another, which he calls Criticism or, synonymously, Idealism: that the validity of our knowledge does not depend on the existence of external things.

Having restored Dogmatism once more, in an idealistic form, Fichte's argument led him to revive Rationalism too. If things-as-they-really-are do not provide the material of our knowledge, then this material (if we still want to call it that) must, he thinks, all be produced by the form of the knowledge alone, taking 'form' here, on Reinhold's lines, as that which is proper to knowledge as knowledge, apart from any further or external *things*. On this view no material is given to us to know; the content of every item of knowledge is due to the creative activity of the knowing subject. This is Rationalism in its most extreme form. On this view, all knowledge is *a priori*. For it is a consequence of the axiom of Idealism that there can be no knowledge *a posteriori*. Another way of putting this, which Fichte himself employs, is to say that the distinction between *a priori* and *a posteriori* knowledge breaks down. With regard to modality, all knowledge is of one type. For the distinction of modes is supposed to rest on a

---

* Of his numerous works the following are our particular concern: *Foundation of the whole Scientific Theory* (1794–5, 2nd ed. 1802), and a series of articles of the year 1797. In his collected works these are called *First and Second Introduction to the Scientific Theory*; they are now available as a separate volume, in the Medicus edition.

distinction in the relation of knowledge to its object. But for absolute Idealism this relation is the same for all knowledge. This removes any distinction of modes within our knowledge. A further and more important consequence flows from this. If all knowledge is of the same type as philosophical knowledge, then the range of validity of the ultimate principle postulated by Reinhold for philosophy must be extended to include the whole field of science of any sort. All science must ultimately stem from philosophy. So we are not now seeking the highest principle of a particular science, philosophy, but the highest principle of any and every science, indeed of all knowledge whatever. For all knowledge is of one type, so it must have the form of a single, unitary system and must be derivable from a single principle. The science whose task it is to derive our knowledge from this highest principle Fichte calls 'Scientific Theory' (*Wissenschaftslehre*). This theory is to provide not only the form but also the content of all knowledge and of every science.

This approach will obviously lead to an explicit demand for a general criterion of material truth: which, as Kant showed clearly and irrefutably, is to ask for the impossible.

All this follows quite naturally from combining Jacobi's misconception of the Critique of Reason with Reinhold's postulate of Basic Philosophy. In addition to this Fichte takes up the attacks of the *Aenesidemus* on Reinhold, attacks which, in his view, showed only that Reinhold had not been consistent enough. Fichte therefore used Reinhold's fundamental idea all over again, arguing that the dispute over his Basic Philosophy must be due to the fact that Reinhold's principle was still not universal enough. There had to be some yet higher principle, discovery of which would settle the dispute.

Fichte took over another point from the *Aenesidemus*: that the Basic Philosophy, as presented by Reinhold, is circular. For the metaphysical concepts whose original derivation it undertakes to provide are really presupposed by the propositions of this same philosophy; for instance, the concept of *a cause*. In constructing his Scientific Theory Fichte therefore tries to ensure that none of the metaphysical concepts still to be deduced occur in it. He himself remarks that in order to draw any further inference from his first principle he must at least presuppose the validity of the laws of logic, although it is part of the task of the Scientific Theory to give a derivation for these. He resigns himself to this, explaining that as this circle is unavoidable one will just have to go round it.

His argument runs more or less like this:

The most general concept, laid down by Reinhold as the foundation for his Basic Philosophy, and from which he derived the law of consciousness, was the concept of *idea* or *representation*. Fichte correctly points out that the concept of *representation* is by no means the most general of all, for representing is just one particular variety of mental activity, alongside other mental activities. The higher concept, which is clearly fundamental at this point, is that of *activity*. Activity, then, shall be the most general concept of the Scientific Theory.

Now this activity must not be thought of as belonging to an acting subject; for that would be to apply a Category to activity. In thinking of it as belonging to an acting subject we should already be employing metaphysical concepts. We must therefore think of it as pure activity, mere action or doing. This action, for Fichte, is the *I*. The *I* is thus the fundamental concept of the Scientific Theory. For Fichte it is the point at which subject and object are united. It was indeed the aim of the Scientific Theory to bring subject and object together; how else could it justify the validity of our knowledge! Here, as in Reinhold's Basic Philosophy, the problem is the relation of knowledge to its object. How do we get from subject to object? That is the problem of the Scientific Theory.

The solution of this problem is based on the idea that the mysterious difference between subject and object is clearly absent in the case of self-knowledge, for here subject and object are identical. The *I* is simply an activity turning back on itself, as Fichte puts it. And as we have found the identity of subject and object in the *I*, the answer must be for the Scientific Theory to trace all knowledge back to the self-knowledge of the *I*.

The influence of one of Kant's mistakes is evident here. In his Subjective Deduction Kant sought a basis for the Categories in what he called the unity of transcendental apperception. As I showed earlier, under this phrase Kant confused two things: the identity of formal apperception, which is the basic idea of objective synthetic unity, and the identity of the subject of representations, the identity of the *I*. This confusion is perpetrated in his phrase: unity of transcendental apperception.

Kant's discussion of this point is comprehensive and profound, but Fichte arbitrarily picks out from it this one mistake. He thus makes the identity of the *I* the basis for an account of metaphysical knowledge and so of all knowledge whatever.

This *I* must not, he says, be confused with the individual *I* of a particular person; for clearly that would introduce psychological concepts. The Scientific Theory is not a science of inner experience, but a philosophical science. It does not depend, as Reinhold's Subjective Dogmatism did, on facts of consciousness, but develops out of pure thought. It can therefore have nothing to do with the individual I of inner experience. No; we are seeking the absolute subject, the highest metaphysical principle, and this can be found only in what Fichte calls the pure I, in a universal and super-individual I.

The identity of the pure I thus provides the content of the highest principle of the Scientific Theory: that $I = I$. From this, the whole of knowledge is to be derived.

By what method does Fichte propose to develop his Scientific Theory from this principle? He conceives of the method like this. We first establish the highest principle. We then find that this principle could not hold good, did we not also make a certain other assumption. For if we do not make this other assumption, there will be a contradiction in the principle established first. To resolve this contradiction, we must add a second proposition. This second proposition of the Scientific Theory in its turn leads to a contradiction, unless a third proposition is adopted, which resolves the new contradiction. And so on. This is the method of contradiction, by which one advances to ever more remote conditions for the validity of the propositions already found.

1. Passing to criticism, I shall begin with a preliminary treatment of the method of the Scientific Theory. The contradiction to which the highest principle of the Scientific Theory is supposed to lead must either reside in that principle itself or else must consist in this principle contradicting some other principle. The former alternative would really mean that this proposition was self-contradictory and therefore false. In the latter case, where the highest principle does not contradict itself, but does contradict some other proposition, then one at least of these two propositions must be false, either the highest principle or the other one. Which one of them is false cannot be decided at this stage. There is a further point. For such a contradiction to be discovered between the first principle and the other one, this other proposition must at least be known. Yet its discovery is alleged to be based on the detection of that contradiction!

The means for resolving such a contradiction must, whether we like it or not, be obtained from elsewhere, and not from the contradictory principle itself; for the proposition which involves a contradiction cannot also contain its resolution. This must therefore be sought outside the system of established propositions. At least one would have to know that a contradiction found in the system does have a solution. The assertion that the contradiction can be resolved cannot itself be part of the self-contradictory system. The same holds for the resolution too, unless indeed the contradiction is only apparent, in which case all one need do is to show that what is alleged to be contradictory is not really so. But then an exposition correct to begin with would not lead to contradictions at all; so we would lose our principle and never progress beyond our starting-point. In no case, then, can this new method provide what it promises, but only bogus results.

There is another point which should help to make this clear. The method of contradictions is supposed to reveal the conditions under which the propositions already established can hold good. But such conditions must be propositions logically superior to those already established, so they cannot also be their consequences. Clearly Fichte is here confusing the regressive method of the Critique, which really does discover conditions of that sort, with a procedure of logical proof.

(Here let me remark in passing, that one can say, with a certain air of profundity—and the remark would apply not only to the Scientific Theory but to every systematic science—that there is an apparent contradiction between the first two propositions of a science, which can be resolved only by adding a third proposition which sets out the conclusion inferred from the first two.

An example will make this clear. I say, that the two propositions 'All men are mortal' and 'Socrates is a man' are in contradiction unless and until we adopt a certain third proposition; and the principle of scientific progress rests on the establishment of this contradiction. If only we can find this third proposition, we can use it to resolve the contradiction. I then claim to have found the third proposition which does this: the proposition 'Socrates is mortal'. The fact is: *if* we took this proposition to be false, so that Socrates was not mortal, then from the proposition 'All men are mortal' it *would* follow that Socrates is not a man. And from the proposition that Socrates is a man it would follow that not all men are mortal. *This* contradiction can be resolved by discovering that Socrates is mortal.

(VI) Syllogism and 'Contradiction'

Socrates is not mortal

All men are
mortal

Socrates is
a man

Socrates is
not a man

Not all men
are mortal

Socrates is mortal

It does indeed hold true in general that denying the conclusion involves a contradiction with the premises. For it is on this very fact that the force of the inference depends.)

2. As this discussion shows, Fichte modelled his method on the ideal of Logical Dogmatism. The result is a pure Logicism, which aims to create a content for science from the logical form of deduction, and from that alone. There is no positive source of knowledge here, from which the content of the Scientific Theory could be evolved, but only the ultimate principle itself. Yet this ultimate principle is for Fichte an empty analytic judgment, so no material content at all can be evolved out of it. It is moreover intended as the highest principle of all science, which must therefore hold good on its own, without any further justification. So it must just be put forward arbitrarily, as Fichte admits in so many words when setting up his principle. There is no reason which can compel us to acknowledge the principle of the Scientific Theory as true. All justification must presuppose some unprovable premises. Fichte here adopts the logicist prejudice that all justification must take the form of proof and concludes that the starting-point of philosophy will have to be an axiom set up dogmatically at the head of the system. Which philosophy one chooses, he says, depends on what sort of man one is. It is a question of character, not of scientific insight, whether or not one acknowledges the principles of the Scientific Theory. Fichte does not realize that this is really an admission that reflection alone cannot provide the material for derivation of the Theory. In effect, he is acknowledging the arbitrary and empty character of mere reflection. This fact forces him more and more to abandon his Logicism and to take refuge in another and original source of knowledge.

3. Such, he proclaims is intellectual intuition. For the knowledge in question must in his view be an intuition, if it is not after all to arise from reflection alone. At the same time it must be intellectual and not empirical, as the science to be derived from it is supposed to be rational in character.

Fichte does not content himself simply with postulating this intellectual intuition, but tries to prove its existence by means of examples. He refers to the intuition of the activity of the *I*. This, he says, is not a sensible intuition, as it is concerned not with an external entity but with an internal activity. So it must be an intellectual intuition. But the distinction between external and internal to which Fichte here appeals is clearly a distinction of objects, not of the modality of our knowledge of those objects. He takes the contrast between external and internal perception or intuition for one between sensible and intellectual intuition.

The mark of the intellect is generality and necessity. But perception or intuition of our internal activity is really just as much sensible as perception of external, physical entities. For both concern the particular and factual. The occurrence of a particular mental act at a certain time is just as much a contingent and empirically given fact as any particular phenomenon of external nature. Fichte thus confuses two contrasts, that between internal and external intuition, and that between intellectual and sensible intuition.

As well as pointing to the example of internal intuition, he refers to items of knowledge which really are intellectual in character, for instance to the consciousness of duty that we find in ourselves. The obligation of duty is a universal law, and so can come to us only in knowledge of an intellectual variety.

Fichte also refers to our consciousness of the effect of a resolve upon our thinking. It is a matter of immediate experience that when we resolve to think of some particular thing, then the thought really does occur because of this resolve. All that sensible intuition shows us in this case is that the thought occurs subsequently in time to the forming of the resolve. But we experience something more, the causal effectiveness of the resolve. We know that the thought arises by means of the resolve. Sensible intuition could not show us this, therefore, Fichte concludes, we acquire this knowledge by intellectual intuition.

This inference involves another confusion. We do have an immediate consciousness, as Fichte calls it, of duty and also of the effect of a resolve on our thinking. But as a more precise self-observation would reveal, this 'immediate' consciousness is not intuitive or immediately clear, but is intrinsically obscure. It is only indirectly, by means of concepts, that its content can be made clear. This immediate consiousness is what I earlier called the feeling-for-truth— and this can be conceptually analysed, which shows its non-intuitive character. As I pointed out before, confusing this feeling-for-truth with a form of intuition results in an illusion which can easily promote Mysticism (cp. Vol. I, pp. 88–92). Fichte is a case in point.

4. There is another false assumption which Fichte made at the outset of his enquiries, owing once again to an error of self-observation, an assumption implicit in the very topic of the Scientific Theory.

The problem of the Scientific Theory is this: How do we come to suppose something objective, the object, an entity, to correspond to the subjective, which is only in ourselves? According to Fichte the difficulty here described does not arise in the case of self-knowledge, but is supposed to arise in the case of our knowledge of the external world.

This way of posing the problem is based on a particular factual assumption about knowledge. It assumes that external knowledge, unlike internal, does not apply to its object directly. In our knowledge of external things, certainty that the object exists is supposed to be a mediate addition to our idea of it. But external perception is as immediate as inner perception, as Kant showed in his refutation of Idealism—thereby confuting this prejudice, which since the time of Descartes had become traditional. It is quite the wrong approach to ask how certainty of the object's existence is added to our idea. This certainty is an original part of the idea. It is not added to it indirectly by means of some inference to the cause affecting our senses, as Fichte supposes from his inadequate self-observation. The situation is not, as he describes it, that we find in ourselves a sensation of red, sweet or cold and thence infer an object outside us as cause of our being thus affected. What happens is just the reverse: we perceive the red, sweet or cold directly and argue back from this to our mind being affected, a matter of which we have no direct knowledge at all.

5. Why is it that the relation of knowledge to its object seems to Fichte less problematic in the case of knowledge of oneself?

Self-knowledge, as the name implies, is a knowledge whose object is the knowing subject himself. So subject and object of the knowledge here coincide; they are identical. Now if one does not make a sufficiently clear distinction between the relation of knowledge to its object and the relation of the knowing subject to the object, the illusion arises that the knowledge itself is identical, in the case of self-knowledge, with the object of the knowledge; that knowledge and object are one and the same. This was the illusion that misled Fichte here. In fact, knowledge is no more identical with its object in the case of self-knowledge than in the case of knowledge of the external world. Even where the object of knowledge consists of an item of knowledge, still the item of knowledge thus known is distinct from the item of knowledge in which it is known. Every item of knowledge is a knowledge *of* something, and the something which is known cannot itself be the knowledge in which it is known. This point can be made another way. In order to know an item of knowledge we need a new and extra item of knowledge, by which to know the item given. Otherwise, if an item of knowledge were itself sufficient for knowledge of that item of knowledge, this would hold equally for knowledge of the knowledge, and so on to infinity; so that there could be no knowledge which was not also object of that same knowledge.

Fichte, however, argues from the identity of subject and object in self-knowledge to the identity of knowledge and its object in self-knowledge, thus achieving a pseudo-solution to the epistemological problem of the relation of knowledge to its object. That is why he undertakes to derive all knowledge from self-knowledge, assuming that in this case no problem can arise of the distinction between knowledge and its object.

6. Let us now look in more detail at Fichte's solution to his epistemological problem. It turns out, inevitably, to be idealistic in character. For on his assumptions objective knowledge occurs only in the form of self-knowledge. The existence of external things, by contrast, is an extra supposition, over and above the fact of our mind's being affected. We are indeed compelled to make this extra supposition. Scientific investigation would, however, show that this supposing of external objects has no objective validity, for the simple reason that it is due to a subjective compulsion leading us to imagine that there are things external to ourselves.

Whether or not this view is tenable in other respects, there are on this point only two alternatives; either the compulsion mentioned by Fichte really does occur, in which case it is clearly impossible even for the author of the Scientific Theory to exempt himself from it, and it is impossible even for him to recognize the assumption of external objects as a fiction; or, alternatively, it is possible to recognize this assumption as a fiction, in which case it follows immediately that compulsion is not in question here.

7. According to Fichte, Being is to be regarded as the creation of the pure *I*, which as he rightly says is distinct from the mere *I* of the individual. Individual personality, like external objects, results only from the creative activity of the pure *I*. If external objects, then, are a creation of the pure *I*, that does not stop them being different from the individual *I*. So it is easy to see that this supposed solution of the epistemological problem, i.e. the question of the relation of the *I* to the non-*I*, only shifts the problem, for it really returns the question to us in another form, still unsolved. We started with the question of the relation of the *I* to things external to it. It is no answer to this question to explain that the external things are ideas of a super-individual *I*. For the things which were contrasted with the individual *I* do not, by becoming ideas of a super-individual *I*, cease to be different from the ideas of the individual *I*. Now this difference was the original problem which Idealism was supposed to solve. The sup-

posed solution leaves the difficulty precisely as it was and simply
gives it another name. It now runs like this: How does one idea of the
super-individual *I*, namely the individual *I*, come to make a contrast between itself and things external to itself, i.e. other ideas of the
super-individual *I*? To put it another way: How is it that the ideas
of the pure *I* include ideas of external objects as well as ideas of the
individual *I*, the former being ideas of the latter ideas?

Finally, we could put it the other way round: How does the pure *I*
come to have not only ideas of external objects but also ideas of those
ideas? Whichever way we dress it up, this question is just another
way of posing the original question which Idealism was meant to
solve.

8. How does Fichte come to assert this universal super-individual
I in the first place?

He is led to it by a false abstraction. If we abstract from the individuality of the *I* we come to the concept of *I-ness*, a concept applying
not only to our own *I*, but also to that of everyone else. Fichte confuses this general concept of *I-ness* with an object, an *I* which is
universal and distinct from the separate *I* and so is non-individual. A
mere concept could not perform any activity, such as Fichte undoubtedly ascribes to the pure universal *I*.

There is, however, another and more particular reason which led
Fichte to the assumption of this universal *I*, or at any rate encouraged
him in his false abstraction. The reason is that he fell into a further
confusion by requiring that a subject be sought which is not in its
turn object of any knowledge, but is subject absolutely. That which
thinks is, he says, contrasted thereby with that which is thought and
so is distinct from the object. So it cannot, he concludes, itself be an
object. It cannot be any individual *I*, for this is the object of inner
experience. So it must be a super-individual subject which is the
ground of the possibility of all objects whatsoever.

'The absolute *I*', says Fichte, 'is not any thing; it has no predicate,
and can have none' (*Foundation of the whole Scientific Theory*, 2nd
ed., p. 29). He does not notice the absurdity in which this explanation
lands him: that he thereby makes the absolute *I* object of a judgment,
and attributes to it the predicate of not having any predicate.

Here Fichte once more confuses the contrast between thinking and
thought with that between thinker and thought, though his inference
in this case is just the opposite of the fallacious conclusion he previously drew from this confusion. He argued earlier from the identity
of subject and object in self-knowledge to the identity of knowledge
and object in self-knowledge; but here he argues just the other way,

from the essential distinction between knowledge and object to the essential distinction between subject and object. As he rightly remarks here, the object of knowledge must be distinct from that knowledge. Knowledge of an object is not itself that object, but only a particular idea of it. From this distinction between knowledge and its object Fichte here argues to the distinctness of knowing subject from object known. But this inference, just like the other, depends on tacitly equating the relation between knowledge and object with that between knowing subject and object. Even if knowledge is essentially distinct from its object, still the knowing subject can very well coincide with the object of knowledge; which is what actually happens, in the case of self-knowledge. So Fichte's assumption of the super-individual I is really based on the tacit presupposition that self-knowledge is impossible.

9. There are other serious confusions in Fichte's work. Not only does he confuse the relation of knowledge to its object with that between subject and object of knowledge, he also substitutes for this the relation of internal to external being or, as he puts it, the opposition of matter to intelligence. The contrast between Idealism and Dogmatism, which he had set at the head of his system and which depends on the one deriving from the subject and the other from the object, thus becomes for him a contrast between Spiritualism and Materialism. For he equates the subject with intelligence and the object with matter.

Finally he confuses this contrast between matter and intelligence with a quite different one between freedom and natural necessity. Having wrongly equated the object with external nature he then confuses it with nature in general, and persuades himself that in the distinction between intelligence and matter he has already found the contrast between freedom and natural necessity. He imagines that a release merely from external nature raises him above all nature—to metaphysical freedom. Kant had distinguished psychological freedom from the metaphysical Idea of freedom. Fichte confused the two again, mistaking independence of laws of external nature for independence of all laws of nature whatsoever. He thus finds it an easy task to prove that metaphysical freedom is possible.

For this purpose he employs another and equally sophistical argument, appealing to the Idealism of his theory of knowledge, by which he thinks he has shown that nature is only a product of the I. This proof is supposed to establish that the I is independent of all nature. But it was the superindividual or universal I that was supposed to be creator of nature. So in offering this proof for the freedom of the will he is evidently replacing the universal *I*, which ranks for him as creator of nature, by the individual *I*. For it is the latter whose will he alleges to be free. By this underhand method the freedom of the first *I* is transferred to the second one.

10. Fichte starts from the *I* and then goes on to nature; and he sees this as 'starting from freedom'. This procedure presupposes that we have a positive idea of freedom, from which we can then derive our knowledge of nature—an assumption which Kant's Critique of Reason showed to be quite unjustifiable, and which Fichte can pretend to justify only, as I showed, by improperly substituting for the negative concept of *freedom* the positive concept of *intelligence*, which he derives from inner experience. Our positive knowledge is restricted to knowledge of nature; and this goes for our self-knowledge too. Self-knowledge is possible for us only as knowledge of inner nature. We can raise ourselves above nature only in Ideas, by denying the general limits on our knowledge. Fichte's manner of philosophizing assumes the opposite: that we can have a positive knowledge of freedom, as opposed to nature, and so of the eternal as opposed to the finite. That explains how he can set himself to derive the finitude of nature from the eternal.

11. Our discussion of Fichte's enterprise in the Scientific Theory has so far been concerned with the epistemological preconception which he inherited from Reinhold and adopted as the starting-point of his speculations. We have seen how this preconception led him to take the identity of the *I* as the ultimate principle of the Scientific Theory—and finally, as owing to his Idealism the *I* is also for him the ultimate ground of existence, to derive philosophy from a positive knowledge of the Absolute.

On what means of knowledge does he rely to fulfil such elevated claims?

This brings us back again to the question of Fichte's method. In order to settle this fundamental point, let us see just how Fichte moves on from his first principle. We shall have to look into this if we are to explain satisfactorily why it seems as though his Scientific Theory *could* be worked out and developed from that principle.

The method of the Scientific Theory is the progressive solution of contradictions. How does Fichte obtain these contradictions?

His train of thought goes more or less like this: The *I*, which according to the highest principle poses itself ('*I* = *I*'), is on the other hand opposed to a non-*I* ('Non-*I* ≠ *I*'). The non-*I*, then, is opposed to the *I*. But as the non-*I* is opposed to the *I*, the posing of the non-*I* cancels the posing of the *I*. This is the 'inference from opposition to

F

non-Being' (*Foundation of the whole Scientific Theory*, 2nd ed., p. 22). There thus arises a contradiction between the posing of the I and that of the non-*I*.

Under the indefinite expression 'opposition' plain difference is here confused with contradiction. To put it another way, a mere formula of comparison is confused with a judgment. Fichte says: that which is opposed to an *A*, being non-*A*, is the opposite of *A* and so contradicts *A*. 'It is not, what *A* is' (p. 20).

Let us just apply this to a simple example. Gold is opposed to silver. As non-silver, gold is the opposite of silver and thus is contradictory to silver, so that the positing of gold annuls that of silver! Now the proposition 'Gold is not = silver' is a correct comparison-formula, but if one infers from this that gold is not what silver is, i.e. that a property belonging to silver (e.g. the property of being a metal) cannot belong to gold, then one is substituting a false judgment for the correct formula of comparison. This is what happens when Fichte infers from a mere difference between two objects to a conflict of their properties and existence. This mode of inference comes out very clearly when he says: 'The non-*I* must, simply because of the opposition, possess the opposite of everything possessed by the *I*' (p. 21) and 'to posit the non-*I* is, *pro tanto*, not to posit the *I*' (p. 24). Now the truth is that positing of the non-*I* is not positing of the *I*. That is a correct comparison-formula. But Fichte replaces it by a false judgment when he goes on to say, 'For the *I* is eliminated completely by the non-*I*' (p. 24).

That is how he comes to decree a contradiction between his second proposition and the first. The second proposition, 'The *I* is opposed to a non-*I*', is supposed to annul the first, which expressed the positing of the *I*. This is the contradiction which the Scientific Theory purports to solve by a third proposition, in which the items opposed, *I* and non-*I*, are equated once again, yet without eliminating the opposition between them. By equating the opposed items we thus come to the new proposition '*I* = non-*I*' (p. 25). 'The *I* should be identical with and yet opposed to itself' (p. 30). How does this 'union of opposites' (p. 31) come about? 'How can *A* and non-*A*, being and non-being, reality and negation be combined in thought, without annihilating and cancelling each other?' (p. 27).

This is how the trick is done. Although *A* is not *B*, if there is some *x* which is the same as both *A* and *B*, then to that extent *A* and *B*, though opposed, must be the same (p. 33). 'For example, gold and silver are equally included in the concept of metal' (p. 42).

This apparently profound discussion thus reduces to the truism that different objects may be so far alike as to come under a common concept. For example: gold and silver are opposed, for after all they are different. But gold is a metal, and silver is one too. So gold is the same as silver. So gold is not silver and yet gold is the same as silver. The contradiction between gold and silver is thus resolved, but without eliminating the opposition between them.

For Fichte, this is a profound philosophical discovery. He thus resolves the contradiction previously established between the positing of the I and that of the non-I, and so achieves his main aim. For, as he goes on to say: 'Everything which may henceforth arise in the system of the human mind must be derivable from the proposition here established' (p. 31). He does not realize that this simply shifts the original problem, if there ever was one. For if I equate A and B to the extent of equating both with x, then in place of the proposition $A = B$, whose possibility I was supposed to be explaining (for B, after all, is not A), I have now put two other propositions, $A = \mathrm{x}$ and $B = \mathrm{x}$. But in these propositions also subject and predicate are not identical; so if the proposition $A = \mathrm{B}$ involves a contradiction (p. 33), then by the same argument the propositions $A = x$ and $B = x$ will also involve contradictions. The contradiction which was to be resolved is thus replaced by two fresh ones.

We have not, then, really achieved anything after all. All that has happened is that a correct comparison-formula, $A = \mathrm{B}$ (gold is the same as silver—which it is, as both are metals) has been replaced by a false judgment asserting A and B to be identical; and that an equally correct comparison-formula, A not $= \mathrm{B}$ (gold is different from silver) has been replaced by a false judgment asserting that A and B are in conflict. 'The positing of a non-A cancels A' (p. 32).

The fallacy is based on a confusion of concepts with objects. 'Gold and silver', says Fichte, 'are equally included in the concept of metal.' Gold and silver, on this view, are not only identical in that both come under the concept *metal*, they are actually united in that concept. Thus the concept *metal* does not have the logical meaning of a general characteristic which can be attributed as predicate in a judgment both to gold and to silver, but acquires instead the meaning of a general object, an identical entity in which gold and silver are united like different predicates of one and the same subject.

It was the Amphiboly of the Concepts of Reflection that misled Fichte at this point. By discovering that Amphiboly Kant was able to destroy the entire structure of Logical Dogmatism that his predecessors had built up. But all the important discoveries which paved the way for this achievement disappear again in Fichte, without trace. He misclassifies analytic judgments under 'opposition of concepts', and synthetic judgments under 'equating of concepts'. '*A* is *A* so far as *A* = *A*, for that is what the logical copula means' (p. 3). Starting from this gross ignorance and distortion of Kant's distinction between analytic and synthetic judgments, he then goes on to boast that his play with the concepts '*I*' and 'non-*I*' has 'in the most general and satisfactory way answered' (p. 36) the main question of Kant's Critique of Pure Reason: 'How can synthetic judgments be made *a priori*?'

FRIEDRICH WILHELM JOSEF VON SCHELLING

In spite of all the warnings of Kant's Critique, Fichte set himself to derive positive knowledge of the finite from the Idea of freedom, and thus to develop a science from Ideas. Fichte's successor Schelling promptly undertook this task. He openly challenged philosophy to make sense of the finite *via* the eternal. He asserted in express terms that positive knowledge could be had of the eternal, that there could be an absolute science directly concerned with Divinity. But this Absolute from which he proposes to derive the finite is no longer Fichte's *I*, which Schelling replaces by the absolute identity of subject and object. Fichte's starting from the *I* was really due to something quite alien to pure Dogmatism; to that epistemological misunderstanding of Kant's Critique of Reason which he had inherited from Reinhold's Basic Philosophy. Even in Fichte this Kantian relic, this rudiment of Criticism, appearing within Dogmatism only as a sort of pathological phenomenon, was pushed more and more into the background; and it was finally expelled from the system altogether by Schelling. He changed Dogmatism back into its original form by freeing it from the subjective tendency, a tendency which arose from confusing the Critique with the system of philosophy, so that the subjective turn given to speculation by the critical method was taken for a dogma of idealist metaphysics. Once Schelling had dropped the epistemological starting-point, the Scientific Theory naturally shed the hybrid character which it bore in Fichte, leaving an objective Dogmatism similar to that taught before Kant by Leibniz and Spinoza—and distinguished from theirs only by its unsystematic and arbitrary manner of exposition and by its disregard of the maturity achieved in the meantime in scientific research and philosophy.

According to Schelling, the original unity of all things is based on the absolute identity of subjective and objective. From this all finite things must be derived and understood in their individuality and variety so as to fulfil the postulate of absolute knowledge. So the task of philosophy is that of cosmogony, as in the old transcendent metaphysics. The reversion of the Critique to Dogmatism thus takes us back to the fantasies of the early Greek philosophers of nature. Schelling sees his task as that of understanding the world by means of the Godhead, tracing all things back to their origin in the Absolute. This is really an attempt to gain positive knowledge of the Absolute and to build a theory from Ideas. This revives quite explicitly a project which Kant had shown to be impossible. The whole apparatus of the *Critique of Pure Reason* was created specially to prove that, as we have no positive knowledge of the Absolute, there cannot be a science based on Ideas. Yet here we find a renewed attempt at constructing just such a science from Ideas.

For this, as Schelling realized, we would need to possess a faculty of intellectual intuition. It is in fact our lack of this faculty, and the consequent separation of sensibility from understanding in our knowledge, that imposes the nature-form (*Naturform*)* on that knowledge. The only way we can describe the Absolute is by negating the bounds which this nature-form sets to our knowledge. The separation of our sensibility from our understanding introduces an unavoidable incongruence between the form and content of our knowledge, an incongruence which only intellectual intuition could overcome. We can only combine form and content in our knowledge bit by bit, in a progressive synthesis of the manifold given intuitively in experience. But we can never achieve a complete synthesis, an absolute unity of the manifold in experience. The incompleteness of this synthesis makes absolute knowledge impossible for us.

Schelling, however, credited himself with intellectual intuition, inheriting from Fichte the assumption that such a faculty does exist. This intellectual intuition applied, in his view, directly to the absolute identity of all things in God. Philosophy has as its theme the doctrine of God's self-revelation in the world. Here again the epistemological origin of this whole new metaphysic is evident: the finite things of the world come about by the self-knowledge of God. The history of the world is the progressing self-knowledge of the Absolute.

This takes us back to the daydreams of the Neo-Platonists. Demolishing the boundaries between natural concepts and Ideas leads, as every mythology does, to mixing theory up with poetry and to abolishing the distinction between science and religion. This is just what Schelling wants; he wants science and poetry, science and

* cf Vol. I, p. 183.

religion to be identical. He wants an absolute knowledge which will eliminate the cleavage between the scientific view of the world and the religious and aesthetic view. Nature, in his philosophy, is to be conceived directly as a cosmos, as the most perfect work of art.

A project which involves combining Ideas with natural concepts in a theory is bound to lead to contradictions; and these are apparent at every step in Schelling's work. This is no science, nor indeed poetry either, but only a mythology, turgid and botched, satisfying neither intellect nor taste. In itself this mythology would be no worse than the mythological fancies of the old philosophers who did not know what is demanded in scientific speculation. But Schelling has the presumption to claim scientific insight for his daydreams, insight into far more profound truths than a natural science based on mathematics and experiment can attain. With this he combines, finally, an unsavoury attempt to exploit church dogmas for the benefit of speculative mythology, to attribute to them a profound philosophical sense and so to bring them into speculation in the guise of explanations. Thus Schelling makes particular use of the church doctrine of the Fall as a principle of metaphysical explanation, to explain how finite things could have their origin in God.

Here again Schelling is only following Fichte's lead. Fichte had the unfortunate idea of subjecting world-history to a philosophico-religious interpretation, presenting it as a falling away from an original state of innocence into a state of sin and as a rising thence to final sanctification.

I cannot here discuss this speculative mythology in detail. My concern is simply to show that the dialectical foundations for Schelling's philosophical work were all borrowed from Fichte. This dependence on Fichte is clearest in his choice of the ultimate ground of explanation in metaphysics. The highest principle, from which he proposes to derive the finite in all its variety, is to be the identity of subject and object. Schelling would never have come upon this relationship of subject to object had he not followed the detour *via* the epistemological approach in Fichte's 'Foundation of Scientific Theory', and derived by Fichte from Reinhold. This relation of subject to object is not the ultimate relationship for our knowledge quite in general. It is a particular relationship known to us only from inner experience. It is solely from our inner experience that we come to realize that we have ideas by which our subject is related to an object. Thus Schelling, following Fichte, took a particular psychological relationship for a general and metaphysical one. This shows that his dialectic derives from Reinhold's confusion of the psychological critique with the system of metaphysics. As a result Schelling, like Fichte, confused the relation of subject and object not only with that of knowledge to its object, but also with the relation of spiritual to corporeal, and this in its turn with the contrast between freedom and nature. Various contrasts are interchanged at will: subject and object, matter and intelligence, nature and freedom; and all are called the relation of the real to the ideal, a relation which is supposed to explain finite things. For all the differences that we come across in nature are due, according to Schelling, to the varying admixture of real and ideal.

The task of natural philosophy, in Schelling's view, is to exhibit the possible quantitative gradations of this relationship and so to explain the variety of individual things. His natural philosophy thus moves progressively from a relation in which objectivity predominates to one in which subjectivity does. The maximum of objectivity he finds in weighable matter, the maximum of subjectivity in the creations of art. He progresses from the one to the other by a series of gradations in which objectivity gets less and less and subjectivity gets greater and greater; from weighable matter to light, from light to electricity, from electricity to chemistry, from chemistry to organic life. Organism then bridges the gap between corporeal and spiritual. In the realm of the spirit he comes first to morality, then to science, and finally to art. And this juggling with analogies is supposed to offer a better understanding of natural phenomena than mathematical natural science can provide!

Two further circumstances came to Schelling's assistance in working out this so-called natural philosophy. The first was Goethe's misconception of Newton's physics, which Schelling was kind enough to deduce as a discovery of natural philosphy. Secondly he had the aid of his own misconception of Kant's natural philosophy. Kant had demonstrated that the possibility of filling space presupposes certain forces in matter. In his *Metaphysical Foundations of Natural Science* he expounded the distinction between the material property of occupying a space and that of filling a space. For matter to occupy a space is not the same as its filling it. For the filling of space involves resistance by the matter occupying the space to other matter pressing into that space. This resistance presupposes a force of repulsion, and is not, as people before Kant had supposed, a property belonging to matter by definition. Schelling mistakes Kant's quite clear demonstration as meaning that matter is a product of the reciprocal action of forces. Schelling therefore sets himself to explain matter from the reciprocal action of insubstantial forces in nature. He thus arrives at an extended metaphysical application of Fichte's fiction of an act without any acting. In place of permanent matter he puts an endless becoming without any permanent substratum on which to base the change involved.

By excluding dead matter at the outset from natural science he gains the supposed advantage that life has no longer to be explained by the lifeless, as on the physicalist interpretation of nature; instead, the apparently lifeless is explained by life. This interpretation re-establishes the dominance of a teleological conception of nature. Phenomena are to be explained not by laws of nature, but by Ideas.

This all goes to show that Schelling's philosophy, as far as its dialectic is concerned, can be explained by its origin in the dialectical mistakes made by Fichte and so, at second remove, by Reinhold's basic mistakes. Dialectically, nothing here is original; the whole development simply carries on the legacy bequeathed by Reinhold's misunderstanding of Kant's Critique, though this is more and more concealed as arbitrariness and fantasy in exposition of the theory gain the upper hand.

The illusion that this philosophy of nature can be worked out from its speculative principle is due simply to the mystical mode of abstraction brought in by Fichte, and to the resulting play with empty formulae of comparison. The same abstraction which leads Fichte to his *I* brings Schelling to his world-soul as the highest principle of explanation in metaphysics. For Schelling arrives at this world-soul only by confusing the relation of individual souls to the general concept of *soul* with that of parts of the whole, just as Fichte confused the relation of the individual *I* to the general concept of *I* with an identity of individual spirits in the absolute *I*. By abstracting from individuality Schelling thus obtains not a general concept of *spirit*, under which individual spirits are subsumed, but a general object in which individual spirits are united as parts. Schelling thinks that the individuality of a particular soul arises only by its relation to a certain body, and that the removal of this relationship to a body abolishes the individuality of the spirit as well. The soul then returns to God: which here means, that its individuality is dissolved and dispersed in the world-soul.

The apparent fruitfulness of the proposal to establish a science of the Absolute rests simply and solely on this confusion of concept with object and on the consequent confusion of comparison-formulae with judgments. The principle by which explanations are given in that science is expressed in Schelling's statement 'That which is natural is free'. He not only wants to make a negative contrast between freedom and nature—as it was nature, after all, from which he had to start—but also to achieve a positive recognition of their identity. The proposition that the natural and the free are identical does of course follow automatically from the presupposed identity of subject and object, once one has confused the relation between subject and object with that between nature and freedom. This proposition, however, explains nothing, but only puts into words the confusion of a correct comparison-formula with a false judgment. There is a certain sameness between what is natural and what is free, between appearances and things-as-they-really-are: for that which appears in nature is the thing-as-it-really-is. The natural and the free can to this extent be described as identical. But for this to show us the way to an absolute science, by which to recognize positively the identity of the free and the natural, that which is intrinsically free would have to appear to us as nature, and, further, the judgment would have to hold good that nature itself already is the free. This judgment, however, is not merely false, but self-contradictory. For it is as good as saying that what is subject to laws of nature is not subject to laws of nature.

The speculative constructions with which Schelling wants to replace inductive natural science all turn out in the same way to be empty formulae of comparison. Thus, when in his philosophy of nature he sets up the supposed law 'Positive magnetism = positive electricity', or again 'Heat = expansion', these assertions are not laws of nature, but mere comparison-formulae. Before these can be used to give a definite explanation of anything we must first know in what respect the things compared are the same. But it is precisely these qualifications that are lacking in Schelling's philosophy of nature. The mere assertion that two things are the same is, of course, always correct, and so is the assertion that they are different. Hence the apparent paradox and profundity of speculations of this type, and their real emptiness.

GEORG WILHELM FRIEDRICH HEGEL

Philosophizing in this manner was carried on further by Hegel. His reputation then, as now, was immense; and it is for this reason that I shall give a somewhat detailed discussion of his theory—not so much to add one more to the series of philosophical systems with which this history is concerned, but rather to make possible an understanding of the age in which we ourselves are living. For one can understand an age and make one's own position towards it firm and clear only if one knows the minds chosen as leaders by that age. And Hegel is in the front rank of the spiritual leaders of the present age.

In framing his philosophy Hegel was very much influenced by Fichte and Schelling. He turns Schelling's absolute identity into an identity of thought and being. Thought and being are identical: for the being of things consists in the Absolute's thinking-of-itself. This thinking-of-itself by the Absolute is the origin of the world. Hegel therefore sees world-history as a dialectical process, and accordingly turns back from the principle of intellectual intuition to a purely conceptual treatment of philosophy. As to its object, philosophy is to be a science of the Absolute; as to its form, it is once again a knowledge from concepts alone, evolved out of pure logic. So just as Schelling's philosophy embodies, among the post-Kantian systems, the type of extreme Neo-Platonism, so Hegel's embodies the type of extreme Scholasticism.

1. Logicist metaphysics was refuted by Kant by his distinction between analytic and synthetic judgments and his discovery that mathematics, the very science whose possibility and fruitfulness had tempted men into the adventures of logicist metaphysics, consists in fact of synthetic judgments. It is therefore no accident that this discovery of Kant's, so decisive for the whole fate and future of philosophy, was rejected by Hegel.

The 'axioms of mathematics', he expressly declares, 'are simply propositions of logic', which in their turn 'are to be derived from universal and self-determining thought, which can in consequence be treated as their proof' (*Encyclopaedia of the Philosophical Sciences*, Vol. I, § 188, note).

Let us linger a little over this assertion to assess its meaning and importance. Let us consider the example which Hegel himself gives of such a proof, and on which he bases his own view as opposed to that of Kant. This example concerns the axiom, which Kant also discussed,* that a straight line is the shortest path connecting two points.

'That this definition', says Hegel characteristically, 'is analytic can easily be seen from the fact that a straight line reduces to simplicity of direction, and simplicity, considered with regard to quantity, determines it as least in quantity, i.e. in this case as the shortest path' (*Encyclopaedia*, Vol. II, § 256).

The obvious fallacy in this proof has been neatly described by the mathematician Schloemilch (in *Philosophical Aphorisms of a Mathematician*).

* 'That the straight line between two points is the shortest, is a synthetic proposition. For my concept of *straight* contains nothing of quantity, but only of quality. The concept of *the shortest* is wholly an addition . . .' *Critique of Pure Reason*, B. 16.

Firstly, Hegel has forgotten, in his proof, what he was really trying to prove. For the axiom asserted is not concerned, as the proof is, with the relation between straight and curved lines in general, but only with the relation between possible paths joining two points. No mention is made of this limitation in Hegel's proof. He would therefore prove too much; viz. the proposition, which in its generality is false, that any straight path is shorter than any curved one.

Further, the proof requires a major premiss, which in its turn is taken for granted as an axiom, that what is qualitatively simple must also be quantitatively simple. This proposition, however, is undoubtedly synthetic. It is also, and just as certainly, false; this too can be seen from the fact that it would prove too much. For if, as Schloemilch suggests, we replace the word 'line' by the word 'jacket', 'straight' by 'white', and 'curved' by 'motley-coloured', we obtain the surprising result that a white jacket is always shorter than a motley-coloured one.

This is how Hegel dismisses one of the fundamental discoveries of Kant's Critique of Reason.

2. He rejects, indeed, the whole programme of the Critique of Reason. He expressly refuses to adopt the critical method, using an argument which has some interest in this connection.

'One of the main points of the critical philosophy is this: that before setting out to know God, the being of things, and so forth, enquiry must first be made into the cognitive faculty itself, to see if it is capable of providing such knowledge.' 'But', replies Hegel, 'enquiry into knowledge can take place only by way of knowing; in the case of this so-called instrument, enquiring means just the same as knowing. But wanting to know before one knows is like the old schoolman's wise resolution not to venture into the water until he had learned to swim' (*Encyclopaedia* Vol. I, § 10).

This demonstration is remarkably similar to that discussed already, concerning the geometrical axiom. For here also the particular limitations in the assertion to be proved are ignored in the proof, making it easy to show the proof to be absurd. By ignoring that limitation Hegel fathers on the Critique of Reason the problem of whether any knowledge at all is possible, i.e. the programme of epistemology. Pointing out the obvious circularity of this programme, he thinks he has shown that the task undertaken in the Critique of Reason is a futile one, and that this justifies a return to dogmatic speculation.

For a proper understanding of the task of the Critique of Reason, however, everything depends on paying due attention to that limitation, as Hegel himself hints at the outset when he says 'that before setting out to know God, the being of things, and so forth, enquiry must first be made into the cognitive faculty itself, to see if it is capable of providing such knowledge'. The question here is not whether it is capable of knowledge at all, but whether it is capable of that particular knowledge, of which knowledge of God and of the being of things are here given as examples. Now the distinguishing feature of this knowledge, which causes the difficulties and gives rise to a previous and critical enquiry into the possibility of such knowledge, is that it is metaphysical; metaphysical knowledge, however, cannot in its abstract form be conceived with that certainty, self-evidence and unanimity which the concrete use of the understanding is capable of. Hence the proposal made in the critical method to start from this concrete use of the understanding, and then, with this as guide, to go on to its abstract use.

All the dogmatic systems in the history of philosophy have met with the same fate. This had made the inadequacy of Dogmatism so abundantly clear as to suggest that a change of method was required. Even if Kant had not set this change in motion, it would surely soon have forced itself on some independent mind. It was not just whim or fancy that gave Kant the idea of carrying the game of philosophical doubt to extremes and, instead of labouring on at the metaphysical problems bequeathed by his predecessors, of asking whether it was possible to know—this is what Hegel falsely imputes to him. No, it was the fact that, even in the most competent hands, the dogmatic approach had not been able to set metaphysics on the path of science. It was this that forced Kant to realize that this task could be discharged, if at all, only by abandoning the dogmatic method. It was this that moved Kant to set out on the Critique of Reason and to persevere in the endless labour it involved. Hegel cannot see the urgent need, flowing from the very nature of the case, for the critical procedure worked out by Kant; as becomes evident when he tries to make fun of it as an absurd proposal for knowing before one knows, and to dismiss it with slanders about 'shallowness', and 'insipidity', about 'conceit' and the 'emptiness of a merely critical labour' (*Encyclopaedia* Vol. I, 2nd ed., xxxviiiff.).

The Critique of Reason is not in fact touched by Hegel's polemic. Enquiry into the faculty of knowledge, to see whether it is capable of that metaphysical knowledge (e.g. of God and of the being of things), is a psychological undertaking, involving only the concrete use of the understanding. It is not in consequence affected by the difficulties which beset abstract metaphysical knowledge. That the faculty of knowledge is here itself made the object of knowledge does not make the task impossible; for the task did not have to be completed 'before one knows', but only before one sets up metaphysical abstractions. If Hegel wants to prove the Critique of Reason impossible from its requiring knowledge to be known, on the grounds that it is as absurd to want to know before knowing as to learn swimming before entering the water, then he could in the same way have shown language-teaching impossible, for it involves speaking the language, and it is as absurd to want to speak before speaking as to learn swimming before entering the water.

3. The Critique of Reason justifies the universal principles of metaphysics without offering proof for them or employing think-tactics of any other variety to conjure them up out of nothingness. It justifies them by actually pointing out in our reason the immediate knowledge on which they are based. The existence of such immediate knowledge was denied by Hegel simply on the grounds that we are not immediately conscious of it and that, even if we were, it would be wrong to reason from the subjective fact of consciousness to the universal validity of the knowledge we are conscious of (§71).* In this, however, Hegel is confusing immediate knowledge with immediate consciousness of that knowledge. The intention of the Critique of Reason—to point out such immediate knowledge, as a fact—is thus confounded with the epistemological enterprise of proving that knowledge to be valid.

Having denied the existence of this immediate knowledge, Hegel quite consistently goes on to deny the mediate and originally empty character of knowledge obtained by thought. He therefore proclaims the creative might and sovereign independence of pure thought (§75). This abrogates Kant's distinction between mere logic and metaphysics.

'Logic therefore coincides with metaphysics' (§ 24).

The knowledge generated by pure thought, being knowledge from concepts alone, is logic; but being knowledge of the reality of the Absolute, it is at the same time metaphysics.

'The most perfect form of knowledge', says Hegel, 'is that in the pure form of thought' (§ 24, note 3).

This annuls all the critical limitations on claims to metaphysical knowledge and, in general, undoes all the critical boundary-drawing laboriously undertaken in Kant's Critique of Reason. Not only does it destroy the distinction between the logical and the metaphysical

* The remaining references to Hegel are all to Vol. I of the *Encyclopaedia*.

forms of our knowledge, between the forms of judgment and the Categories, it also removes that between the forms of pure thought and the forms of pure intuition:

'Pure intuition is exactly the same thing as pure thought' (§ 63).
'Abstract thought and abstract intuition are one and the same' (§ 74).

The law of the immanence of human knowledge is thus abolished, together with the distinction between Ideas, as having significance only in the determination of boundaries, and Categories as having constitutive significance.

'So if', says Hegel, 'the science of logic deals with thought in its activity and productivity, then its general content is the super-sensible world' (§ 19, note 2). 'The formulations of logic are pure spirits' (§ 24, note 2).
'That the form of thought is absolute, that in thought truth appears just as it really is—this is what philosophy asserts' (§ 24, note 3).

4. The reasons given by Hegel why there could be absolute knowledge through thought alone derive from two different arguments. One is familiar to us from Fichte: that knowledge and its object are identical in self-knowledge. All separation and mediation between knowledge and object consequently disappear, and so, here, do all bounds to knowledge too. Fichte's *I* does indeed turn, in Hegel, into thought:

'We could say: *I* and thought are the same, or, more precisely, the *I* is thought as a thinker' (§ 24, note 1).

From this the unlimited or 'infinite' nature of thought follows for Hegel automatically:

'*I* or thought is therefore infinite, because in thought it is related to an object which it itself is.' 'Thought as such, in its purity, has therefore no limits in it' (§ 28, note).

The other argument is aimed directly at Kant's Transcendental Idealism. If, as Kant's theory asserts, our positive knowledge is limited to mere phenomena, then according to Hegel it must also be impossible for us to achieve knowledge of this limit to our knowledge. So if we are able to recognize a limit to our knowledge, that proves that we can overcome that limit, so that absolute knowledge is possible:

'Something is recognized as a limit or defect only when one has already gone beyond it.' 'Limit or defect in knowing is determined as a limit or defect only by comparison with a present idea of the universal, of a perfect whole' (*des Allgemeinen, eines Ganzen und Vollendeten*) (§ 60).

The truth is this: only by comparison with a present idea of a perfect whole is our reason able to recognize its own limits. But the mere idea of the perfect whole, as criterion for the limited character of our actual knowledge, is not the same as a positive knowledge of the perfect whole itself. The confusion between these two becomes quite obvious as Hegel continues with his fallacious inference:

'So it is plain stupidity not to see that to describe something as finite or limited proves the real presence of the Infinite and Unlimited. We can have knowledge of the limit only if the Unlimited is *on this side* in consciousness' (§ 60).

5. By discovering the Antinomies Kant showed that our knowledge is inevitably limited. They are in fact the direct consequences of the conflict between the basic forms of all the knowledge that is open to us and that Idea of the whole and perfect which alone enables us to conceive of reality-as-it-really-is. Kant had therefore good reason to argue back from the fact of the Antinomies to the falsity of the assumption that we can get to know things-as-they-really-are, and thus to his Transcendental Idealism. For it is only by taking away that false assumption that the Antinomies themselves can be removed. Now Hegel attributes a deeper meaning to these Antinomies of Kant's: in them, rightly—as he thinks—understood, he finds the real starting-point for his own metaphysical dialectic. But in this he is far from even understanding Kant's thought. He does not understand that Kant's distinguishing thing-as-it-really-is from phenomenon really does resolve the Antinomy and so removes the contradiction. He supposes that Kant used it to shift the contradiction he had come upon from things-as-they-really-are to phenomena.

'The solution is that the contradiction does not come in the object as such, as it really is, but belongs only to the knowing mind' (§ 48).

As one could expect, this solution then does not satisfy him. For once one allows contradictions to hold good at all, it is far from clear why one should not also allow them to hold for the being of the things themselves. So Hegel goes all the way:

'There is nothing whatsoever in which it is not possible, and indeed necessary, to point out a contradiction, i.e. opposite determinations' (§ 89).

While Kant gives up the claim to absolute knowledge for the sake of the Law of Contradiction, Hegel gives up the Law of Contradiction for the sake of the claim to absolute knowledge. Kant's discovery of the Antinomies merits high praise, in his view, for it was a step towards the discovery that reality itself is contradictory. Yet he thinks

Kant is to be blamed for the shallowness of his attempted solution, that is for his inability to recognize the reality of the contradictions: a weakness revealed, as Hegel says, in Kant's false 'fondness for worldly things':

'This broaches the suggestion', continues Hegel in the passage quoted about Kant's Antinomies, 'that it is the subject-matter itself, namely the Categories as such, that leads to the contradiction' (§ 48).

The true position is just the contrary of this: It is not the Categories as such that lead to the contradiction, but their twofold application to phenomena: the application on the one hand of Categories limited by the forms of Pure Intuition, and on the other hand of Categories thought in an absolute manner through Ideas. The Antinomies arise only from the incompatibility of these two modes of application, of the mathematical schematism and the Idea of the Absolute; that is why distinguishing these two really does yield a solution and does not merely shift the contradiction elsewhere. For anyone who has understood this solution any further mystery that might be sought in these Antinomies has disappeared. Hegel, however, tries by tracking down this mystery to unveil the true and underlying meaning, the approach to which had been barred by the narrowness of Kant's solution:

'The true and positive significance of the Antinomies,' he says, 'consists simply in this, that everything real contains within itself opposed determinations, so that to know and, indeed, to conceive an object just means to become conscious of it as a concrete unity of opposed determinations' (§ 48, note).

6. This already shows the peculiarity of the method by which Hegel wants to see pure thought developed as knowledge of the Absolute. He calls it the 'dialectical method', thus contrasting it with what he calls 'Dogmatism', into which (as he says in so many words) the old metaphysics was bound to relapse because it assumed 'that of two opposed assertions one must be true and the other false' (§ 32).

'Dogmatism', so he explains, 'consists in holding on to one-sided determinations of reason to the exclusion of their opposites. In general, it is this strict Either-Or.' 'Truth or Speculation, by contrast, is that which admits no such one-sided determination by itself, but includes within itself, united as a totality, those determinations which in separation Dogmatism regards as definite and true.' 'The struggle of Reason is to overcome the rigidity imposed by the Understanding' (§ 32, note). 'In the dialectical stage these finite determinations supersede themselves and pass into their opposites.' 'Dialectic is this immanent outgoing, in which the one-sided and limited nature of the determinations of the Understanding shows itself for what it really is, viz. their negation. All finitude is self-annulment. Dialectic therefore constitutes the life and soul of scientific progress and is the only principle by which the subject-matter of science acquires an immanent connection and necessity; for it is in dialectic that a genuine, as opposed to external, superiority to finitude is found.' Indeed, he goes even further, saying: 'Dialectic is the principle of all movement, of all life and activity in the actual world.' 'Everything around us can be taken as an example of dialectic' (§ 81, with note 1).

But as dialectic, unlike the formal logic of abstract and reflective understanding, does not rest with mere negation, but holds firm to what is negated, along with its negation, or, as Hegel puts it, 'includes it in itself as suspended (*aufgehoben*)', it leads to 'speculation' or 'Mysticism':

'that which includes in itself as suspended those oppositions with which the Understanding rests satisfied', and is thus 'the concrete unity of those determinations which hold true for the Understanding only when distinguished and contrasted' (§ 82, note).
'Speculative matter can therefore never be expressed in a one-sided proposition' (§ 82, note). 'The form of the proposition or, more precisely, of the judgment' is 'clumsy, for expressing speculative matter: the judgment is by its form one-sided, and so far false' (§ 31).

In this dialectical method of Hegel's we are unmistakably confronted with the method of contradictions, familiar from Fichte's time. In Fichte an assumption which leads to a contradiction thereby entails a new assumption, for removing that contradiction; and this new assumption in its turn occasions fresh contradictions, which have to be resolved in the same way, until the circle of contradictions is complete. The same thing happens in Hegel. In his case the dialectical process comes about by one concept veering round into its opposite, and these two opposed concepts then being united in a third, according to Fichte's scheme: Thesis, Antithesis, Synthesis or, as put in the monotonously repetitive triplet of Hegel's dialectical treadmill: In-itself, For-itself, and In-and-For-itself.

7. The concepts, however, which form the foundation of this mystical process are not supposed to be what the old logic, founded by Aristotle and still adhered to by Kant, understood by concepts (§9, §160). The concepts of Aristotelian logic are general characteristics which we derive from intuition by means of abstraction, in order to use them as predicates of judgments—characteristics which in consequence assert nothing on their own and have no independent

G

significance for knowledge, much less indicate any independent entity like the intuitively known particulars which we range under them in the form of an affirmative or negative judgment. The precise contrary of all this holds true for the concepts of Hegelian logic: they are not obtained by abstraction from intuition, but produced spontaneously by pure thought; they yield independent knowledge, not dependent on the form of the affirmative or negative judgment (§ 33); they lead an existence of their own, without dependence on any thinking individual; indeed they form the true being and creative basis of all particular existent things. The concept, says Hegel, is the

'endless creative form, including in itself and at the same time releasing from itself the fullness of all matter' (§ 160, note). 'The concept is what dwells within the things themselves, by which they are what they are' (§ 166, note). 'Really it is the concept that comes first, and things are what they are by the activity of the concept which dwells in them and reveals itself in them' (§ 163, note 2).

It is no coincidence that Hegel calls his concepts 'Ideas'—in a distinctive sense. The philosopher arrives at these Ideas when he rises above the ordinary mode of sensible representation and so above the finite concepts of the ordinary abstractive understanding. He thus acquires the notion of the Concrete-Universal, which unlike the Abstract-Universal of finite concepts not only covers individual actuality, but includes it in itself (§ 164). This Concrete-Universal is therefore not the predicate, under which the particular actual things given in intuition are ranked in the judgment, but is itself the truly actual and real.

'Although it also is abstract, yet it is concrete, and is indeed the absolutely concrete, the subject as such' (§ 164).

In the totality of this Concrete-Universal the oppositions of actuality are to be reconciled, the contradictions which Hegel finds in the variety of things are to be annulled.

Hegel's logic, which sets forth this dialectical development of the concept, is just Fichte's Scientific Theory, with all the reminiscences of Kant removed and worked up into the most extreme form of Scholastic Realism. To put it another way, it is the consistent execution—if one can speak of consistency in this connection—of the non-Aristotelian logic postulated by Fichte, a logic revolving around the problem which Fichte put like this:

'How can A and non-A, being and non-being, reality and negation be thought together, without destroying and cancelling one another?' (Fichte, *Foundation of the whole Scientific Theory*, § 3, B 5).

8. We shall understand the secret of Hegel's dialectical conjuring-trick better if we examine more closely the way in which he comes to set himself this task. Nor is it such a very mysterious matter to get at this secret, as Hegel himself, in the introductory section of his *Encyclopaedia*, gives his own simple-hearted account of how it came about, this result which his admirers have always regarded, and still do regard, as the really unique creation of his speculative genius. If we will only take the trouble to do the reading first and the admiring afterwards, we shall find that this speculative profundity has quite another origin than the general admiration would allow one to sus-pect—admiration, that is, which comes before the reading, not after-wards.

We may recall that logic, being objective, is indeed to deal with thought (§ 19), and moreover with that very thought which itself is Being. Its thoughts are 'objective thoughts', viz. 'the essence of things' (§ 24). How is one to interpret this? The matter is simple enough. 'That understanding or reason is in the world' will not, of course, be disputed. This, however, 'says the same as the expression "objective thoughts"'.

The only 'inconvenience in this expression is that "thought" is commonly used only as belonging to mind or consciousness, and "objective" for its opposite'. 'If one says that thoughts, as objective thoughts, constitute the inner nature of the world, this could seem to be the ascribing of conscious-ness to natural things' (§ 24, and note 1).

It could indeed seem so, as long as one abides by the sense which the words have in common usage. But what does that matter to the philosopher? When a philosopher speaks of 'thoughts', he does not mean the thoughts which a thinking mind thinks and finds that it is conscious of, he means 'thought-determinations' (*Denkbestimmungen*). But what are 'thought-determinations'? We could comprehend this easily enough if it were meant as an objective designation of that which is thought, as opposed to the thinking of it—as, say, the truth thought of; for Hegel himself says a little later:

'The expression "objective thoughts" signifies Truth, which must be not merely the aim, but the absolute object of philosophy' (§ 25).

As I said, we could understand this explanation well enough; but it occurs on a different page. In the present passage, however, we are told something else:

'Logic must be sought for as a system of thought-determinations in which the opposition between subjective and objective (in its usual meaning) disappears' (§ 24, note 1).

So he is not referring subjectively to the thinking, nor objectively to that which is thought. Then what is he referring to? Well, as he said, to thought which constitutes the substance of things, 'the substance of external things' just as much as 'the universal substance of mind'. That must make it clear at last:

'If thought is taken as the true universal of everything natural and of everything spiritual, it extends beyond all this and is the basis for everything.' 'Logical thoughts . . . are the self-existent ground of everything' (§ 24, notes 1 and 2).

Yes, indeed! Who will deny that if by 'thinking' we mean 'the basis of everything', then thinking is the basis of everything.

The dialectical transition from being to thought, in the ordinary sense of this word—or, in Hegel's language, from objective to subjective thought, can only be made by playing on the double sense of the word 'thought'. If this ambiguity is avoided that transition also breaks down. Hegel makes this dialectical transition from objective to subjective thought (in ordinary language, from being to thought) by a move from being-in-itself to being-for-itself:

'Man is a thinker, and is universal, but he is a thinker only so far as the universal exists for him. The animal also is, in itself, universal, but the universal as such does not exist for it.' 'Nature itself does not bring the νοῦς* to consciousness, man is the first so to duplicate himself as to be the universal for the universal. This happens when man knows himself as "I".' ' "I" is pure being-for-itself.' 'We could say that "I" and thought are the same, or more precisely: "I" is thought, thinking. What I have in my consciousness, exists for me.' 'The animal cannot say "I", but only man, because he is thought' (§ 24, note 1).

Now the statement that someone is or is not conscious of something could also be expressed by saying that it is or is not present 'for' him. But one requires independent knowledge of what it means to be 'conscious' of something in order to understand the word 'for' in the sense intended here. If we did not know from our inner experience what it is to be conscious or to think, we could not fathom it out of 'being-for-itself'. In the dialectical world of the Concrete-Universal man may very well be 'the universal for the universal', but this item of wisdom is not of the slightest help to us in finding out that he is a conscious and thinking being, in the sense which that expression bears elsewhere—the only sense in which its use is of any interest to us. That man in this sense is the being-for-itself of the universal, Hegel has not proved. For even if one wanted to define the concept of

* Spirit, mind.

man by means of this concept, without worrying where one had got it from, and it is of course *a priori* open to one to define it in this way, still this would only postpone the question how we are to decide whether such men exist and whether the beings which are on other occasions known to us by this name are 'men' in the sense so defined. On this point the dialectical explanation that man is the universal for the universal leaves us completely in the lurch; to settle it we must still, as before, refer to experience.

In this case, then, it is the misuse of arbitrary verbal definitions that hides the shifts of meaning, thus enabling the play on 'in-itself' and 'for-itself' to produce results.

9. We have not yet, however, adequately indicated the real source of the speculative discoveries which this metaphysical logic confers on us. For this purpose we must discuss in greater detail Hegel's theory of the concept.

Let us begin by considering the statement 'Man is universal. The animal also is, in itself, universal'. Let us enquire how Hegel came to this discovery. He tells us himself, in these words:

'A better example is the fact that when we speak of a particular animal, we say it is animal (*wir sagan: es sei Tier*). The animal as such cannot be pointed out; all one can ever point out is some particular animal. The animal as such does not exist, but is the universal nature of individual animals, and each existent animal is something much more concrete and definite, a particular. It does however, belong to a particular animal to be 'animal', the class or universal, and this constitutes its particular essence. If we abstract from "dog" the being an animal, no-one could say what it would be. Things do in general have an abiding inner nature, and an external presence. They live and die, they arise and pass away; their essential nature, their universality is the class, which is not to be thought of merely as a common characteristic' (§ 24, note 1).

In this passage Hegel really does unveil the secret. Now we can see where he gets that profundity from which all his speculative wisdom is fashioned. He gets it from plain ignorance of the basic grammar of his mother tongue. If we are speaking of a particular animal, and if we have learnt how to speak at all, we do not as Hegel asserts say 'it is animal' (*es sei Tier*). Instead we say, it is an animal (*es sei ein Tier*). The animal which we have before us is in fact a particular animal, not animal (*Tier*), i.e. the concept *animal*. This meaning which in the grammar of our language belongs to the article, viz. the referring of the concept to objects which come under it but are not identical with it—this meaning of the article is unknown to Hegel. In his logic, in consequence, the grammatical form of a simple proposition does not signify a judgment, i.e. the subsuming of objects under concepts, or of the subject under the predicate, but the equating of the two, so that the distinction between subject and predicate, or concept and object, is completely lost—unless indeed the functions of both are just exchanged.

Hegel does in fact retain between the universal concept and the individual things a quantitative distinction which is merely gradual.

'Each existent animal', he says, 'is something much more concrete and definite' than the 'animal as such' or 'the universal nature of individual animals' (§ 24, note 1).

This, however, by no means fits the distinction between the animal itself and the concept *animal*, but only that between specific concepts more particularly defined, as against the general concept *animal*. But however far we may go in adding further particular specific differences, we shall never arrive at the individuality and actuality of a particular animal, but shall always remain in the realm of mere concepts. No process of making the concept more concrete can lead us from there to the individual itself; the one and only way to that is by the immediate knowledge which we gain in perception. And this is precisely what the article refers to, when put in front of the concept-expression. We can thus see how Hegel's complete confusion in grammar prevented him from grasping how concepts are related to perception and why perception is an indispensable prerequisite to knowledge.

10. The immediate result of this confusion was that Hegel got the relationship of individual beings to the class-concept mixed up with the relationship of a concept to a defining property contained in that concept. 'If we abstract from "dog" the being an animal, one could not say what it would be.' This is clearly meant to say more than just that the concept *animal* is presupposed in the concept *dog*, so that the concept *animal* could not be removed without that of *dog* disappearing too, or in brief, that the concept *animal* is one of the defining properties of the concept *dog*. For it is not Hegel's intention at this point simply to discuss the meaning of the word 'dog', but that which, as he stresses, constitutes the 'essential nature' of the particular animal, its 'abiding, inner nature', as opposed to its 'external presence', to that in it which comes to be and passes away. According to Hegel this essential nature of the particular animal is the class 'animal', which can therefore be known, in its essential nature, from its concept; for the concept determines what 'the animal as such' is.

But the fact is that if we concentrate on some particular animal, there is nothing special to give precedence to the concept *animal* in relation to it, rather than to any of the other concepts which also belong to it; nothing requiring us to seek the 'nature' or 'essential character' of the individual before us in the concept *animal* and not, say, in the concepts *carnivore* or *living creature* or *thing having non-retractible claws*.

When Hegel contrasts the concept as abiding and universal, or as the 'nature' of things, with their coming-to-be and passing-away, it becomes clear that he is confusing a concept with a law. The nature of the thing is in fact just the sum total of the universal laws applying to the existence of that thing and enabling us to explain the phenomena connected with it. It is in laws of nature, not in concepts, that the reality of the universal is really to be found. Laws, unlike concepts, do not occur in the predicate of a judgment; that is, they cannot be attributed categorically as properties to the objects which come under them, but determine those objects only by the form of a judgment which presupposes some other predications as already made, i.e. through a judgment made up of simple predications (a hypothetical or a divisive judgment). To put it another way, they do not link a concept to an object, but link together two such object-concept linkages. Thus it belongs to the nature of quicksilver, for instance, that it expands when heated. But if we say 'Heat expands the quicksilver', the heat is not an object to which the expanding of quicksilver is attached as a general property. No, this is really a hypothetical judgment and would be more precisely expressed as one, by saying 'If quicksilver is heated, it expands'. To establish this law we must combine two categorical judgments, which can be known, whether separately or together, only by perceptual observation: it would therefore be futile to try to derive this knowledge from the concept *quicksilver*.

Hegel's logic knows nothing of all this. Essence, as that which is important or noteworthy for some purpose, is there substituted at random for 'being' in the sense of substance, for the class-concept, and for the 'nature' of an object, in the sense of a law. If scientific workers had been able to make progress even before the discovery of the Concrete-Universal, they owed this, according to Hegel, to the 'instinct of reason which suggests that this or that empirical determination is based on the inner nature or the class of an object, and encourages further reasoning therefrom' (§ 190, note).

Hegel is quite seriously suggesting that the nature of things is their class, which can therefore be known from the concept, and so by means of thought alone! (§ 21).

11. Although it is a serious matter, I shall not at this point go into the shameful nonsense of Hegel's eccentricities in the field of natural philosophy. It is to be hoped that the deplorable collapse which attended the exaggerated claims made in his speculation in this field, right from the beginning, will never be forgotten. Anyone who would like to inform himself on this matter may refer to the excellent book by Schleiden, the botanist: *Schelling's and Hegel's Relation to Natural Science* (Leipzig, 1844). I shall concentrate on the general dialectical basis of Hegel's theory, for here even after the obvious nonsense and mere puns have been removed there is plenty left that is false and misleading but not transparently so. Its corrupting and delusive appearance is always liable to tempt people astray, even if Hegel's influence in natural philosophy was destroyed long ago.

12. As we saw, Hegel confuses the nature of things with our concept of them. This leads him to assert the reality of general concepts, or classes, and to hypostatize these as entities existing in their own right. Here we meet once more the scholastic distinction between essence and existence, and the idea that philosophy should use the concepts of things to work out what their nature is. 'The deeper (philosophical) significance of truth', he says, 'is not that our representation agrees with the object, but that the objects agree with their concept' (§ 24, note 2).

Let me cite a few more passages:

'Truth is reality agreeing with the concept—not external things agreeing with my representations; these are just correct ideas which I have of it. The Idea is not concerned with this, nor with representations, nor with external objects. Everything actual . . . owes its truth entirely to the Idea. Individual existence is one aspect of the Idea, for which further actualities are needed, which also seem to have an existence all their own; and the concept is realized only in their joint existence and relationship. The individual as such does not agree with its concept; for the limited character of its existence ensures its finitude and its fall' (§ 213; cf. § 24, note 2).

'The Absolute is the One and universal Idea which . . . particularizes itself into the system of particular Ideas.' And so 'to start with the Idea is only the One universal substance, but its developed and proper actuality is to exist as subject, and so as mind' (§ 213).

'It is through the concept alone that things come to exist in the world' (§ 213, note).

'The general is, in fact, the ground and basis, root and substance of the individual' (§ 175, note).

'God alone is the true agreement of concept and reality; all finite things involve some untruth, they have a concept and an existence which are incommensurable. For this reason they inevitably go to ruin, that the incommensurability of their concept and their existence may be evident. The animal, as an individual, has its concept in the species; and its death sets the species free from individuality' (§ 24 note 2).

'What is living comes to death, for its very being is a contradiction; in itself it is the general, the class, yet its immediate existence is as an individual. In death the class shows its power over the immediate individual' (§ 221, note).

I have quoted these passages at length, as they show clearly the metaphysical consequences of the logical fallacy which I mentioned earlier. As I remarked then, the threat to logic involved in ignorance of the form of judgment is not just that the distinction between objects and concepts may be lost, but that these may even exchange roles: a swop which brings us to the final secret, the metaphysical summit of Logical Mysticism. Without this secret we would merely be deprived of the means of distinguishing objects from concepts which was provided in Aristotelian logic by the designation of the subject of a judgment: but with it we obtain something the Aristotelian logic could never provide, a way of transforming concepts into objects or of evaporating objects into concepts, any time we like, thus outbidding empirical knowledge by a speculative knowledge of the Absolute, and dissolving the actual facts of experience into mere appearance.

Our critique will therefore be complete only when we have laid bare the dialectical foundations of this Logical Mysticism.

13. To get this matter really clear, let us return to the previous example: 'It belongs to the individual animal *to be animal* (the class, i.e. universal); that is what gives it its own peculiar nature' (§ 24, note 1). The swop is already evident in this quotation.

The generality of the concept *animal*, which is used as predicate of the judgment, 'belongs', says Hegel, 'to the particular animal'; that is, he ascribes it to the subject of the judgment. This is of course quite logical if the fact that the subject comes under the concept of the predicate is once equated, as Hegel equates it, with its being the predicate. As he says explicitly, 'The animal is in its essence universal'.

The concept *animal* as a general object thus comes to take the place of the subject, which was previously occupied by the individual object falling under it, the particular animal. The concept *animal* is indeed the 'peculiar nature', the genuinely existent aspect of the individual animal. The animal itself is then reduced to a mere manifestation or phenomenal form of the concept.

The concept is

'the altogether concrete, the subject as such. The Absolute-Concrete is Mind—the concept, so far as it exists as concept. Every other concrete thing, however rich, is not so heart-and-soul identical with itself, and so is not in itself so concrete. And what people commonly regard as concrete a manifold extrinsically conglomerate—is the least concrete of them all' (§ 164).

This brings us to Hegel's theory of judgment, which is the real key to his whole dialectic.

According to Hegel the essential nature of every judgment consists in this, that 'what the subject is, is stated only in the predicate' (§ 31).

'In itself the subject is a mere representation, an empty name; only in the predicate does it acquire its specific character and content . . . It is the predicate which first says what the subject is' (§ 169).

This account of the matter is clearly ambiguous. It is true that the quality of the subject is stated only in the predicate. But it by no means follows that the subject is 'in itself an empty name.' Of course, if we were seriously trying to spin knowledge out of mere ideas we should be without objects for the subject of our judgment to name; for such objects can be got only from perception. But Hegel draws the wrong conclusion from this when he claims that the subject acquires definiteness only in the predicate of the judgment. The right conclusion is that on those conditions one could never get around to judging, being for ever stuck with the predicate on its own, and quite unable to relate it to any object. That is quite apart from the question of how we could have ever got the predicate.

On Hegel's view the subject is determined solely by the predicate not only in respect of the quality which the judgment is determining, but even as plain subject. As he says:

'some such statement is expressed in every judgment: that the individual is the universal, or more precisely, the subject is the predicate (e.g. God is absolute Mind). Admittedly Individuality and Universality, Subject and Predicate are distinct classifications, but the general fact still remains, that every judgment asserts their identity' (§ 166).

'The copula "is" derives from the nature of the concept, which is, to be identical with itself even in parting with its own (*in seiner Entäusserung*)' (§ 166).

'The copula states the identity of subject and predicate' (§ 171).

Hegel thus finds in the 'is', the copula, an expression of identity. If you start out with this idea, his further assertions follow naturally, and so does his entire metaphysic of Logical Mysticism.

The truth is that the predicate is a general concept; so if subject and predicate are identical, this general concept is itself the subject, and the subject 'in itself', i.e. apart from that concept, is 'an empty name'. Individual objects given in perception do not qualify for a place as subject of a judgment; the only real thing about them is the general concept, their class. In and by themselves they are just illusory appearance. The concept (e.g. *animal*) has, however, this peculiar property: it manifests itself in separate objects (e.g. dogs), thus 'emanating' some such illusory appearance.

This is the relationship expressed in the judgment: or rather, which is itself the judgment. So it is quite consistent of Hegel to conclude:

'All things are a judgment, i.e. they are individuals which essentially are an universality or inner nature, an Universal, which is individualized; in their case universality and individuality, though distinct, are at the same time identical' (§ 167).

For it is not we who in a judgment subsume an object as subject to a predicate, but—

'the predicate is the Universal, obtaining of its own whether or not this subject exists . . . and subsumes it under itself' (§ 170).

Consequently what in the traditional logic stood as predicate now becomes the proper object of knowledge, 'Substance, or the nature of the subject, the concrete Universal, the class' (§ 177). By contrast, what had previously appeared as the object to be known now retreats to the position previously occupied by the predicate; for we know it now 'in the particularity provided by its concept', as a 'specialization of the concept', 'due to the concept's own activity' (§ 166, note). We thus get an even more definite formulation:

'All things are a categorical judgment, that is, they have a substantial nature, giving them a firm and unchangeable basis. Only when we look at things from the point of view of their class, and treat them as determined by this necessarily, only then does the judgment begin to be genuine' (§ 177, note).

Hegel's logic thus expressly teaches 'the exchange of meaning between the two elements in the judgment' (§ 169, note).

14. The metaphysical fertility of this logical juggling which, as we saw, depends in its turn on ignorance of the basic grammar of the language, will now be evident. Mystical logic has here a convenience which Aristotelian logic always lacked, an aid to dreaming up the actuality of the Absolute, and for dissipating the facts of experience into mere appearance.

This makes it perfectly clear why, as Hegel says,

'the form of the statement or more precisely of the judgment is a clumsy one for expressing what is concrete or speculative: its form makes the judgment one-sided and, to that extent, false' (§ 31).

The fact is that its form allows every actual judgment only to be either affirmative or negative; the affirmative form excludes the negative, and conversely. Once the form of judgment is removed, however, the limitation to these two alternatives also disappears. Questions like: should a predicate be attributed to an object (in the sense of the Aristotelian logic) or not? have no meaning at all in this (new) logic. Here the copula does not signify the subsumption of a subject under a predicate, but rather that the two are identical, that is, that they coincide. No genuine judgments, in consequence, can occur here, with the result that the Law of Contradiction also is without application.

Consider once again the dog, which Hegel says 'is animal'. This assertion, which equates dog with animal, clearly does not exclude the other which states them to be distinct. Otherwise one would be driven to say that there could not be any other animals besides the dog, and further that the dog could not be anything beyond just being animal—so that the concept *animal* would exhaust the dog, even though the dog is also a carnivore, a living being, and many other things. Hegel explains this quite clearly in another instance:

'If we say: this rose is red, the copula "is" implies that subject and predicate coincide with each other. But the rose as a concrete thing is not just red, but also has a scent and a certain shape and various other determinations not included in the predicate "red". Moreover this predicate, being an abstract universal, does not belong only to this subject. There are other flowers too, as well as objects of a quite different sort, which are equally red' (§ 172, note).

The enigma of the dialectical method is here dissolved, without remainder. What at first seemed paradoxical, nay quite ridiculous, is now seen to make quite good sense, indeed to be self-evident. For it comes down to this: 'There is nothing whatsoever which' on this method 'contains no contradiction, i.e. in which it is not both possible and necessary to discern opposite determinations' (§ 89).

Now if this is self-evident, it is very far from self-evident how the application of such a method is going to lead to anything informative about how things actually are.

To conclude our consideration of this question, let us consider the use to which the dialectical method is put, in particular when Hegel starts on the systematic construction of his logic; an application which forms the centre-piece of this metaphysical logic and provides the foundation for absolute knowledge itself.

The foundation is to be found in the statement: God is Being (§ 86).

An axiom by no means strange or arbitrary to the dialectician, but virtually self-evident!

The first and highest concept, from which the dialectical development derives, is that of Being, for it is the most general concept under which everything existent falls. So all things are at one with regard to this concept, if, that is, they *are* at all. So if the essence of things lies in concepts, and if the concept of Being is the highest concept, and if the highest Being is God, then God is Being.

As we also know, pure Being is on Hegel's view pure Mind: Mind as it is in itself, as distinct from individual finite minds. This is an abstraction, like that by which Fichte reached his absolute *I*. For Fichte, this *I* was quite indeterminate, i.e. could not be determined by any predicate (Fichte *Foundation of the whole Scientific Theory*, § 3, C. 1). For Hegel, likewise, Being is no other than this Indeterminate: the concept-as-it-is-in-itself, before it has any particular content (§ 84).

This explains the next step in the dialectical development. Being, being quite indeterminate, is the same as Nothing. Hence the statements: God is Nothing (§ 87) and, Being and Nothing are the same thing (§ 88).

Being, however, is not *mere* Nothing; it is Nothing only to the extent that it is not any definite existent. So alongside the identity of Being and Nothing we must set the difference between them (§ 88); so we cannot say simply that Being and Nothing are one and the same, but only that they need uniting in a new concept.

This is the concept 'Becoming'. Becoming is just one Being stopping and another one starting. Here Being and non-Being coincide.

This first instance, of Being and Nothing, shows clearly what bungling rubbish the so-called dialectical method is. When Hegel says 'Being is Nothing' he is right to this extent that the general concept of Being is not any determinate individual existent. By attributing 'being' to an object I do not determine it qualitatively at all; the predication of 'being' leaves it entirely undetermined in respect of its qualities. For Being is not any particular property of an object. In this sense one can say that Being is Nothing. But that does not lead us to the contradiction proclaimed by Hegel and soluble only by the intervention of a new concept. The apparent contradiction here is due to Hegel's failure to distinguish between a comparison-formula and a judgment. If we mistake the statement 'Being is Nothing' for a judgment, then we really shall arrive at a contradiction; for if we say of the objects falling under the concept 'Being' that they 'are Nothing'—if we say of something existent that it does not exist— then we do obtain a self-contradictory judgment. The right conclusion is that the concept 'Being' provides no qualitative determination. Hegel smuggles in in place of this the statement 'What is, isn't'; which is a false and self-contradictory thing to say.

Hegel's fallacy could also be explained by saying that he confuses two different concepts of Nothing. In one of these the word expresses a qualitative negation; in the other, a modal negation. Denying a particular quality is qualitative negation; but modal negation is denying the existence of the object. Hegel confuses the two by taking his very first statement 'Being is Nothing' as asserting a contradiction. (His extreme fondness for the Ontological Argument for the existence of God (§§ 51, 193) is evidence of his inability to understand the distinction between qualitative and modal affirmation.) If I ascribe Being to an object, I do not thereby determine it qualitatively in any way at all, but I do modally affirm its existence, so I do contradict myself if at the same time I deny its existence.

16. As this instance shows, Hegel did not know the difference between the philosophical concepts he introduced, such as those of *Being*, *Nothing*, and *Becoming*, and non-philosophical concepts. He had not understood Kant's transcendental guideline. In consequence he was without an epistemological principle by which to construct a proper system of philosophical concepts. For the concept *Becoming* is not a philosophical category at all, but a pure-intuitive schema. Becoming is different states succeeding one another, one phenomenon replacing another with the lapse of time. In other words, it concerns the concept of *change*, which is a pure-intuitive schema (cp. Translator's Note), and not a metaphysical concept at all, as Hegel wants it to be.

This piece of verbal smuggling, again, is due simply to the abuse of an arbitrary verbal definition. Clearly there is nothing to stop us defining Becoming as the unity of Being and Nothing (§ 88). But we could not give any positive meaning to the expression 'unity of Being and Nothing', did we not tacitly introduce with it the concept which in ordinary usage is associated with the term 'Becoming', which is familiar to us because of intuition; for the concepts *Being* and *Nothing* on their own contain nothing from which we could even infer the possibility of uniting them, much less that uniting them results in what is known to us from intuition as Becoming. Not an iota of information about this sort of Becoming is provided by the account of it as the unity of Being and Nothing. But this is precisely what Hegel's account does claim, since he makes no bones about drawing the most far-reaching conclusions from it: for example,

'But the concept of Presence (*Dasein*) actually involves change, and change is just the manifestation of what Presence in itself really is. What is living dies, and for this very reason that as living it bears death in embryo within itself' (§ 92, note).

On this account, which is unambiguous, the concept *change* should really be purely logical in derivation, for it follows simply from the concept *Presence*. But how do we acquire this concept *Presence*? Well, on Hegel's account 'Presence' is 'the Being which is identical with Negation' (§ 89), which is precisely how Becoming had just previously been defined; a definition which, apart from its arbitrary character, contributes nothing towards the development of a concept of *change*.

'Presence' is also said to 'result' from Becoming (§ 89). But even if one could extract the concept *change* from the concept *result*, itself not further expounded and so still quite empty of content, even then the question would arise, as Hegel himself remarks, 'of how Becoming comes to have a result'. To this question he returns a profound answer—though without revealing whence the inspiration came—that Becoming is 'the ultimate in restlessness, though unable to continue in this abstract restlessness'.

But if we *did* know that Becoming has results—which we christened 'Presence'—we should in the last analysis be able to conduct a purely logical enquiry into the nature of its result. And we are, in fact, on the brink of a new discovery:

'Presence is Being with some definiteness, which being immediate or existent definiteness, is Quality' (§ 90).

Here, then, is yet another piece of information: Becoming has a result, and that result is Quality. This is how the 'dialectical method' conjures concepts up for us out of the abyss of nothingness: a variety of nothingness, admittedly, which in this case is not pure and simple nothingness, but only the absolutely Indeterminate. So it really isn't nothingness at all, since it presupposes the concept of *quality*, for example, which was supposed to be derived from it. For if the concept of *definiteness* is supposed to arrive along with Quality, and if nothingness, as the absolutely undetermined or Indeterminate, is defined by negating definiteness of every sort, then the concept *nothingness* in its turn must really presuppose the concept *quality*.

17. The dialectical development of concepts continues always in this strain. In each case we are fobbed off with empty verbal definitions and formulae of comparison with no opportunity to apply them to real experience. Here are two more examples:

Consider the explanation on which depends the transition from idea to nature (and so that from logic to 'natural philosophy'): 'Nature is the Idea, in its other-being'. Now apart from the fact that by nature Hegel here means merely material nature, and that he takes Idea as a synonym for Mind, thus like Fichte confusing the contrast material/spiritual with that between nature and freedom, quite apart from this all we have here is an empty formula of comparison. The distinction between nature and spirit is asserted and at the same time their oneness, but without saying in what respect they are similar, or in what they differ. The result is that this definition never touches, much less explains, that which is known to us otherwise as nature.

Or take that notorious statement: 'What is rational, is real, and what is real is rational.'

Absolute knowledge, if postulated, would imply that no distinction could be made between the rational and the actual, between what ought to be and what is. An absolute knowledge would involve an immediate grasp of the actual as necessary, leaving no scope for things to be otherwise than they are or, consequently, for things which ought to be otherwise. Here a contrast of Ought with Is would have no meaning. There could be no gulf between the necessity of existence and the necessity of value; being would be the same thing as being worth while. In this sense, Hegel's famous statement is genuinely significant and has a rightful place in the system of absolute knowledge.

But what about *our* knowledge? If we go by the testimony of experience, which is not, of course, very philosophical, we are bound to realize that the rational is very often not actual, and that lots of things are actual which we cannot really recognize as rational. That is why we set ourselves to alter actuality, in its irrational aspects, so as to make it rational; a task which on Hegel's account would be meaningless. That statement of his expresses a boundless optimism, for which whatever seems bad is really meaningful and right, and we have no right to be dissatisfied with things as they actually are and to go round trying to improve on them. We should simply try to understand their rationality and treat them with due respect. And if we take Hegel's statement in its context, which is that of the preface to the *Basic Outlines of a Philosophy of Rights*, it must bear this quietistic sense. This comes out anyway in the same passage, where Hegel denounces his colleague Fries for his allegedly subversive speech at the Students' Union Festival on the Wartburg.

In spite of this legal and political quietism Hegel's political and legal philosophy still has a high reputation. His political philosophy, in particular, is praised for having introduced the concept of organism. This does suggest an analogy which can be more or less cleverly applied in various aspects, and which certain schools of economic, sociological and legal theory have been particularly keen to emphasize. But one would have to be quite besotted with Logical Mysticism to imagine that any fresh scientific insight can be obtained in this way. For it is merely an analogy and so offers no explanation of the facts, as is quite evident from the fact that an organism is itself something far from self-explanatory; so how is the analogy with it to cast light on the nature of the State? In any case this 'discovery' does not in my view derive from Hegel, but is considerably older. If my information is correct, this example comes down from good old Menenius Agrippa of ancient Rome, who—so the story goes—used this comparison to persuade the Plebs, who had revolted and decamped onto Mons Sacer, to return to Rome, urging them as members of a social organism not to go on depriving its stomach of the necessary nourishment. There may be a similar intention in Hegel's comparison. Certainly his political philosophy does in general encourage the pious preservation of what has happened, and it almost always ends by glorifying naked power-politics; a deification of power whose tragic consequences are today plain for all to see.

In sum: it is no good trying to patch up this philosophy. We must throw the whole thing out. It is of no benefit to science.

Hegel's philosophy was itself to suffer the dialectical fate of being turned upside down. His deification of Spirit and his theory that world history is the evolution of the world-spirit were immediately transformed into their opposites, being replaced by an extreme Materialism. Indeed it was Hegel's own pupils who brought this about. Not that the transition from Hegelianism to Materialism was very difficult to arrange. All it needed was that the Hegelian conceptual world be seen for what it was, a world of mere concepts. That was enough; the reality of this world was then denied, thus leading to a pure Materialism. This step was taken by the so-called left-wing Hegelians, Feuerbach, Stirner and Strauss, to name but a few, and also by Marx and Engels. Once conceptual Realism is dropped, Hegelian philosophy is left with nothing but material existence, as concepts and minds are the same thing for him. Nor need one abandon

H

the claim to absolute knowledge; one can still assert the identity of thought and being, thus reaching the statement that only matter is real. This only shows how basically irreligious and purely materialist Hegel's system really is, the contrary appearance being a façade due only to puns. According to Hegel, God is just the most general and so the emptiest concept, which is why he expressly equates him with Nothing (God is Nothingness); and God is realized only in the consciousness of humanity. From which the only logical conclusion is, that God exists only as an idea in the minds of men and is a complete illusion.

Feuerbach was the first to draw this frank conclusion, with the corresponding complete reversal in his view of history. Hegel saw history as the world-spirit gradually achieving consciousness and irresistibly working out its plans, human thought and decision being a merely phenomenal aspect of this dialectical process of the coming-to-consciousness of the world-spirit; so that on Hegel's view of history this impersonal spirit is the only real agent in history, and men are under an illusion if they think of themselves as effective agents in history. Now if you delete this impersonal world-spirit, as an empty concept, all that is left is the external material events. Everything else falls away as illusion, an illusion on which men stay their hopes in vain.

EXCURSUS ON THE MATERIALIST CONCEPTION OF HISTORY

What is usually called the Materialist Conception of History, or Historical Materialism, is a refinement on Hegel's theory, worked out by Marx and Engels. On this view—if one is to enshrine this much disputed theory in a brief formula—the only decisive influence on the course of history is that of the existing economic relationships: more precisely, of the relationships of production. Everything else— Rights, Constitution, Art, Science, Religion, Morality—these are mere accompanying phenomena, mere forms of expression, reflections in men's minds of the evolution of those economic relationships. They all belong to what Marx and Engels call the superstructure, as opposed to the basic realities, the relationships of production.

The importance and fertility of this new conception of history is due to its contrast to the so-called idealistic conception which had hitherto been dominant. By an idealistic conception of history I mean one in which the ideas of men are thought to have a decisive influence on the course of events, quite apart from the material conditions and in particular the economic relationships of the time. On this view—

to put a finer point on it—human ideals realize themselves in history. It is precisely this 'idealist' approach to history that we find in Hegel: on this view 'ideas are not powerless' as he puts it; 'reason rules the world', achieving its ends in the march of events, without regard for the decisions or activities of men. This approach was certainly not adequate for a sound, empirical and scientific treatment of history. For history too needed a purely scientific and empirical method. Only then could events be studied quite realistically, without dragging in mysterious powers whose activities are not subject to observational control. Only then could the changes which occur in history be explained by the interplay of forces actually present within history and empirically detectable—by power-relationships in society. Only then would the way be open to genuinely impartial historical research. Marx and Engels were the pioneers here. It was indeed a considerable achievement on their part to have directed attention to economic relationships, previously neglected, and to the role these play in historical development. To put it more precisely: what the Material-ist Conception of History did achieve was to point out, emphatically, successfully and for the first time, the decisive influence on the course of events of class conflicts in society, and their influence also on the history of ideas, on the development of the ideological superstruc-ture. As Marx and Engels put it in fragmentary form in one of their manuscripts:

'The class which controls the means of material production also controls the means of spiritual production, and those who lack the latter are usually subject to that class even in the realm of ideas. The ruling ideas in a given state of society depend on the interests of the ruling class in that society, which in virtue of its control over the means of production also controls thoughts, and can decide what is to be thought in the rest of the society just as it can decide what the rest of society is to eat.'

There is an important discovery here, but not one that we can discuss in detail, as we are not concerned with history but with philosophy. What is the philosophical significance of Marx' and Engels' theory? One cannot overlook the one-sidedness and over-emphasis which enabled this view of history to appear as a sort of philosophical system. But the confusion and futility of the debate over the Materialist Conception of History is mainly due to the chameleon-like fluctuations in its original presentation. One thing is clear straight away: that the degree of influence of this or that circumstance on the course of historical events cannot be worked out from any general axiom, nor by the analysis of any concepts or so-called categories of history, but simply and solely by means of empirical research into the detailed historical facts. But the Materialist Conception of History takes on in Marx—and even more in Engels, and more again in their disciples and followers—the form of a philosophical axiom, which is then used to impose a more or less forced interpretation on the facts of history—exactly as Hegel had done earlier.

If we enquire into the mistakes which lead to this distortion of experience and so once again to an unscientific approach to history, we shall find the same causes for them as we did in Hegel's case, however great a gulf there may be in other respects between this Hegelian Left, as it was called, and the master himself.

One easy way, for instance, of introducing the Materialist Conception of History axiomatically is to define society, for which alone it is supposed to hold, as the totality of relations of production. One can then so readily forget that the object so defined is not the real object which we were going to consider, but a mere concept, whose applicability to particular cases will require empirical demonstration on each separate occasion. Take for example the opening statement of the first section of the *Communist Manifesto*, that the history of all previous society is the history of class struggles. It does not say, all previous history, but, the history of all previous society, so that everything depends on how society is defined. Now the word 'previous' does not accord with the generality and demonstrative form in which such assertions are made—and which, one would think, can be verified only in particular instances by reference to historical actualities. But this expression is typical; it is always coming up. This law, if it really is a law, should not apply only to *previous* society. But if it does hold only for previous society, then it certainly cannot be discovered from the mere concept *society*. So the alleged generality and demonstrative character of the statement disappears in the haze.

There is a more general point to be made here. While combating that conception of history in which ideas operate as independent forces and even determine the course of events, its opponents went so far as to deny that ideas have any effect at all. They refused to regard ideals in themselves as independently existing forces influencing events, and in consequence they also excluded the ideas which occur in the minds of men, denying that the notion or awareness of an ideal could have any historical effects. This was the real issue in the battle carried on by Historical Materialism against so-called Utopianism. The result was an unholy confusion of the two theses. The so-called scientific socialists (i.e. socialists who accepted Historical

Materialism) made a real contribution by diverting attention from the mere ideal of Socialism to the question of how it could be realized, thus showing clearly that an ideal for society can be attained only by fighting for possession of power in society, and that the means for realizing goals of this sort do not, as the phrase goes, 'come straight out of one's head', but must be based on actual historical facts and so involve research into these.

This correct and fruitful idea is, however, here combined with the claim that the goal can itself be derived from the facts of history and can thus be seen to be necessary and (as it says in the preface to *Capital*) to be based on a trend which operates with the necessity of a law of nature.

For a more detailed discussion of the theory of Historical Materialism we shall have to refer to some particular formulation of this theory. The most suitable, in my view, is that neat, clear and brief little work of Engels', *Socialism, Utopian and Scientific*.

The thesis of this book is quite general in character. We should therefore expect to find its proof general too. And we do find more or less conscious attempts at a general proof for a general statement.

'The Materialist Conception of History', says Engels, 'starts from the proposition that the production of the means to support human life and, next to production, the exchange of things produced, is the basis of all social structure; that in every society that has appeared in history, the manner in which wealth is distributed and society divided into classes or orders, is dependent upon what is produced, how it is produced, and how the products are exchanged. From this point of view the final causes of all social changes and political revolutions are to be sought, not in men's brains, not in man's better insight into eternal truth and justice, but in changes in the modes of production and exchange. They are to be sought, not in the *philosophy*, but in the *economics* of each particular epoch' (p. 45).

Now if the Materialist Conception of History starts from the proposition that production is the basis of all social structure, this involves the assumption that production or, in its more general description, the economy, is obviously something purely material. This fits in with the other main passage explaining what Historical Materialism is, which says that the actual economic structure of a society is the material basis from which in the last analysis the entire superstructure, justice and all the other notional aspects of any given historical period are to be explained. Here we have a materialist conception of history formulated, showing how to explain men's consciousness from their existence, instead of their existence from their consciousness, as was done before. For the idealist conception of history, as Engels remarks in this context, knows nothing of a class war based on material interests, indeed it does not refer to material interests at all. Material interests, then, are taken as the motive force, the real power behind historical development. But what are material interests? The word 'material' can here be taken only as signifying the object of the 'interest'. An interest in food, in clothing, in shelter could be 'material'. But that does not make the interest itself something material. Now if this interest is itself no more material than any other interest, then what distinguishes this particular interest as superior to all the other interests?—a question not answered here, or even asked. Then again, consider the concept of an economy, or even of production. We talk of production when men deliberately, that is by working, provide means for satisfying their needs; which they do, of course, only because they do not come across these means all ready for use. Their action, then, is done for the prudential consideration that they must work to provide these means, if they are not to go hungry. But prudence, imagination, thought and decision undoubtedly belong to human consciousness, to the mental realm. The economy is ruled by the attempt to provide as much as possible of the means for satisfying needs, with as little cost as possible. The guiding principle here is an activity of the human mind, not any purely material forces. So the controlling element in the economy belongs to what on Engels' view is the superstructure; for it is here that human ideas and human consciousness belong.

Something like a general proof of Historical Materialism may be found in Marx' and Engels' critique of the Hegelian system.

'Hegel was an idealist', it says in Engels' book. 'To him the thoughts within his brain were not the more or less abstract pictures of actual things and processes, but, conversely, things and their evolution were only the realised pictures of the "Idea," existing somewhere from eternity before the world was. This way of thinking turned everything upside down, and completely reversed the actual connection of things in the world. Correctly and ingeniously as many individual groups of facts were grasped by Hegel, yet, for the reasons just given, there is much that is botched, artificial, laboured, in a word, wrong in point of detail. The Hegelian system, in itself, was a colossal miscarriage—but it was also the last of its kind. It was suffering, in fact, from an internal and incurable contradiction. Upon the one hand, its essential proposition was the conception that human history is a process of evolution, which, by its very nature, cannot find its intellectual final term in the discovery of any so-called absolute truth. But, on the other hand it laid claim to being the very essence of this absolute truth. A system of natural and historical knowledge, embracing everything, and final for all time, is a contradiction to the fundamental law of dialectic reasoning. This law, indeed, by no means excludes, but, on the contrary, includes the idea that the systematic knowledge of the external universe can make giant strides from age to age.

The perception of the fundamental contradiction in German idealism led necessarily back to materialism' (*Socialism, Utopian and Scientific*, pp. 37–8).

But how can the perception of the fundamental contradiction in German Idealism lead necessarily to Materialism? By Idealism is here meant the view that actual particular things in the world are mere copies of general ideas existing in their own right, i.e. of general concepts, so that the reality of the thing resides in the concept. Now if one infers from a fundamental contradiction in this view to the necessary correctness of Materialism, i.e. of another view on which matter alone has causal efficacy and anything mental is a mere copy or appearance of something material, then one will commit just the same fallacy as Hegel did when he confused concepts with minds. For in concluding from the non-existence of concepts to the sole existence of matter one is assuming that concepts and minds are the same. If the mental is not actual, then it can't act either, so it cannot engage in any activity in history. But then what happens to Historical Materialism? —to the theory that what men think must be explained from what they are, rather than *vice versa*, as before. If thinking is not actual, then it will not really serve to explain any historical event; for what is not actual cannot act. But how, in that case, is what men think to be explained from what they are? For the effect of Being is then not Thought, but only Matter. If X is to be, or at least to become, an effect, X must first be actual or at least able to become actual; just as X cannot cause or act unless X is actual. There are only two alternatives: (i) Thought is an effect of Being, in which case it also must belong to Being, and so must, like all other being, be actual; (ii) Thought does not belong to Being, and so is not, of course, actual, in which case it cannot be an effect either. Explaining Thought by means of material Existence is a bogus undertaking. For if X does not actually occur, there is no need to explain how it comes about.

There is a further point. We saw what was true in the Materialist Conception of History, namely the discovery that the ideas of an age depend on the interests of its ruling class; that the ruling ideas in any age are not formed according to the truth they contain, but according to the degree of interest which the ruling class has in their formation.

Marx and Engels, however, take this one step further, saying there is no absolute truth in human ideas at all, but that they are just the reflections in men's heads of existing economic relationships. All truth, they say, is relative. Now a relative truth would be one that does not exclude its opposite; and if one takes this strictly, the epithet 'absolute' would really be superfluous, and it would be clearer and simpler to assert that there is no such thing as truth. For the point of the word 'truth' is to exclude the opposite of what is true. Every statement expresses an assertion and so lays claim to truth; and the intention is to exclude the truth of its contrary—and this will have to apply to the assertion expressing the Materialist Conception of History. For instance, if I say that all human ideas simply reflect existing economic relationships, and that no idea is true absolutely, then this is an assertion which lays claim to truth, and so excludes the contrary assertion that ideas do more than reflect existing economic relationships, that they are true absolutely. The theory that truth is relative thus destroys itself. For the statement of the Materialist Conception of History is itself intended as universally valid, as expressing an assertion which applies to all history, so it must certainly exclude the contrary of what it asserts. It's meaning, if it means anything at all, must be one laying claim to absolute truth. On this strict interpretation, then, Historical Materialism is self-defeating. If human ideas belong only to the ideological superstructure, as opposed to the real foundations (the economy), then the word 'ideological' must imply that there can be no question here of absolute truth and that the claim to such truth is illusory. The entire superstructure has no real significance. It belongs to thought, not to fact. Its reality is a mere illusion. All that remains is the material basis. The world of ideas is illusion pure and simple. That is the only proper way to take the term 'Materialist Conception of History'.

Let us now examine this concept of 'ideological superstructure' a little more closely and ask whether the alleged illusion is really possible. The assumption clearly is that all that is necessary, for an illusion to occur, is that what seems-to-be is not there in fact. But is that enough? For instance, is it sufficient in order for lightning to seem to flash that it should not really flash? From this it would follow that the illusion of a lightning-flash would occur (i) only when it is not flashing and (ii) on every such occasion. Clearly something more is needed, before an illusion can occur, than the non-existence of the thing which illusorily appears to occur: namely, that it should be imagined to be real, that the mistake should be made, that there should be the idea—untrue, admittedly—that something is there which is not really there. So for any such illusion to occur, ideas or something like them must be real. If there is any illusion at all, then the theory that the existence of ideas is quite illusory must be illusory.

Let us now see what can be saved from the wreck of Historical Materialism, once we have recognized that it must logically lead to the denial of any real world of ideas and so to the denial that there could even seem to be such a world. What then remains of the ideological superstructure whose origin and historical development the theory of Historical Materialism offered to explain? There are no thoughts left, anyway; for our assumption rules them out. All we have left to satisfy the requirements of Realism are the signs of speech, the words, usually taken as signs of thought and material in nature. We can thus take Historical Materialism as a theory by which to explain the origin and development of a world of signs. In place of the world of ideas we now have a world of signs, of tangible material objects. Can this interpretation be carried through? I answer, No. For the question would arise how we are to tell that something is a sign; how, in other words, we are to tell whether it belongs to the ideological superstructure or to the material substructure. We have no means left by which to decide this point. For a thing is a sign just so far as it designates a thought, and no further: just so far as some thought is combined with that oral or written sign—and our assumption forbids this as impossible. We could never tell whether any given object was a sign or not. Perhaps the moon is a sign; we cannot tell, any more than we could for a book. So there is, and can be, no criterion by which to classify any object as belonging to substructure or to superstructure.

I have already mentioned another version of Historical Materialism on which it is really concerned with something simple and illuminating: that the means for changing social relationships must be sought in the circumstances of the present age and not dreamt up out of one's head. But this correct and helpful notion is almost always combined with the claim that the end which these means are supposed to subserve must itself be derived as a necessary consequence from the material circumstances and indeed from the circumstances of economic development. Historical Materialism thus reduces to an attempt to exclude ethics from the business of deciding on goals in the social life of men; as is more or less clear in Marx's well-known remark that the working class has 'no ideals to realize but to set free the elements of the new society with which old collapsing bourgeois society itself is pregnant' (*The Civil War in France*, p. 44).

This idea is the basis of what people have come to call 'Scientific Socialism'—another pernicious consequence of Hegel's dialectic. Scientific Socialism (as Marx wrote to Arnold Ruge in 1843) is supposed 'to deduce from the particular forms of existing reality the true reality which they ought to be and will finally become'. It is like listening to Hegel on the rationality of the real, which has only to be uncovered by stripping off the superficial exterior, the merely contingent existent.

Here is another comment from Engels' book *Ludwig Feuerbach and the Outcome of Classical German Philosophy.*

'Historical events thus appear on the whole to be likewise governed by chance. But where on the surface accident holds sway, there actually it is always governed by inner, hidden laws and it is only a matter of discovering these laws' (p. 58).

Marx' and Engels' application of this dialectic, which they derived from Hegel, to the theory and history of capitalist society is common knowledge. The capitalist order of society, in which we are living, is supposed gradually to change into its opposite. All we need do is to peel off, in thought, the superficial exterior of this order of society to expose its inner kernel and essence, and there we shall find the germ of the future socialist order of society.

This alleged historical necessity is supposed to work itself out independently of any human contribution. But is that consistent with the appeal to individual interests, to human activities, to act as midwife to the coming order of society? Clearly this is an appeal to prudence. We must act in this or that way, it is said, if we are to reach the end at which we aim. We are also given a reason for reaching that end: viz. we should do this or that 'lest we be destroyed'. The hypothetical nature of the alleged necessity comes out clearly here, for these are prudential commands. The proleteriat is required to carry through the revolution 'lest it be destroyed, sinking to a Chinese coolie-dom'. But what sort of necessity is that? Leaving aside the point whether any such interest in prudence really exists, the question still remains whether men are sensible enough to appreciate their real interest. If I say that certain events will occur if men are rational enough to appreciate where their own interests lie, it by no means follows that the said events really will occur. There is a tacit assumption here—as in this entire theory—that men will always do what prudence recommends on the basis of their interests. Here a further point emerges. The lever which is here applied to disengage the future socialist order from the present order of society is men's insight into their own advantage; now 'men's insight' is an element in the superstructure, not the substructure. The whole fate of the theory depends on this condition that men have insight; if so, it will be fulfilled, if not, not. So the theory of the coming of a socialist society, though based on Historical Materialism, depends for its realization on a condition in the superstructure.

The version of Historical Materialism which I have been criticizing, on which what men are determines what they think, and not the other way about, is closely connected with the account of social development as conditioned in the last analysis by economic forces. This phrase 'the last analysis' is a clear admission that these are not the only forces which are active in social development and may be used to account for it; that in addition to the forces belonging to the material substructure there are others, belonging to the ideological superstructure, which are also active in history, and not just in the last analysis. But this is in effect to abandon the claim that the forces at work in history are all material in character; indeed, it means giving up Materialism altogether; for not only is the reality of spiritual forces conceded, but also their causal effectiveness. We have of course no measure here by which to rank the forces which are at work in history. No such measure is given, or can be given, as the theory requires the elimination of all measures of value. The same applies to the distinction mentioned earlier between the superficial exterior of the historical process and its real core, for again there is no criterion by which to tell the exterior from the core. The same applies to the assessment of historical prophecy implied in the phrases 'ultimately' and 'in the long run', which again removes the assertion in question from the control of experience as to its truth or falsity. If we retain all these phrases, they will always enable us to defend the theory. But this victory has its price; the assertions in question are turned into truisms, verbal assertions of no informative value. The meaning of 'real' is defined along Hegelian lines, and experience loses its control over this 'reality'.

It was Hegel's dialectic that made this retreat from experience possible. I shall now go on to show how it was that Marx, though a great mind and one well up in the sciences of experience, came to employ speculative dialectic in a complete rape of the experience available to him, thus rendering it worthless and barren and devaluing the aim he pursued all his life. Nor was it Marx alone—who once remarked 'I am no Marxist'—but his disciples and successors, the Marxists, who remained wedded to this same dialectic. The more orthodox they were as Marxists, that is, the stronger their desire to remain true to their master's teaching, and the more eagerly they sought for firm ground on which to combat the principles of their opponents—who really were trying to hold fast to experience—the more they imprisoned themselves in this dialectic. No less a man than Lenin, in one of his last essays, expressed the wish that his fellow-workers should not neglect to study Hegel's dialectic. The ground for this advice is deep down in the nature of Marxist theory, as I shall now proceed to show.

Engels says, in his polemic against Dühring (which, after Marx' *Capital*, is the most important source for our enquiry):

'Dialectics, however, is nothing more than the science of the general laws of motion and development of nature, human society and thought' (*Anti-Dühring*, p. 195).

What does the science of the general laws of motion look like? There is such a science, indeed it is unique among all the edifices of thought constructed by the human mind. No other science has such rigidly fixed concepts, such clear and unambiguous definitions, such strictly universal laws, laws independent of time and space and unaffected by circumstance. Some of these traits may be found in other sciences, to a greater or less degree, but they are most clearly and perfectly evidenced by the science of motion, mechanics. That is why it has become a model for all the sciences. And its highest principle is that there should be no contradictions. Note the contrast in every point with the dialectic which stems from Hegel. This is not just a matter of a change in terminology. What Marx and Engels had in mind, and actually used at every turn, was the assertion that contradictions are real, the theory that contradiction is the driving force in the actual evolution of nature and of human history—and not only in evolution, but in every change whatsoever; in short, in every event.

Dühring had rightly recognized this as the essential point in the Marxian theory and put his finger on it in his critique:

'The first and most important statement with respect to the fundamental logical properties of existence points to the exclusion of contradiction' (quoted by Engels in *Anti-Dühring*, p. 167).

That is well and clearly said. And it was against this very proposition that Engels directed his most vigorous polemic.

Marx and Engels, we may recall, had taken over Hegel's dialectic but had rejected his Idealism. That puts Marxist theory in an even more unfortunate position. If one is going to be a dialectician it is much better to go on being an idealist.

An idealist, holding as he does that concepts are real, does at least have the advantage of being able to think of these concepts as negated, having a negative concept available to go with each concept. And if, like Hegel, he is logical enough to go on and hold that each and every thing is a concept, there will be nothing to stop him holding that contradictions are real, and that every judgment is a negation. But someone who holds that concepts are not real, and, further, that men's thoughts simply reflect material relationships and have no significance in their own right as assertions, would at least have to propound 'negative matter' in order to hold contradictions to be real. But that is a phrase which just prohibits thought! No idea whatsoever is or can possibly be associated with it. If anything is a meaningless sign, a piece of mere ideology in the strictest sense of the term, it is the theory that contradictions have a reality in terms of material existence. And the fact that someone manages to entertain such a theory, even for a moment, can be explained only by supposing that its originators are still crypto-idealists and idealists of the purest Hegelian water, seeing that at the same time they reject Idealism as 'a monumental miscarriage' and 'complete nonsense'. In Marxist theory we come across this idealism at every turn. Nor are matters improved by the concepts, which in Hegel's theory came on as spirits, appearing here in a materialist garb.

To show the part played by dialectics in the Marxist theory, let me take the most serious instance, as it forms the centrepiece of the whole theory and so cannot be dismissed as inessential. I am referring to the supposed proof of the necessity af Socialism.

Engels discusses this in his book *Socialism Utopian, and Scientific,* as follows:

'In the medieval stage of evolution of the production of commodities, the question as to the owner of the product of labour could not arise. The individual producer, as a rule, had, from raw material belonging to himself, and generally his own handiwork, produced it with his own tools, by the labour of his own hands or of his family. There was no need for him to appropriate the new product. It belonged wholly to him, as a matter of course. His property in the product was, therefore, based *upon his own labour.* Even where external help was used, this was, as a rule, of little importance, and very generally was compensated by something other than wages. The apprentices and journeymen of the guilds worked less for board and wages than for education, in order that they might become master craftsmen themselves.

Then came the concentration of the means of production and of the producers in large workshops and manufactories, their transformation into actual socialized means of production and socialized producers. But the socialized producers and means of production and their products were still treated, after this change, just as they had been before, i.e., as the means of production and the products of individuals. Hitherto, the owner of the instruments of labour had himself appropriated the product, because, as a rule, it was his own product and the assistance of others was

the exception. Now the owner of the instruments of labour always appropriated to himself the product, although it was no longer *his* product but
exclusively the product of the *labour of others*. Thus, the products now
produced socially were not appropriated by those who had actually set
in motion the means of production and actually produced the commodities, but by the *capitalists*. The means of production, and production itself,
had become in essence socialized. But they were subjected to a form of
appropriation which presupposes the private production of individuals,
under which, therefore, every one owns his own product and brings it to
market. The mode of production is subjected to this form of appropriation, although it abolishes the conditions upon which the latter rests.

This contradiction, which gives to the new mode of production its
capitalistic character, *contains the germ of the whole of the social antagonisms
of to-day'* (pp. 51–3).

Which contradiction? Clearly that involved in combining social
production with a private form of appropriation. The products are
now manufactured or produced socially and not, as in the Middle
Ages, individually. But the products are treated as though they were
still the products of individuals. Production becomes social but
appropriation stays private. This is the supposed contradiction which
gives the contemporary mode of production its capitalist character.

Now anyone who knows what a contradiction is will here search for
one in vain: for *private appropriation* is not the negation of *social
production*, any more than *social production* is the negation of *private
appropriation*. In one case we are dealing with production, and in the
other appropriation; and these two concepts are different. One can
speak of contradiction only if the subject, at least, is guaranteed to be
the same. If we start with the concept *social production*, we can by
negation reach *non-social production*, which we can call 'private
production'. That would be a contradiction. If we start from the
concept *private appropriation*, we can by negation reach *non-private
appropriation*. That would be a contradiction. So there is only an
apparent contradiction, not a real one, in the present case. Now
Engels refers to this contradiction more precisely in the words 'as
the products of individuals'. For previously, when they were still
produced by individuals, they also belonged to the individuals who
had produced them. Now the owner of the means of production
continues to appropriate the product, although it is no longer his.
This is what is supposed to be contradictory: it is his product and it is
not his product. We could say: the product belongs and does not
belong to the capitalist.

The trail becomes clearer if we follow Engels a little further. He
himself speaks of a presupposition negated by the progress of

development: the presupposition of private appropriation—by which he means private production. The presupposition involved in private appropriation, and now negated, is that of private production. But how can X take place if X presupposes Y and Y has been negated at the point where X takes place? Has this presupposition, which seems to lead to the contradiction, any basis in fact? Has the contradiction itself such a basis? Do we find it anywhere among the facts here described?

What Engels does take for granted is this: that personal labour is presupposed in private property. Once again I ask, has this assumption any basis in fact? No. Its introduction is purely arbitrary. We could just as well lay down this law: private appropriation presupposes private possession of the means of production. At once the supposed contradiction disappears!

Suppose we concede to Marx and Engels that property in a product rests upon one's having laboured at it personally. Now why should this form of appropriation and of production, which held sway in the Middle Ages, continue the same when the mode of production changes? Why should they not also change correspondingly? A historical materialist ought to be the first to welcome such an idea! If the mode of possession changes, like everything else, with the mode of production and is dependent on that mode, that is all the more reason, having recognized the original presupposition as applying to the medieval mode of production, to introduce for the modern mode of production a new presupposition, on which property in a product does not depend on personal labour but on private possession of the means of production. What notion could suit the principles of Historical Materialism better than this? And this again removes the contradiction; for the presupposition, which contradicts the new mode of appropriation only if it is itself preserved unchanged, will in fact change along with the mode of production. This is an assumption which we should need good reasons *not* to make, if we were historical materialists. And Marx and Engels, being historical materialists, must have had very good reasons, otherwise they would not have treated this presupposition as unchangeable and universally valid, and left it holding the field when the mode of production had completely changed.

These very good reasons are not far to seek; but they do not fit in with the system. If one cuts loose from that, they lie ready to hand, but within the bound of the system they cannot even be recognized as reasons, for they would blow the system up and annihilate it completely. For we shall find, once we raise the question, that that presupposition conceals an implicit moral assertion; not one based upon the facts of life, but one which expresses a moral evaluation of the facts. For the presupposition is—to put it in unambiguous language—that every man has the right to enjoy the fruits of his labour or that no-one should be compelled to labour for another's enjoyment. It says, in short, that exploitation is abominable.

This is a moral judgment, a statement not at all dependent on the fact; an ought-proposition. Even Engels lets the word slip out, when he says:

'In the medieval stage of evolution of the production of commodities the question as to the owner of the product of labour could not arise' (quoted above, p. 111).

This is by implication to admit that there is an 'ought' about it. And this 'ought' is admitted because it is an essential presupposition of the entire argument.

The moral assertion that every man ought to enjoy the fruits of his own labour appears to Marx and Engels to be so certain, such an established truth, that they take it for granted as self-evident and never think of adapting the truth expressed in this assertion to the change in the mode of production. Instead, they hold precisely the contrary: that this truth remains, whatever change there may be in the mode of production. This is the fundamental stay and support of the entire theory, and it is really a replacement for 'Scientific Socialism'.

JOHANN FRIEDRICH HERBART

Among the philosophers who after Kant revived logical Dogmatism once again there is one whose work deserves particular mention because of its effect upon education.

Herbart was a contemporary of Schelling and Hegel, and like them he carried on where Fichte had left off. He developed Fichte's philosophy further along its original line as a metaphysic of reflection, in the sense of a metaphysic from concepts alone. This takes us back once more to the logical Dogmatism of the scholastics. Herbart was led astray by Fichte's method of contradictions. In his work this method appears in a new form, under the name 'Method of Relationships'. According to Herbart, this method is supposed to lead to a critical assessment of what is given in experience. This reference to experience does ensure that the working out of the theory is not nearly so fantastic in Herbart's case as it was in that of Schelling and

Hegel. On his view, what is given in experience contains contradictions, and it is the task of metaphysics to criticize and resolve these contradictions. This is to be done by making certain assumptions which explain why it is that things should appear to us in that contradictory manner in experience. So Herbart, like Leibniz before him, goes behind intuition and claims a metaphysical knowledge of a world outside our continuous space and our continuous time, a world of monads precisely in Leibniz' sense.

This world of monads is assumed in order to explain why the world appears to us as continuously extended in space and time and consequently as shot through with contradictions. According to Herbart the monads are simple and unchangeable beings which in themselves have no relationships but which do have the tendency to interfere with each other in a certain way, and which react to such interference with certain acts of self-preservation. These acts of self-preservation are ideas. Herbart constructs the mind out of monads which are in this way affected and react in self-preservation, and he then tries to apply a calculus to these arbitrarily assumed acts of interference and self-preservation in the hope of opening the way to a mathematical treatment of psychology. Now from the warnings given in the Critique of Reason we can tell *a priori* that such an undertaking must miscarry and that Herbart's success in the matter must be illusory, since his calculus does not apply to the facts of inner experience but only in a realm of metaphysical fictions. Mathematics cannot be applied to the phenomena of inner sense, for those phenomena are merely intense magnitudes and so are not open to numeration.

Herbart expressly rejects the method of the Critique of Reason. Like Hegel he accuses Kant of arguing in a circle. The Critique of Reason, he says, is an undertaking in the field of human knowledge and so can get to know its object only by applying the Categories. So the Critique of Reason belongs to the science of psychology and must therefore presuppose the metaphysical principles which it is itself intended to justify. Faced with this logical circle one is compelled once more to construct metaphysics on a dogmatic basis.

This approach to the Critique reveals clearly the logico-dogmatic preconception underlying Herbart's views. His objection applies to the Critique of Reason only if, adopting the ideal of logical Dogmatism, one treats the Critique as a science intended to deduce the basic principles of metaphysics from even higher premisses. In that case the Critique of Reason would indeed be bound to move in a logical circle, for the science of inner experience, like every other science of experience, would presuppose certain metaphysical prin-

I

ciples as conditions of its own possibility. This point is quite correct, but it does not touch the Critique of Reason, for the simple reason that the Critique is not intended to provide any proof of metaphysical principles. Herbart says that the enquiry undertaken in the Critique of Reason rests upon a gigantic mistake—the mistaken assumption that it is easier to tell what the Critique of Reason is about than what is the business of metaphysics.

Herbart was encouraged in making this attack on Kant by a confusion which he shares with the philosophers we considered earlier; the confusion between the Critique of Reason and epistemology. This is what we called the epistemological preconception, which interprets the Critique of Reason as intended to provide a theory of the relationship of knowledge to its object in order to justify that knowledge as objectively valid. Now this is not a correct understanding of the task of the Critique of Reason, whose aim is simply to derive indirect or mediate knowledge (which requires justification) from immediate knowledge as its ground. That ground is not a part of the Critique, but is its object—so that the Critique is itself psychological in character. Now we have a choice. One alternative is, following the dogmatic method, to set up straight away some alleged axioms or other and to develop a system of metaphysics from them. The other alternative is to make metaphysical knowledge itself the object of a psychological inquiry and show what immediate metaphysical knowledge actually exists, so as to erect a system of metaphysics on the metaphysical principles thus justified.

Our decision between these two alternatives depends simply on which of them is likely to lead us to our goal more easily. Not that it is in general any easier to gain acquaintance with an item of knowledge than with its object. But the critical method has a more profound advantage, owing to the peculiar character of metaphysical knowledge. As Herbart could have learnt from the history of philosophy, the dogmatic method in metaphysics either does not reach its goal at all or else makes our choice of the metaphysical principles to be set at the head of the system an entirely arbitrary affair, and so in effect a matter of pure luck. He ought, therefore, to have tried following Kant's critical method, which involves a psychological enquiry. That method starts from items of empirical knowledge; its appeal is only to observations; and it does not take any philosophical abstractions for granted. The framing of such abstractions is indeed the most difficult part of philosophy. However difficult an empirical psychological enquiry may be, it is in every respect more open to scientific treatment than are metaphysical abstractions. It can moreover help us to reach those abstractions, by a gradual ascent from experience, with the aid of a reliable guideline.

Herbart does praise Kant for his special contribution in showing that the absence of contradiction is not an adequate criterion of existence, and for this reason he calls himself a Kantian. He also implies by this that metaphysics ought to start from what is given in experience, but he does not himself abide by this principle of method for—missing the point of Kant's law of the immanence of human knowledge—he sets himself with the aid of merely logical criteria to resolve the contradictions which experience is said to contain, by constructing a transcendent world. He rejects perception, on account of its supposed contradictions, and raises himself above it by the aid of a metaphysic from concepts alone. But perception by itself contains no contradictions at all. Contradictions can occur only in judgments. We have a contradiction only where the same state of affairs is asserted both affirmatively and negatively. But perception only supplies situations, not negations; so no contradiction can occur in it. And even if we grant that perception might contain a contradiction, still pure thought would not be in a position to resolve it, for we should first of all need a criterion by which to resolve the contradiction in favour of one or the other of the two assertions allegedly contained in perception. The law of non-contradiction would in this case decide nothing. Reflection by itself, mere logicality, is empty; it has no information to offer us. Yet Herbart attempts by mere logic, using the mere absence of contradiction as a criterion, to decide about the existence of transcendent things. He tries to make positive progress beyond experience by means of pure thought. Little does he realize that the difficulties he is struggling with—difficulties about the simple and the continuous, continuity and discontinuity, which he thinks he meets with in perception—that it was precisely these difficulties that Kant resolved in his theory of the Antinomies.

Herbart cannot be considered a genuine Neo-Platonist, for he does not lay claim to an intellectual intuition. In contrast to the Spinozist views of Schelling and Hegel, Herbart holds fast to the plurality of things, so he does not make the fantastic claims which they did. Nevertheless, he does commit fundamentally the same dialectical fallacy as that on which Neo-Platonism is based. For Herbart, too, holds that what is given is contradictory; though in his case the contradictions are supposed to be resolved by formal logic, which he does regard as valid.

For instance, Herbart regards the possibility of change as contradictory. A thing which changes is the same and yet not the same,

There is clearly a confusion here between individual and type. A thing which is undergoing change remains the same thing in spite of the change of its states. Nevertheless, it varies in its type with the variation in its states. At one time it possesses one quality and at another time another. The object itself remains numerically the same throughout, only its qualities change. Now in order not to get involved in contradictions at this point, we shall clearly have to take some account of time. There is no contradiction in a thing having a quality at one time which it does not possess at some other time. All that is happening here is that a thing possesses two characteristics: first, that of having a quality at a certain time and second that of not having that quality at another time. The only difficulty here is how a thing can possibly possess a variety of characteristics. Now Herbart finds this possibility contradictory. On this alleged contradiction all Herbart's 'difficulties' depend.

Is there really any difficulty in one thing having a plurality of characteristics? How can one and the same object possess various different characteristics? An object, for example an apple, is round. It is also red. But red is not round. So it must be round and yet not-round, and this is said to be a contradiction.

This is an instance of the principle 'Realities conflict'—the counterpart of Leibniz' principle that 'Realities do not conflict with each other'.

One characteristic is different from another. The concept *red* is not the concept *round*. If one confuses this variety with conflict, then there does seem to be some contradiction in a thing possessing several characteristics. The formula of comparison given here is correct: Red is not round. From that it does not follow that something red cannot be round, i.e. that an object which comes under the one concept cannot, for that reason, come under the other. Variety is not the same as conflict. But anyone who has not payed attention to the Amphiboly of the Concepts of Reflection may well confuse the two. This confusion is the basis of Herbart's theory of contradictions.

I remarked that Herbart does not revert to Spinozism, as Hegel and Schelling did, but retains the plurality of things in his world of monads. Nevertheless, it is clear from what I have said that Herbart's theory of monads is based on the same dialectical fallacy which underlies the metaphysic of Schelling and Hegel. The difference between them lies only in the application of this fallacy. Schelling and Hegel tend always to infer from logical simplicity to metaphysical identity, whereas Herbart concludes from logical variety to a real conflict, and thence to the impossibility of one thing having several different characteristics. That is to say, he infers from logical variety in the characteristics of things to their metaphysical plurality. That is the same fallacy differently applied.

Bolzano also revived Leibniz' theory of monads, in a way very similar to Herbart's. He is in general the most loyal representative of the Leibnizian spirit in philosophy. So it is no surprise to find that his philosophy is much less arbitrary and fantastic than that of his romantic contemporaries. The Amphiboly of the Concepts of Reflection, at any rate, is less in evidence in his work than in that of Herbart. Being a mathematician, he is much too practised as a thinker to commit this fallacy in a gross form, though it is hidden in the background of all his philosophical work. It is the reason for his return to Leibniz and for all his misunderstanding of the Critique of Reason. Yet his work does deserve serious consideration, if only for his contributions to mathematics and to logic. The example of Bolzano is an instructive one. It shows how easy it is to fall prey to the above-mentioned dialectical fallacies and how misleading this dialectical illusion is. Otherwise a thinker who in other respects is so acute as Bolzano would not have been misled by it.

Herbart and Bolzano bring us to the end of a series of representatives of Rationalism after Kant. Our concern here has been to examine those philosophers who became famous in the history of metaphysics after Kant and to see to what extent they had progressed beyond Kant's metaphysics or regressed behind it. As we have seen, these famous representatives of post-Kantian rationalist metaphysics— the empiricists still remain to be considered—all depend on Fichte for the dialectical basis of their philosophy, and so all come indirectly under the influence of Reinhold. For it was Reinhold, as we showed, who provided Fichte with the fundamental dialectical premises for his philosophical theorems. Our main aim in discussing the regress in philosophy after Kant was to get this point clear.

These historical results are not, however, sufficient on their own. We must now review this entire development of thought. This will be done systematically, from several points of view.

A Review of the History of the Transcendental Preconception

The systematic character of this review may be indicated by giving it the following sub-title: Epistemological Rationalism and the Amphiboly of the Concepts of Reflection.

Let me go back to my remark that this whole development of

thought which we have been discussing derives from the fundamental idea of method in Reinhold's Basic Philosophy, and so depends on Reinhold's misunderstanding of the Critique of Reason as an epistemology, i.e. as a science supposed to contain the ultimate premisses for philosophical knowledge. This was in fact the intention of his Basic Philosophy; it was to be the science of the faculty of ideas. The fallacy in this is already familiar to us. It consists in confusing the content of the Critique of Reason with its object, i.e. with the ground sought for philosophical knowledge itself; and that ground is taken to be the object of epistemology. This confusion recurs again in Fichte. He starts from the notion that the activity of the *I* is the ultimate basis for the unity of all knowledge. This activity gradually turns into an axiom for him, an axiom from which all human knowledge is supposed to flow as from its ultimate premiss. So Fichte, like Reinhold, confuses the constitutive principle of metaphysics, which can be determined only psychologically, with a logical principle. He confuses immediate knowledge with a judgment, the judgment which has that immediate knowledge as its object. The results of Reinhold's preconception thus become quite clear.

In Schelling's case, the ultimate basis for metaphysical explanation was found in the relation of a subject to an object. But how does Schelling come to give this content to the ultimate metaphysical principle? Simply and solely because of the way in which Fichte's Scientific Theory had posed the problem of epistemology. Fichte's Scientific Theory was intended to enquire into the relation between subject and object and to trace it back to the identity of both in self-consciousness. Only if the epistemological problem is posed in this way can one see how a purely psychological relationship could be made by Schelling into the ultimate principle of metaphysical explanation.

And what happens in Hegel's case? In this philosopher we find a conscious and explicit rejection of the Critique of Reason. Let us, however, remember the reason he gives for this rejection. His objection to the critical method was that it is impossible to know before one knows. This objection in its turn makes sense only if the Critique of Reason is confused with epistemology, i.e. only if one supposes that the Critique was meant to show how knowledge is possible *in general*. Thus Hegel's diversion of philosophy from epistemology back to objective Dogmatism is explicable only from Reinhold's misunderstanding of the Critique of Reason as an epistemology.

The same may be said for Herbart and for Bolzano.

Reinhold's misunderstanding thus takes us back, lock, stock and barrel, into the pre-Kantian transcendent metaphysics, the refutation of which was the main aim of the Critique set in motion by Kant.

Now, as we showed earlier, certain defects in Kant's philosophy did contribute to Reinhold's misunderstanding and so to the reconstruction of dogmatic metaphysics. Kant's proof that there could not be a transcendent metaphysics, independent of its relation to the objects of experience, was inadequate, for it was based on Formal Idealism and on the transcendental proof. As we saw, both these sections of his theory are unsatisfactory. We also saw that the method of the transcendental proof must logically lead to the enterprise of epistemology. And we saw, lastly, that Formal Idealism must logically lead to abandoning completely the distinction between phenomena and things-as-they-really-are and thus to giving up the distinction between knowledge of experience and a transcendental mode of knowledge which goes beyond the bounds of experience. The line which Kant had drawn between a concept of nature and an Idea was thus inevitably obscured once again. This led to the rejection of his insight that all human knowledge must be naturalist in form. A further factor was that mistake in Kant's Theory of Ideas with which we have so often been concerned. The mistaken theory that Ideas could find a regulative employment in natural science led Kant to leave a loophole for teleology in science, a teleology of nature and also of history. This theory of the regulative employment of Ideas was the breach in the wall by which fanaticism could once more gain entry into philosophy. Kant's mistake of method lent itself to this abuse— all the more as Kant's warning against a constitutive employment of Ideas went unheeded. Thus the regulative employment of Ideas in natural science, which is really inadmissible but had been permitted by Kant, led immediately to a constitutive theory of Ideas. This was bound to lead to conflict with scientific research based on experiment and on mathematics. Hence the well-known dispute between natural science and post-Kantian metaphysics.

As we saw, there was a reason for all this in Kant's own work. The ultimate reason was Kant's transcendental preconception, his assumption that critical knowledge (which he also described as transcendental and which has *a priori* knowledge as its object) must itself be a form of *a priori* knowledge. On this mistaken assumption the Critique itself was bound to appear as yet another instance of transcendent metaphysics. This first became quite clear in the attack of the *Aenesidemus* on Reinhold and so indirectly on Kant. Transcendental knowledge thus reverted immediately to a form of transcendent knowledge. In place of the Critique of Reason, which was intended to reveal the conditions under which experience is possible, we once more have a transcendent metaphysic, offering knowledge which transcends the bounds of possible experience.

It must be said, however, that in spite of this defect in Kant's Critique, which was responsible for the regress to transcendent dogmatic speculation, Kant's own work contains a sufficient refutation of all the post-Kantian attempts at a transcendent metaphysic. Sufficient equipment, indeed, for such a refutation is to be found in Kant's theory of the Amphiboly of the Concepts of Reflection. For any and every attempt at a transcendent metaphysic is bound to be ensnared in that same mistake, whose basis Kant pointed out in the Amphiboly of the Concepts of Reflection. In this discussion Kant had Leibniz in mind, as the typical example of a metaphysic of that sort, so his discussion is directly concerned only with the metaphysic of Logical Dogmatism—for this metaphysic alone sets out to construct a transcendent knowledge out of concepts. Its application to a metaphysic of intellectual intuition is less direct, for this metaphysic appeals to a source of knowledge which is independent of concepts. So one might think that the Amphiboly of the Concepts of Reflection could be avoided in this way. But what Kant's discussion really shows is that the only reason why transcendent metaphysical knowledge is not available to us is that we do not possess an intellectual intuition. It is only because sensibility and understanding are distinct, in our knowledge, that the principles of metaphysics can have no further significance for us than as formal conditions of possible experience. For this reason the protagonists of a metaphysic of intellectual intuition are not directly affected by Kant's critique of the transcendent metaphysic of Logical Dogmatism. As, however, we do not in fact possess that superior organ by which to achieve a metaphysic independent of concepts, a metaphysic of intellectual intuition, reflection is the only remaining means for transcending experience. So metaphysical Mysticism, when closely examined, turns out in every case to be merely a frustrated and concealed form of Logical Dogmatism, and so is still open to Kant's Critique of transcendent metaphysics. For Mysticism also and inevitably falls prey to that error, which it was intended to avoid, of attempting to extract a substantial metaphysical science from mere reflection. That is why Kant's theory of the Amphiboly of Concepts of Reflection really applies to every attempt at transcendent metaphysics, to those of mystics as much as to those of the scholastics. So if we start from this point we should be able to give a complete explanation of the error involved in the post-Kantian renewal of rational metaphysics described above, by availing ourselves of the aid provided by Kant in his theory of the Amphiboly of the Concepts of Reflection.

There is another reason why that error needs to be explained. There is a deep inner connection between these two sources of error which led to the renewal of rationalist metaphysics, between the epistemological preconception and the Amphiboly of the Concepts of Reflection. It is indeed possible, as history abundantly illustrates, to construct a rationalist metaphysics which falls prey to the Amphiboly of the Concepts of Reflection *without* becoming involved in the epistemological preconception. The reverse, however, is impossible. Every exposition of rationalist epistemology depends on a misuse of concepts of reflection. For the concepts of reflection are the only source from which rationalist epistemology can derive its material. Empirical concepts are forbidden goods for Rationalism, right from the start. Intellectual intuition is something we do not possess. If we appear to, that is solely due to an epistemology conjured up on the side from mere concepts of reflection. The apparent fertility of rationalist epistemology is thus always due to the Amphiboly of the Concepts of Reflection. For epistemology—rationalist epistemology, anyway, which is all we are discussing at present—has to be generated from empty reflection. Its aim is to prove that knowledge is in general both possible and valid, and to prove this *a priori*. So it cannot set out from some knowledge already established, but is compelled to start by deriving all knowledge from something which is not yet knowledge, from ideas inherently problematic. But where else can these be obtained—loans from experience being not allowed—if not from mere reflection? So the whole question is whether one can achieve a transition from mere reflection to a substantial metaphysic, a transition from problematic to assertoric ideas, from analytic judgements to synthetic ones.

The dialectical illusion that this undertaking can be carried through is, and must be, rooted in the Amphiboly of the Concepts of Reflection. Only when this source of error stands completely exposed shall we be able to derive due profit from all our occupation with error and sophistical theories. For we are here concerned with typical aberrations of the human spirit, whose appearance in the history of philosophy is not a matter of chance and which are not met with at this point alone. We are concerned with a very deep-rooted error, which is always springing up again. We can never be secure against its return until we have brought its origin right out into the light of day. That is why it is so important to criticize the dialectical basis of this rationalistic speculation.

One part of such a critique is the investigation of the reason for the plausibility of such a theory, for it was this that led to the mistake. If we are successful in this we should also be able to assess the theory in question as fairly as can reasonably be required. For this purpose we shall have to take a slightly longer run and engage in a general inquiry into questions of logic.

The Logic of Aristotle and Kant and that of Neo-Platonism and Fichte

The contrast between two basically different ways of philosophizing becomes apparent in discussion of the first principles of logic. Even at this point the two philosophical factions separate and become mutually hostile. There would seem to be no prospect at all of reconciling starting points so radically opposed. So we must first formulate clearly the contrast between these two ways of thinking, before seeing what can be done about a reconciliation. The division into two seemingly irreconcilable forms of logic and of thought in general becomes apparent first of all in the mode of abstraction practised, and then in the construction of judgments.

Let us first consider qualitative and quantitative abstraction.

In the logic of Aristotle and Kant there are two ways of abstracting. Using an expression coined by Fries, whose treatment I am following at this point, one could distinguish them as qualitative and quantitative abstraction. Qualitative abstraction consists in separating out a characteristic common to different things and treating it as predicate of possible judgments. This sort of abstraction concerns a universal, with a view to ranking under it what is particular in individual objects. Quantitative abstraction is entirely different. In this case we do not arrive at predicates of possible judgments nor at a universal under which particulars are to be ranked, but at a whole, reached by abstraction from its parts. Now the relationship between a whole and its parts must not be confused with that between a universal and its particulars. A whole includes its parts, whereas particulars are included *under* a universal, and not *in* it. Qualitative abstraction leads to an idea of analytic unity, but quantitative to one of synthetic unity. If we rank various objects under one and the same concept, we are unifying them in a merely logical manner, in a class. If for example by ranking gold under the concept *metal* I unite it with other objects—silver, say—in a class, just so far as these other objects come under the same concept *metal*, then the result is a merely logical unity of these objects. These objects are not thereby related in a genuine community, I just unite them subjectively, in my own thinking, under one and the same concept. Now quantitative abstraction is quite another matter, for it leads to the idea of a whole. If I represent various objects as just spatially connected, for instance the various parts of a piece of gold, and then conceive the shape of the whole in which they are united, for instance the shape of a disc, the result is quite a different relationship. I now have various parts in a real connection, combined into a whole, and my thought concerns that whole. In this case the parts stand in the real relationship of propinquity or succession or perhaps in one of mutual penetration. The objective form of the whole is one either of combination or of connection, and in both cases the resulting unity is synthetic and not analytic.

We may now ask whether there is any point at all in forming the notion of a merely logical unity, if no real relationship between things is to be known thereby. This question must in the end be answered by reference to the fundamental obscurity of metaphysical knowledge—what could be called its non-self-evidence. The basic metaphysical notion of an objective synthetic unity is not intrinsically clear, nor, in consequence, is the notion of connection. It does not resemble any perception. We recognize it only in the abstract form of lawlikeness, that is indirectly, by the aid of concepts in a judgment. So before we can come to think of objects as connected objectively, we must first conceive those objects whose connection is to be recognized in the form of concepts. That is the only way in which we can think of them as connected in a lawlike manner in a judgment, which we must do if we are to have a clear conception of this connection. It is only by such a judgment that we can come to think of the objects as synthetically unified in an objective way. So the detour by way of analytic unity was essential in order that we should come to think of them as synthetically unified. If we possessed an intellectual intuition, metaphysical knowledge would not have this fundamental obscurity, but would be intrinsically clear, apart from reflection and from the form of the judgment, and in that case we would not need to make this detour. For the objective synthetic unity of the universal would in that case be immediately evident to us. Our perceptual knowledge of particular facts would in that case enable us also to perceive their necessary connection. There would be no need to rank particular facts under general laws. Even the construction of general concepts—by which we may cleverly reunite in judgment what abstraction had put asunder—would become unnecessary.

This then is the meaning of abstraction in the Aristotelian logic.

The mystical mode of abstraction of the Neo-Platonists is something entirely different. Logical Mysticism admits no distinction between quantitative and qualitative abstraction, but regards abstraction as leading straight to absolute unity. This absolute unity is not conceived in the way that analytic unity was conceived in the Aristotelian logic, as a general quality separated out from particular objects whose consequent unification in a class subjects them to it; nor is it conceived along the lines of synthetic unity, as the combination of a manifold into the form of a whole. Instead, logical Mysticism regards the particular objects as literally unified, as simply and directly *one*. It therefore conceives of this unity not as something marked off in any way from the manifold, but simply as that in which different objects are one. For this school, particulars are not ranked under a universal, but are equated with other particulars. So the differences between the various particulars are not eliminated in the universal, as in the qualitative abstraction of Aristotle, but are retained, as in Aristotle's quantitative abstraction, like parts in a whole; yet in this whole the different objects are equated, as in the qualitative abstraction of Aristotle. Logical Mysticism thus avoids all the complications of the synthetic unity of the judgment, the detour *via* lawlikeness and analytic unity on the way to synthetic unity. Regarding the separated manifold itself as one, as absolutely identical, it requires no special form of connection to unify the manifold synthetically, neither the mathematical form, combination, nor the metaphysical form, connection. Mathematical combination and the connection effected by a law of nature are both unnecessary digressions for this school. It possesses absolute unity directly in every manifold, quite apart from the form of the judgment. It therefore admits no distinction between analytic and synthetic unity. On this theory the unity of the manifold does not depend on a special form of connection, but simply on the equating of different things.

The difference between these two modes of philosophical thought will become even clearer if we follow it out in their theories of judgment.

Judgment, if we can use the term at all here, meant one thing to the followers of Aristotle and something quite different to the mystics. According to the Aristotelian logic the statement $a = b$ (a is identical with b)—if taken as expressing a judgment—means that the two things a and b are one and the same thing, and so do not differ in any respect. It would therefore strike an Aristotelian as pure nonsense if someone proposed to assert at the same time that $a \neq b$, or that a is equal to not-b. Logical Mysticism, however, finds no difficulty at all in putting these two assertions together, setting them forth as true and regarding them as correct. The reason is that for this school an expression like $a = b$ means simply that the two things a and b are alike in some respect or other, which clearly does not prevent their being different in some other respect. Properly understood, an expression of this sort is not a judgment in Aristotle's sense. The distinction here is between genuine judgments and mere formulae of comparison. Comparing concepts is not judging. One may call such formulae judgments, on the Neo-Platonist theory; but an essential difference remains. The word *is*, taken as expressing the copula, does not carry the meaning of equating. And the word *not*, taken as negation in a judgment, does not carry the meaning of contrast. An affirmative judgment is not the assertion of identity either between concepts or between objects. And a negative judgement is not the assertion of difference either between concepts or between objects. Before we can speak of a genuine judgment, there must first be two notions which occur inside the judgment in quite different roles. The word *is* acquires its proper sense—that which it bears as copula— only if the roles played by the two notions in the judgment are kept distinct; the same applies to the expression *is not*. In order to mark the different roles which these two notions play in the judgment, we call one the subject and the other the predicate. The copula *is* presupposes that the judgment applies to an object. For example if I say 'this table is black' I do not mean that an equality holds between the concepts *table* and *black*, between what I call 'table' and what I call 'black'. For in that case I would really have to say 'the table is not black', since no such equality in fact obtains. What I do when I say 'this table is black' is to subsume an object, this table, under the concept *black*. So I have here on the one hand the idea of a particular object, and on the other hand a general concept. The relation of the object to the general concept is expressed by the copula *is*, which shows that the object in question is being ranked under the concept.

The relating of the judgment to the object is what in Aristotelian logic is called the reference (*Bezeichnung*) of the judgment. In our example this reference comes out expressly in the word *this*. By putting the word *this* in front of the term *table*, I refer to the object, thus making it explicit that I am not concerned with the concept *table* but with a particular individual object which comes under this concept. Where such a reference is lacking, there remains only an empty comparison-formula, and all knowledge of the things equated disappears. For to achieve such knowledge it is not enough to establish that this and that are the same or are different; if knowledge is to result, then one has to discover in what respect the two things are the same, and in what respect different. This decision presupposes some perception of the objects. Apart from perception one could equally well say that any things you like are the same, or are different. However different they may be in other respects, if they were not somehow the same they could not be compared as things at all. And however similar they may be, if they were not different in some way, they would really be one and the same thing and not several. We shall never get to know things just by equating or distinguishing them, but only when we know in what way they are the same, and in what way different. And for this purpose perception is essential. You can just as well say 'gold and silver are the same' as 'gold and silver are different'. For example they are the same in both being metal, and they differ in their specific gravity. But if we want to know this, we must go beyond mere concepts and take account of perception of the objects to which those concepts refer.

This logical theory about the form of judgment has the most serious consequences in metaphysics. The most profound metaphysical insights turn out on closer inspection to depend on their originator's insight into the nature of the form of judgment. I have shown that the mystics do not regard an expression like $a = b$ as excluding $a = $ not-b, as the Aristotelians do. We can go even further. Even with the identical proposition $a = a$, a mystic is bound to assert the opposite. He must be able also to assert $a = $ not-a, which is the opposite of the first statement. For if $a = b$, but b is plainly not equal to a, then $a \neq a$. For example: gold is a metal, metal is not gold, therefore gold is not gold. We are thus compelled to abandon the law of identity as well as that of contradiction. Nor should we be surprised at this, for these logical axioms derive their meaning from the form of the judgment, which as judgment must be either affirmative or negative, and affirmation and negation are mutually exclusive. But we are not in this case dealing with judgments at all, neither affirmative nor negative, as these are understood in Aristotelian logic. How then can the axioms of that logic be applied here?

Aristotle himself made the position very clear. He discussed this matter in his theory of fallacies, using the well-known example 'Coriscos is Socrates'. To any unprejudiced person this statement must appear nonsensical, yet nothing is easier than to show its validity according to the rules of mystical logic. For Coriscos is man, and Socrates also is man, so it follows that Coriscos is Socrates. To Aristotelians this conclusion is patently absurd. How then is it reached? By confusing mere formulae of comparison with properly formed judgments. This confusion is due, in its turn, to the failure to distinguish subject from predicate in the judgment. The fact is that Coriscos is a man, and Socrates also is a man. It follows that Coriscos and Socrates are the same, and from that the mystics' assertion follows, for them automatically. The statement 'Coriscos and Socrates are the same', is correct as a formula of comparison, for they are the same as men. But under the cover of this correct comparison-formula 'Coriscos and Socrates are the same' logical Mysticism smuggles in a false judgment, replacing the similarity of the mere comparison-formula by the identity of two objects equated, thus asserting that the two men are in fact one man. As Aristotle showed, the term *man* denotes a general concept, not an object with which the object *Coriscos* and the object *Socrates* could be equated.

Along with this equating of what is different we also find a corresponding contrasting of things which are really the same. We could indeed say, ambiguously, that a thing (maybe everything) is something different from itself. Alongside the identity of a thing with itself we can also assert its difference from itself, in the sense that everything which comes under the subject concept of a judgment is also determined by qualities of some other sort. Suppose the subject-concept is a, then an object coming under a can also come under another concept, concept b. Gold, in addition to coming under the concept *gold*, can also come under the concept *metal*. But metal is not gold. Metal and gold are different concepts. Yet the same object which comes under the one also comes under the other. So it is to that extent something different from itself. But this does not really mean that an object is different from itself, in the sense of not being identical with itself, but only that it possesses qualities which differ from each other. Just as we found previously that several objects can possess the same quality without being for that reason identical, so now we see that the same object can possess different qualities, without for that reason being different from itself.

This explanation was given by Aristotle in his criticism of the theory of judgment of his master Plato. The logical relationship concerned seems to us today perfectly simple, but Plato was quite unaware of it, so by discovering it Aristotle really did become the founder of logic.

These discoveries of the Aristotelian logic, concerning the distinction between subject and predicate in the judgment, and the resultant theory of the referring function of the judgment are not, however, sufficient in themselves to destroy the basic error in logicist metaphysics and provide complete protection against this fallacy. We must also consider the differences between forms of judgment in respect of relation, a distinction which Aristotle did not come across, and which was first correctly expounded by Kant. This distinction concerns the relationship between simple and complex judgments, where the simple judgments are in every case categorical, but the complex judgments really bear an entirely new form, quite distinct from the categorical. To get this point clear we must first look more closely at the logic of Plato, against which Aristotle's criticisms were directed.

Although Plato was involved in the confusion from which the mistake of mystical logic springs, the ultimate metaphysical consequences of that logic were first drawn by the so-called Neo-Platonists. To avoid doing an injustice to Plato, and even appearing to make him responsible for the fantastic nonsense of the Neo-Platonists, I shall mainly concentrate on Neo-Platonism, in order to contrast it clearly with Aristotle's logic. But the fact remains that the basic dialectical error which ultimately led to Neo-Platonism was originally committed by Plato. This error underlies his whole discussion, and in particular was responsible for the failure of his Theory of Ideas.

Plato's Theory of Ideas is based on the apparent possibility of a positive knowledge developed from Ideas, and this is what brings his theory to grief. The absolute synthetic unity in the being of things, which we all the time cheerfully presuppose in our concept of *the world*, is for us merely an Idea, in the strict Kantian sense of the term; i.e. this absolute synthetic unity in the being of things cannot be given to us as a definite item of knowledge. Definite knowledge is possible for us only through experience, in the form of a judgment. Now judgment, to use Neo-Platonist terminology, is concerned with the uniting of opposites, thus achieving the synthetic unity of the Variety or Manifold of perception. The judgment accomplishes this connection of the Variety of perception by means of a form of synthetic unity possible only in thought. But this task of unifying the Variety of perception into knowledge of the objective synthetic unity of the actual is one that we can never complete. We can take the synthesis of the Variety of perception only as far as our experience reaches; as our perception is of a form which cannot achieve completeness, a complete synthesis of the Variety of actuality is beyond us. The illusion that it might be possible to derive positive knowledge from Ideas, that it might be possible after all to conceive the absolute unity of actuality in a scientific manner, this illusion is due simply to the Neo-Platonist confusion of the ultimate metaphysical principle of the theory of Ideas with the most general and empty formula of comparison; to confusing the statement 'every actual Manifold is subject to the law of objective synthetic unity' with the statement 'all things are logically one'.

The philosopher after Kant mainly responsible for the reintroduction of the Neo-Platonist logic is Fichte. That is why I refer to the logic of the Neo-Platonists and Fichte, in contrast to that of Aristotle and Kant.

Let us see how Fichte came by the general principle of his so-called Scientific Theory, his universal or pure *I*. He got it by means of an authentically Neo-Platonist abstraction, for he took the universal concept of *I*-ness, under which all individuals are logically unified in a class, and hypostatized it as a basis of being, an entity from which individuals in all their variety are to be derived. Moreover that well-known principle of the Identity of Indiscernibles, which expresses the fundamental interchangeability of comparison-formulae and judgments and brings out its metaphysical significance, that principle reappears as Fichte's Method of Contradictions, by whose aid he was able to build up his so-called Scientific Theory. The so-called contradictions which are here brought forward and supposedly resolved are in fact mere formulae of comparison, empty oppositions expressed in comparison-formulae. These comparison-formulae are then confused with judgments, for the categorical relationship of subsuming an object under a concept on the basis of qualitative abstraction is confused with the relationship of parts to a whole—which is divisive in character. So underlying it all is an ignorance of the distinction between categorical and divisive judgments. Gold and silver, says Fichte, are equally included in the concept *metal*, just as you and I, as particular individuals, are equally included in the general concept *I*. Gold and silver are therefore equal, not simply in that one like the other comes under the concept *metal*, but because both are united in the concept *metal*. Here the concept *metal* no longer has the logical significance of a general characteristic which can be attributed to gold or to silver as predicate in a categorical judgment or, as subject of a divisive judgment, can form the basis of division for the extent of this concept; on the contrary the concept *metal* here obtains the significance of a general object, an identical entity, in which gold and silver are unified like different predicates of one and the same subject. Fichte indeed imagines that this equating of what is different explains an affirmative judgment, and that the contrasting of what is the same explains a negative judgment. He states his basic error very openly when he says '*a* is *b* means the same as $a = b$'; for this, as he says explicitly, is the significance of the logical copula—this, which Aristotle showed was *not* the significance of the logical copula! Fichte's formulation of the principle of method

K

of his Scientific Theory follows the same lines. He puts it like this: 'That which is contrary must be brought together, so long as anything contrary remains, until absolute unity is achieved.'

The vague expression 'unifying of opposites' here transforms the task of recognizing, in judgments, the synthetic unity of the Variety into something quite different, that of merely resolving alleged contradictions. This is a very clear case of confusing analytic with synthetic unity, mere comparison-formulae with judgments. Any remaining doubt is now removed. We can see clearly that the whole secret of this philosophy is the disregard of the theory of reference in judgments. One could really say that Fichte gave the error of mystical logic its clearest formulation. Fichte's Scientific Theory could be described as the classic attempt at systematizing mystical logic. I have already pointed out how far Schelling's so-called Philosophy of Nature, particularly his theory of the World-soul, is due to the same error. I should like to mention here as another fact of historical interest that it was this mystical mode of abstraction, as opposed to the proper method of scientific research, which made Schelling's Philosophy of Nature attractive to Goethe. Goethe's immense authority thus assisted in the spread and final triumph of this romantic manner of philosophizing. Newtonian physics was as repugnant to Goethe as it was to Schelling and Hegel, and his own scientific writings contain ideas similar to theirs, though his sound sense of realism prevented him from getting completely lost in such abstruse ideas and, as he put it, spoiling his stock of phenomena.

The fallacy of this wrong mode of abstraction, which we have discussed, comes out most clearly in Goethe in his concepts of the Original Phenomenon (*Urphänomen*) and of the type. The Original Phenomenon, for example the Original Plant, is made a principle of explanation in botany, leading some people, quite wrongly, to see Goethe as a forerunner of the modern biological theory of evolution. Goethe's Original Plant (*Urpflanze*) is not intended as an individual entity which precedes in time those forms of plants which developed later; it is the concept *plant* hypostatized to a general entity. This provides no way at all of relating the original phenomenon to the particular entity which it is supposed to explain and which comes before us in perception; all it offers us is the mystical relationship of a manifestation, emanation, attribute, or whatever else the Neo-Platonists like to call it. This similarity of ideas explains Goethe's well-known liking for Spinoza.

Let me at this point return to my earlier statement that Kant's discovery of the Amphiboly of the Concepts of Reflection enables us not only to refute Logicism, which is what he had in mind when making this discovery—especially as expressed in Leibniz' metaphysics—but also makes possible an adequate refutation of rationalist Mysticism. The proof is that mystics, unlike logicists, have no right to appeal to an intellectual intuition. The illusion of possessing such an intuition, and so of being spared the detour by means of concepts, simply stems from the failure to distinguish formulae of comparison from judgments, or categorical judgments from divisive ones. One who fails to make these distinctions seems justified in asserting that his philosophy has no need of judgments. For he is going to make do with mere formulae of comparison, without any denotation for the subject concept, and so without either affirmation or negation, that is without the form of a judgment at all. In the symbolism of antiquity the seer became a seer only when he lost his earthly sight. And all one needs to become a rationalist mystic is a touch of logical blindness, so as not to see the distinction between concepts and objects, between categorical and divisive judgments. Nothing further is required; all one need do is to miss that distinction and imagine oneself in possession of an intellectual intuition, and so to think oneself justified in passing over, without the extra reasons which the form of the judgments could have provided, from formulae of comparison to the corresponding judgments, to a corresponding metaphysical assertion. Once this transition or interchange is permitted, one has all that is needed to make that metaphysical assertion genuinely self-evident. For those formulae of comparison are quite unimpeachable and irrefutable, and this carries over to the corresponding metaphysical judgment, which at once becomes self-evident.

My treatment so far has been partly historical and partly systematic. In conclusion I would like to illustrate it by an historical parallel, for an analogous development can be found in classical Chinese philosophy, which certainly neither influenced nor was influenced by European philosophy. There is in fact a Chinese Neo-Platonism.

The conquest of Neo-Platonism is a great achievement in the cultural history of Europe, although as yet incomplete, but its significance in the development of the Chinese mind is even more remarkable, for Chinese writing, unlike European, does not have any single sign corresponding to our copula, to the word *is*. The interchange of a judgment with a mere formula of comparison is therefore even easier over there. For Chinese is not written with letters, as European languages are; it is a concept language, i.e. each sign stands directly for one concept, and the sign is not itself composed from a finite number of letters, so that it is not possible, as it is in our languages, to denote all concepts by means of different combinations of letters. Instead each concept really has a new sign. There is therefore nothing at all in Chinese writing to designate the copula, this just has to be guessed by various artificial means. This makes the question all the more interesting: however did the Chinese come to develop a science like our logic?

The main contribution, here as elsewhere in Chinese thought, is found in the theories of the two classical writers, Lao-tze and Kong-fu-tze or Confucius. Their contributions were, however, very different, for in this as in most things they were poles apart. As is well known, Taoism, the theory of Lao-tse, is the speculative theory that all things originate in non-being, and as practical teaching offers salvation by non-action as the way to redeem mankind. Non-action corresponds on the practical level to non-being on the speculative. Already in this preference for negation as a basic principle of meta-physics we can see a tendency towards logical Mysticism. Thus Lao-tze for instance says: 'All things arise out of Being. Being arises out of non-Being.' And in another passage: 'Non-Being exists undivided from Being . . . One could call it mother of the universe, I call it Tao.'

Contrasted with Taoism there is Confucius' theory of the rectification of concepts. Such rectification enabled one not only to achieve theoretical clarity but also to get one's bearings right in practice. But what was meant by 'rectification of concepts'? This was the great puzzle for the Chinese philosophers who followed Confucius. In the Chinese language there was as yet no distinction between concepts and mere names, and in Confucius the same expression serves for both. So his phrase could mean 'rectification of names'. These concepts or so-called names were chosen by Confucius in a way very similar to Plato's, chiefly from qualities which admit degrees, i.e. a quality reckoned in degrees towards an ideal, so that one could easily follow Confucius in speaking as if a thing shared in a certain concept to a greater or less degree, just as in Plato's theory of μέθεξις (sharing, participation).

The theories of Lao-tze and Confucius were bound to confront subsequent thinkers with the problem of the significance of concepts. The main point for our purposes is that a thinker arose forthwith whom we must describe as the father of Chinese logic, in the way that Aristotle is the father of European logic. This was Mong-tze or Mencius, or as he was also called, Mo-ti. He is the Chinese Aristotle, and he was in fact a contemporary of Aristotle's. Not only was he an important logician; he also worked as a moralist, evolving a moral theory very similar to the Christian, with love of mankind in general as the ideal. Mencius was the first Chinese thinker to recognize the distinction between the subject-concept and the predicate-concept in a judgment. He taught people to distinguish between what is predicated and that of which it is predicated. This discovery led him to a fairly clear formulation of the requirement that all subject concepts should be reduced to subject ideas which can be shown in perception—a demand which, if fulfilled, would be quite enough to defeat logical Mysticism. We ought not of course to be surprised that Mencius' work did not achieve this result, for Aristotle's work has not achieved it in Europe even yet. Instead—and this should be a comfort for many Europeans in the twentieth century—logical Mysticism flourished even more after Mencius. This is clear from the growing power acquired by the mystical mode of abstraction of Taoism. The literature also offers us a very striking parallel to the so-called sophistical fallacies dealt with by Aristotle. We may hope, however, that it will be easier for modern Chinese philosophy to return to the theories of its founder Mencius than it is for Europeans to return to the theories of Aristotle.

To bring the present enquiry to a satisfactorily systematic close let me now try to set out as a system the fundamental way in which mystical logic can be critically applied, I mean according to principles and with some claim to completeness, so forming a sort of axiomatic system.

Our basic concern here is with the metaphysical reinterpretation of the logical form of the copula. Everything therefore depends in the end on the relationship between subject and predicate in a categorical judgment, and so on the Concepts of Reflection which come under Quantity and Quality. In the moment of Quantity we have (in Kant's terms) the two Concepts of Reflection, unity and variety; and in that of Quality we have agreement and conflict. Under Quantity we compare objects in respect of their likeness or difference. Under Quality we compare characteristics in respect of their agreement or conflict. But in order to form judgments we must relate our concepts to perception. Perception must provide us with qualities in respect of which we can judge objects to be similar or different, and also with objects in respect of which we can judge our concepts to agree or to be in conflict. Objects are similar if they agree in any one characteristic; they are different if they disagree in respect of a characteristic. Characteristics in turn agree if they can be combined as characteristics of one object; they are in conflict if they exclude each other as characteristics of one object. As we know, one cannot say that objects are in themselves similar or different, or that concepts as such agree or conflict; for it must first be determined in respect of what concepts we are comparing the objects, and in respect of what objects we are comparing the concepts. But in the mode of philosophical thought which we have been considering it is assumed, on the contrary, that objects can be known by thought alone and that reality can therefore be completely determined by means of mere concepts. The yoke of perception is thrown off. Objects are now to be determined by the Concepts of Reflection themselves. So one must be able to assert that objects are similar absolutely or absolutely different, and that concepts are in agreement absolutely or absolutely conflicting.

There must at this point be a hidden transition from a formula of comparison to a judgment. Perception cannot perform this transition, for the whole point of it is to get rid of perception. Whence, then, comes the dialectical illusion that such a transition can be made? Kant has resolved the mystery for us. This illusion is due to the interchange of logical concepts of comparison with the corresponding basic concepts of metaphysics, which Kant called Categories. The concepts of comparison which come under Quantity are exchanged with the Categories of Quantity, and those which come under Quality are exchanged with the Categories of Quality. This effects the transition from the empty analytic unity of the concept to the real synthetic unity of the object. Kant's discovery, which disperses all the mystical haze surrounding the mystery, appears even clearer and more remarkable in the light of a clever remark made by Apelt. In his *Metaphysics* there is a very good discussion of the Amphiboly of the Concepts of Reflection. He there demonstrates that in order to apply the Categories, and so to achieve knowledge from concepts, we should need some criterion showing us to which things to apply a particular Category and which Categories to apply to a particular thing. And he points out that in the attempt to derive knowledge from concepts alone, the Concepts of Reflection play the part of such a criterion; that is, they must appear as related to the Categories rather as the mathematical schemata are, in empirical knowledge—those schemata or pure determinations of time whose combination with Categories, yields the real principles of metaphysics—as Kant showed in detail in his Critique of Pure Reason. Once the Concepts of Reflection lay claim to this role of providing their own Schematism of the Categories, there results an illusion of metaphysical knowledge gained from mere formulae of comparison. The upshot is that what is thought of as similar by means of a formula of comparison is now conceived of as one in the sense of the Category of unity, and what is thought of as distinct in a formula of comparison is regarded as plural in the sense of the Category of plurality. The same goes for the Concepts of Reflection which come under Quality. The mere concept of agreement, without relation to any particular object, is used as a schema for the Category of reality. And the mere concept of conflict, again without reference to particular objects, is used as a schema for the Category of negation.

Enough has now been said about this principle of method. Let us see what metaphysical statements result from it. For this purpose we shall first have to set out the formulae of comparison to which the individual Concepts of Reflection do quite properly lead. These then become logical axioms.

Let us take the moment of Quantity first. A correct application of the Concepts of Reflection which come under Quantity leads us to the principles 'all objects are similar' and 'all objects are different'. However paradoxical and absurd these statements may appear when treated as judgments, as formulae of comparison they are entirely unobjectionable and by no means mutually exclusive. There is of course a price to pay for this, namely that they do not lead to any definite knowledge, as the reference to perception is lacking. They do not and cannot determine in respect of which characteristics objects are similar, and in respect of which they are different. For all their profundity, these statements are no use to us, as knowledge.

Corresponding statements can be obtained in the moment of Quality. Here we have just as good or bad a right to say that realities are in agreement with each other as that realities are in conflict with each other. As formulae of comparison these statements are not mutually exclusive; but for the same reason they offer no positive knowledge. In application *to what objects* is there this agreement or conflict?—this point would need to be settled first. As a mere matter of logic, from the perspective of mere thought, and apart from any objects which may be determined in perception, we can only say that identical characteristics are in agreement, and that contradictory characteristics are in conflict with each other. But, again, that is no help in getting to know actuality; for that purpose the relationship of one reality to another would have to be determinable as agreement or conflict:—actual combination in application to an actual object, or actual mutual exclusion in application to an actual object. Now this relationship occurs neither in the case of identity of characteristics, nor when they are contradictory. If, however, we take the Concepts of Reflection, in the way already explained, as criteria for the applic-

ability of the corresponding Categories, and consider them as schemata
of the Categories, we then arrive at synthetic judgments, which—
having originated from mere concepts—appear here as metaphysical
axioms. Synthetic judgments from concepts alone! To what statements of this sort does our principle of method lead us? The answer
can be given quite mechanically, simply by reading what is set out in
Table VII.

(VII) Axioms Drawn from Concepts of Reflection

Moment	Concepts of Reflection	Categories	Logical formulae of comparison	Metaphysical Axioms	Consequences
Quantity: Subject (object or thing)	Similarity	Unity	1. All objects are similar	1. What is similar is one and the same thing	Everything is one
	Difference	Plurality	2. All objects are different	2. What is distinguish-able is plurality	Indiscernibles are identical
Quality Predicate (concept)	Agreement (inclusion)	Reality	1. Identical characteristics agree	1. Non-con-tradictory concepts agree and determine an object	The sum of realities: realities never conflict
	Conflict (exclusion)	Negation	2. Contradictory characteristics conflict	2. Non-identical concepts con-flict; and cannot determine an object	Herbartian theory of monads: realities do conflict

One basic point must be remembered in using this table: it is here
assumed that objects can be determined by means of thought alone.
Once this is presupposed, the only criterion left for the unity of an
object is that of logical similarity. The merely logical concept of
comparability thus determines the unity of an object. Whatever is
similar is one thing, one and the same thing; that is our first metaphysical axiom in the moment of Quantity. And having assumed that
objects can be determined by means of mere thought, the only
criterion we have left for the plurality of objects is the mere concept of
difference, understood as a matter of logical comparison. So having

assumed that concepts on their own are sufficient to determine objects, we take a merely conceptual distinguishability as schema for the plurality of objects. All and only those things that are conceptually distinguishable form pluralities. Here the unifying of a plurality of given things in thought under one predicate-concept, in the usual way, is confused with the unifying of a plurality of given determinations in the unity of a single thing. The one is a logical similarity, in respect of a concept, and the other is a real unity, the identity of an actual thing. If one confuses the two, conceptual similarity becomes the schema for objective unity, and conceptual distinguishability that for objective plurality. A Concept of Reflection thus does duty as schema for the corresponding Categories. It is the necessary and sufficient condition for applying the Categories. The two concepts which are combined into a metaphysical axiom, the Concept of Reflection and the corresponding Category, are interchangeable concepts, i.e. their denotation is the same. So in the moment of Quantity we have two metaphysical axioms:

1. 'What is similar is one and the same thing'. Mere similarity is here taken as sufficient criterion for the unity of an object. In other words, noncomparability is taken as a necessary criterion for plurality. This leads to the metaphysical consequence that all things are really one thing: in brief, everything is one. This statement of the unity of all things (numerical unity) is the axiom of the metaphysics of Spinoza.

2. 'What is different is a plurality'. Conceptual distinguishability thus becomes a necessary criterion for objective plurality. To put it another way: conceptual indistinguishability becomes a sufficient criterion of unity. This brings us straight to Leibniz' principle of individuation, which states that the individuality of objects depends on their conceptual determination, and that if any objects have all their conceptual determinations the same, then they are identical. That is only to be expected if we assume that general concepts are sufficient to determine reality, for on this assumption plurality is possible only as a result of conceptual distinguishability. Now these two axioms are mutually exclusive. They are no longer compatible, as were the formulae of comparison from which we began. For the first eliminates, and the second admits, the plurality of things.

What metaphysical axioms do we reach in the moment of Quality? To discover these, we must start, once again, from our assumption that objects can be determined by means of thought alone. On this assumption the only predicates which can be thought of as compatible with the concept of an object are those which are logically included in that concept. And conversely the only concepts which can be known through thought alone as conflicting are those which stand in the logical relation of contradiction. So all those characteristics disappear which could belong to an object without being included in the concept of it. Another casualty is the negation of those characteristics which conflict with it without being contradictory to its concept: for the distinction between a logical and a real relationship is here destroyed. So the correct statements that contradictory concepts conflict with each other and that identical concepts are in agreement, are replaced, owing to the Amphiboly, by the false statements that whatever does not agree is contradictory and that whatever is not in conflict is identical. Or—which comes to the same thing—whatever is not contradictory agrees and whatever is not identical is in conflict. Metaphysically these statements signify that we are using Concepts of Reflection (agreement and conflict) as schemata for Categories (reality and negation), but that—as in the Amphiboly of the Concepts of Reflection—agreement is sought in the mere absence of contradiction and conflict in mere difference, in the non-identity of concepts. So we could quite well express the metaphysical axioms of Quality like this:

1. Non-contradictory concepts are in agreement, i.e. they determine an object.

2. Non-identical concepts are in conflict, i.e. they cannot determine any object.

This brings us to the principle that distinct positive realities do not conflict with each other if they are not contradictory to each other, an idea brought out in Leibniz' theory of God as the Sum of realities. We also come to the principle that distinct positive realities must of necessity be in conflict, simply because they are not identical. We thus obtain Leibniz' well-known law that realities do not conflict, and also the axiom of Herbart's theory of monads that realities must be in conflict. The two metaphysical axioms are thus mutually contradictory, unlike the formulae of comparison from which we derived them. For according to the second axiom distinct realities are in conflict, while according to the first the same realities cannot be in conflict. The common element in the two conceptions is this: synthetic agreement and conflict found in perception are excluded. Those characteristics of an object which are neither contained in its concept nor contradict that concept are confused either with those which contradict it or with those already contained in it. If one combines Herbart's axiom that a thing cannot possibly combine several qualities with Spinoza's axiom that there cannot possibly be several things—his principle of the unity of substance or of the numerical unity of all things—one obtains the final consequence of the Neo-Platonist theory of unity: not only are all things one, but there can only be one predicate. One reaches the Eleatic theory that there is one Being, without any differences.

To complete our axiomatic treatment we must ask what internally consistent, complete, and mutually independent systems seem possible, on the basis of the insight we have now obtained. We have seen that in both the moments—in that of Quantity as well as in that of Quality—the two axioms exclude each other and so cannot be combined in one and the same system. All that remains is to combine an axiom in one moment with one of the two in the other moment, thus producing internally consistent, complete, and mutually independent metaphysical systems. If we call the axioms of Quantity A^1 and A^2, and those of Quality B^1 and B^2, we obtain the following four possible combinations: A^1 with B^1, A^1 with B^2, A^2 with B^1 and A^2 with B^2.

If we combine A^1, the axiom that everything is one, with B^1, the axiom of a Sum of reality, that all realities must agree, i.e. determine an object, we get a perfect embodiment of Spinoza's metaphysic. This rests on the two axioms 'everything is one' and 'non-contradictory concepts agree'. Here we find the postulate of the unity of things combined with that of the plurality of characteristics, corresponding to the absolute and universal single Substance of Spinoza's theory and its infinite attributes.

If we combine A^1 with B^2, i.e. the axiom that everything is one with that which declares distinct concepts to be in conflict, we obtain a metaphysics combining the postulates of the unity of things and the unity of characteristics, the metaphysics of the Eleatics, the theory of the single Being without any difference.

If we combine A^2 with B^1, the axiom of the identity of indiscernibles with the axiom that non-contradictory characteristics agree (the axiom of the Sum of reality), we immediately arrive at Leibniz' metaphysics, as those well-known phrases show. Here the plurality of things is preserved along with the plurality of qualities; exactly the opposite of the metaphysics of the Eleatics.

If we combine A^2 with B^2, the axiom which admits the plurality of things with that which excludes the plurality of qualities, we come at once to the metaphysics of Herbart.

Finally we must ask how the concepts and axioms thus obtained stand with regard to the corresponding concepts and axioms in the other moments of the judgment, the moments of Relation and Modality, and especially with regard to the concepts and axioms of Relation. For this moment contains the properly and directly metaphysical principles, those of connection. It is here that we meet those complicated problems raised by the metaphysics of Descartes, which have been the centre of metaphysical interest in modern times, and which look like keeping us busy in metaphysics for some time to come.

If we consider the logical foundation for Descartes' metaphysics, apart from logical Mysticism, we meet under the heading of Relation two main axioms, one asserting the singularity of Substance—which we had already arrived at in our first axiom of Quantity—and the second stating that one substance cannot possibly act upon another. The latter was a principle of Cartesian philosophy of nature and is one still for modern physical theory, which is influenced, more or less unconsciously, by Cartesianism. It really appears to us as self-evident, steeped as we now are in this mode of thinking. After all, we did set out to decide on the basis of concepts alone what is impossible.

Descartes' justification for the statement that no substance can act on another was based on his explanation that the only possible action would be one where the mind could see how it worked.* But the mind is not able to see how such an action could take place. For that is a metaphysical relation, not a logical one. So for a metaphysics based on pure intellect no action will be possible, and in particular no action of one substance upon another. In any case this statement follows from the axiom that there cannot be a plurality of substances. For such a plurality would have to be assumed in order for one substance to act on another. The statement also follows, however, from the opposing metaphysics, which asserts the plurality of things (in accordance with the second axiom of Quantity), at least if one denies that individual things can have a plurality of qualities. For there can be action, within our knowledge, only if there can be change. Change is what action is supposed to effect. But change can take place only if we may assume that there can be several qualities of one and the same thing. A thing which admits of only one quality does not admit any possibility of change nor, in consequence, of action. So in the metaphysics of Spinoza or, we should say, of Descartes, the unity of the world, that ultimate and comprehensive unity which we have demanded for reality under the moment of Relation, can consist—if it is there at all—only in the numerical unity of Substance. Such a unity cannot obtain at all if it is assumed that there are several substances. For if we hold that there are several substances, but deny, with Descartes, that one substance can possibly act on another, then we lose the unity of the world. The system of pre-established harmony

* cp. Vol. I, p. 33.

is still perhaps available, but this really contains as many worlds as there are assumed to be substances thus supposedly harmonized.

This whole metaphysics, then, allows of a unity of the world only on the basis of the singularity of Substance; that is only as a categorical, not as a divisive unity. This matches precisely the findings of our earlier logical enquiry which showed that this metaphysics depends on interpreting as categorical what are in fact divisive judgments. The world and the absolute Substance thus coincide. God, as absolute Substance, and the created world are one and the same and are distinguished and contrasted only by one's perspective, the one as *natura naturans*, the other as *natura naturata*—hence the essential Pantheism of this metaphysic. The real puzzle of this Spinozist theory of unity is how plurality is possible, and the question arises: can we still assert that there is one world? Spinoza's answer refers the unity of the world to the singularity of Substance. All plurality is a plurality of attributes of this Substance.

We also come across, even in Descartes' work, a further axiom which is relevant here, the axiom that substance cannot be caused to exist, that the concept of a substance excludes the possibility of such causation. Descartes describes substance as that whose existence is such that it has no need of anything else in order to exist. This inevitably led him to his idea of substance as *causa sui*, its own cause. This explains his assertion that the dependence of individual beings on God for their existence in the one world is possible only if God is the one and only Substance. Otherwise each individual being, as a substance, would also be *causa sui*, which would contradict its dependence on God's existence, and also the unity of the world. So only one substance can really be *causa sui*, if we are to retain the unity of the world. Yet the conclusion which Cartesianism draws from this, that God is the sole Substance, is fallacious. For this presupposes that a substance cannot be an effect. Without this presupposition there could perfectly well be a single *causa sui*, and still a plurality of substances, if we think of the individual substances as created by the *causa sui*. This possibility is only apparently ruled out by Descartes' arbitrary introduction of a verbal definition of a substance as that which exists in such a way as not to need anything else in order to exist. This illusion is further promoted by the fact that one unconsciously operates already with the mathematical schematism of the Categories, instead of with the pure Categories themselves, disentangled from that schematism, which would be more proper for a metaphysic from concepts alone. For this mathematical schematism derives from our intuition of time, which is forbidden goods. And what appears in this metaphysic as a judgment taken quite harmlessly on the basis of mere definitions really presupposes the synthetic proposition that substance is permanent, the firmly established principle of the natural philosophers that substances cannot arise in time.

This assertion, however, was originally due to perceptual knowledge and holds good only for the concept of substance as applied to temporal perception, and not for the idea of absolute substance. Once this mistake is eliminated the axiom that substances cannot be caused to exist loses its deceptive plausibility. Once set free from the mathematical schema provided by our perception of time, the concept of substance does not conflict with its existence being caused. On the contrary, if we really think through the idea of the unity of the world, and consequently drop the idea of the mathematical schematism, an adequate idea of the unity of the world will really demand that the plurality of particular beings be thought to depend on a single *causa sui*, rather than on non-existent and abstract laws of nature, though within our own empirical knowledge it is the latter alone which make the unity of the manifold objectively thinkable.

We have now explained fully why it is that there should appear to be a source of knowledge for synthetic propositions from thought alone, as metaphysical axioms. Our success in this is really just one more triumph for Kant's transcendental guideline, that discovery of his which not only gives us complete and reliable insight into the system of genuine metaphysical concepts and principles but also, if rightly applied, shows fully and clearly the nature of the various possible errors in metaphysics and thus gives us a safe defence against these errors. Anyone who has understood the rule by which this metaphysic is constructed from mystical logic will easily find his way among the abstruse philosophical theories of Neo-Platonism, and will indeed be able to make up his own theories along those lines. The only equipment needed is that grotesque combination of pedantry and fantasy of which Grillparzer said:

> Pedantry and fantasy
> Misbehaved, I don't know how,
> And planted out in Germany
> The fruits of their misunion.
> A crop without a parallel
> Pedants all fantastical.

6

Systematization of the Psychological Preconception and Reversion of the Critical Philosophy to Empiricism and Nominalism

Our discussion of the regress in philosophy after Kant will concern, finally, the systematization of the psychological (or psychologistic*), as contrasted with the transcendental, preconception; and the resulting reversion of the Critique of Reason to Empiricism and Nominalism. This development, like the other, is a direct result of Reinhold's Basic Philosophy, with its epistemological misinterpretation of the Critique of Reason. So we shall find here the precise counterpart to the rationalistic development which we have traced so far.

This tendency comes out most clearly in Schulz' *Aenēsidemus*, in his attacks on the would-be 'rational psychology' which he thought he had found not only in Reinhold's Basic Philosophy, but also in Kant's Critique of Reason. The movement towards Empiricism went further in Ernst Reinhold, the son of the founder of Basic Philosophy, and appears in a still clearer and more typical form in Beneke, who is closer to Kant than any other empiricist, and who works out more consistently than any other philosopher of this school the psychological and empiricist interpretation of the Critique. The ideas which seem to us typical of modern Empiricism and Positivism were all put forward by Beneke. The positive renewal of pre-Kantian metaphysics which we found in the rationalists is combated in Beneke by a negative metaphysic, by an attempt to abolish metaphysics as a rational science and to build up all knowledge exclusively from experience. But, as the Critique of Reason has taught us, this undertaking is impossible. It can result only in a concealed, and so more dangerous, metaphysics, which does all the more mischief because the positivist does not realize the metaphysical presuppositions which he is employing and so does not consider them critically. Thus he has no guarantee against getting lost in endless and extravagant speculation, just when he thinks he is basing all his theories on experience.

Let us first consider how Beneke stands towards the method of

* see p. 24, note.

Kant's Critique of Reason. The dogmatic rationalists, as we saw, concluded from the *a priori* nature of metaphysical knowledge, whose justification the Critique of Reason was supposed to provide, to the *a priori* nature of the Critique of Reason itself. Here we find the contrary conclusion which, as we know, is equally valid. For if one confuses system with critique, as Reinhold's Basic Philosophy did, and if in consequence one takes critique and system to be of the same type, then instead of concluding from the rational nature of the system to the *a priori* character of the Critique of Reason, one could equally well conclude from the empirical nature of the Critique to the empirical nature of the system. This is Beneke's conclusion. He asserts that there is a contradiction in Kant's attempt to justify metaphysics as a rational science by means of the Critique of Reason, that is by means of inner experience. The Critique, he says, is really a science from inner experience, so metaphysics also must in the end be derived entirely from inner experience. If it is to be a science at all it must be one which follows from psychology and cannot contain any rational knowledge. What we have here, according to Beneke, is simply the result, correctly understood, of Kant's method. Beneke therefore thinks that he alone has developed Kant's philosophy further in a consistent manner.

This shows that Beneke, like the upholders of the transcendental preconception whom he attacked, treated the Critique as logically prior to the system, thus sharing Reinhold's misunderstanding of the critical method. Beneke also took this method as a mode of proof, though he did not adopt Reinhold's view of it as a progressive proof proceeding from a general rational premiss. Rather he regarded it as a regressive conclusion from particular facts of observation, similar to that employed in an empirical science—thus confusing the analytic method of abstraction with the proof-procedure of induction. And having misinterpreted Kant's method in an empirical sense, Beneke also reverted entirely to Empiricism in psychology itself, on which his metaphysic is supposed to be based. In this also he appealed to Kant's authority. Kant's greatest contribution, he thought, was his proof that knowledge cannot be carried further by thought alone; Kant's most important discovery, in his view, was that human knowledge is immanent, for he thought that this law would logically lead straight back to Empiricism. In this he treats the emptiness of reflection, which Kant had admitted, as sufficient proof in itself of the axiom that all our knowledge is empirical in origin. This inference, which is always cropping up, shows clearly the dogmatic assumption that reflection and sensibility form a complete disjunction. For the inference is valid only if one assumes that there is no third source of knowledge apart from these two. This tacit assumption is clearly the fundamental issue in the whole dispute, but Beneke passes it by, as though he were dealing with something quite self-evident. Yet everything depends, for Beneke, on the justification of this statement. His whole philosophy is thus seen to rest on a *petitio principii*.

Driven by this idea, seized by this (in itself quite arbitrary) assumption, Beneke quite logically reverts to pre-Kantian Empiricism. He denies that man possesses anything like a reason in the Kantian sense. For him, there is no *a priori* knowledge. But in saying this he once more confuses two questions: when, and where, the knowledge arose. He appeals to the psychological fact, which Kant did not dispute, that man does not bring with him concepts or judgments of any sort, that all concepts and judgments owe their first development in the human mind to experience. From this correct and quite undisputed fact of observation he concludes that the human mind has no *a priori* knowledge. From the fact that all knowledge comes to conciousness in the course of experience he concludes that all knowledge must be based upon experience. So he does not regard reason as an original faculty in man, but as arising in the human mind in the course of experience. For him, reason is the sum of mental activity carried to its highest pitch of development, and so merely an ideal. It is not there when the human mind starts its development, but really signifies its end and aim. Beneke was thus the founder and most active defender of the famous axiom that man possesses no reason, an axiom treated by empiricist psychologists even today as the most important discovery of their science and defended with tenacious pertinacity as an inviolable sanctuary.

Of particular interest in this psychology is Beneke's theory of judgment. He goes to considerable trouble to construct an empiricist theory of judgment. Judgment, he says, is an equating of similar mental activities. Take for instance the judgment 'this lily is white'. The subject of this judgment, according to Beneke, is a perception, and the same goes for its predicate. These two mental acts are to this extent equated in the judgment that the second is included in the first. The perception of the lily includes the perception of white. That is what the judgment expresses.

This theory of judgment contains several characteristic mistakes. First of all, the subject of the judgment is quite clearly a particular lily, so it is not the perception of this lily. Beneke confuses the object perceived with the perception itself, which certainly is a mental act.

L

Moreover, we are not dealing with two mental acts, a perception of the lily and a perception of white, the second being included in the first, rather we have a single indivisible perception of the white lily. But in that which we perceive we can in thought separate the colour from the shape, by abstracting one or the other. This separation is a work of reflection. This leads in the end to the construction of concepts, which certainly are open to comparison. But the comparison of the concepts thus obtained, in our case of the concepts *lily* and *white*, is not yet a judgment, but only a formula of comparison. And it would be a false formula of comparison into the bargain, if we declared the concept *lily* to be the same as the concept *white*.

Here once again is that same error which we saw to be the basic and dialectically decisive mistake in the rationalist theory of judgment; only in place of general concepts we now have mental acts. The theory of judgment is all the more significant for Beneke's entire discussion, as he tacitly assumes that every item of knowledge is a judgment. What is said about judgments is therefore carried over without further discussion to all items of knowledge quite in general. Hence his assertion that every item of knowledge is an equating of similar mental acts. But in order to equate mental acts we would have to have knowledge of them first. And we have knowledge of mental acts only by means of inner perception. All knowledge—so Beneke rightly infers—must therefore stem from inner perception. Now apart from the false assertion that every item of knowledge is a judgment, which was assumed without justification of any sort, quite apart from that it is easy to see that this account of the origin of all knowledge in inner perception is intrinsically inadequate. For inner perception, to which all judgments are to be traced back, being itself an item of knowledge and therefore necessarily a judgment, would have to depend in its turn on an equating of similar mental acts and so would presuppose other judgments, by which these mental acts could be known, and so on in an endless regress, so that no judgment would ever be able to occur at all.

A theory which proposes to derive all knowledge from sense perception will of course have particular difficulty in showing general judgments to be possible. Beneke does remark that from perception alone only singular judgments can arise directly, so it is a problem for him how general judgments can occur at all. This is the problem of induction, a problem whose solution is all the more important and indispensable for an empiricist theory of judgment, as this theory in the end makes induction the sole mode of proof for general and so also for philosophical truths. The empiricist theory itself, whose defence is here attempted, is only a paraphrase for a general judgment, the judgment that all knowledge derives from sense perception, particularly from inner perception. A cautious empiricism would therefore have to give some account of how it reaches this general judgment that all knowledge derives from sense perception.

To the question how general judgments can occur Beneke gives a reply typical of consistent Empiricism. Someone observes, say, white lilies several times. So he generalizes his observations to a judgment 'all lilies are white'. At first, of course, this judgment is merely a suggestion. This judgment might find confirmation for quite some time in experience; but he is bound to come across an orange lily in the end. So it seems that a general judgment can be meant only as a hypothesis; it cannot claim strict validity. It is always possible for a general judgment to be refuted in this way by later experience, but according to Beneke this does not prevent our maintaining the strict universality of the judgment. Certainly experience cannot guarantee its universality for us. So long as we refer to experience, we must always be prepared for counter-examples. But we can set ourselves free from observation without reintroducing *a priori* knowledge, which is taboo, by taking the predicate of the judgment into the concept of the subject; in our example that means altering the meaning of the word *lily*, so that it not only refers to the shape, as previously, but also includes the colour, namely the white colour. Our judgment will then hold with complete universality, independent of all further observation. For in this way we change a synthetic judgment into an analytic one. And the analytic judgment holds with absolute universality.

In this theory Beneke confuses the concept with the meaning of the word. The content of the subject-concept in a general judgment is not a creature of our whim, as it here seems to be. We cannot change it just when we like; though we can arbitrarily alter the meaning of the word which designates it. In our case we can for example declare that by the word *lily* we shall not mean, as previously, a plant of a certain shape, but a plant of a certain shape and a certain colour. But this alteration in the meaning of the word does not change the content of the subject-concept. It does not change a synthetic judgment into an analytic one; only the same series of words, by which we previously denoted a synthetic judgment, we now use to express an analytic one. This sleight-of-hand does not get rid of non-white lilies. They are still there, even though they no longer have the honour to be called lilies.

Beneke's theory, then, does not succeed in providing an empiricist foundation for induction and so for the sciences of experience. If we could achieve general judgments simply by means of verbal definitions, induction would in any case be superfluous. There would be no need to collect experiences, to set up experiments and make observations, as we could acquire general truths by arbitrary decrees about verbal uses. But it would be a fatal illusion to suppose that the statements obtained in this way apply to experience. In order to apply the general analytic statement 'all lilies are white' to particular actual objects and so to infer their white colour, we must subsume these objects under the concept of the subject of the judgment. But for this we would need—according to the definition here introduced—already to have established their white colour. So we no longer need the general judgment to infer that colour from.

The position is quite different for synthetic general judgments obtained by induction in the sciences of experience. These enable us to ascribe a quality to an object on the basis of another quality known to us by observation, the latter forming the subject-concept in a general judgment and so serving as middle term, enabling us to apply the predicate of the general judgment to the object observed. But synthetic general judgments of this sort would of course not be possible if there were no genuine *a priori* knowledge. This shows that the empiricists' supposed freedom from metaphysical presuppositions is just a *carte blanche* to deny experience its rights and to disregard the claims of empirical science.

Beneke's procedure in the case of genuine philosophical judgments is slightly different, but equally characteristic. He starts from the fact that the generality of these judgments rests on the impossibility of thinking the contrary. Take for instance the statement that everything actual is in time, a statement which Beneke himself produces as an instance of a philosophical universal judgment. Now the universality of this is supposed to be due to the inability of the human mind to think the contrary. So Beneke bases this judgment on its subjective necessity. But this subjective necessity, the necessity of thought, can be known to us only by means of inner experience. This makes it seem as though philosophical general judgments could really derive from inner experience. But this is a mere illusion, due once more to a failure to distinguish two quite different judgments. That I am compelled to think of everything actual as in time, is one judgment; that everything actual is in time, is a different judgment. The validity of the second and philosophical judgment cannot be inferred from the first. The fact that we are compelled to think certain judgments is no criterion for the truth of those judgments.

Beneke's only escape from this criticism lies in his assertion that all the general judgment really says is that we are compelled to treat it as true. But what is it that we are really compelled to think? If what we are supposed to be compelled to think is that same judgment 'everything actual is in time', and if all this means is that we are compelled to think this judgment, we would really have to say that we are compelled to think that we are compelled to think that everything actual is in time. But in this explanation the statement we are trying to explain recurs and so must be replaced once more by its meaning. And so it goes on in an endless regress, so that we can never get back to what this statement really means. The circularity of this definition is obvious.

There is, however, a further difficulty. Beneke's judgment from inner experience, taken strictly, is by no means a mere statement of fact. It concerns what the human mind is in general compelled to think. So it is related to the other general judgment that all men are compelled to think that everything actual is in time. But on Beneke's theory the only way to guarantee such a general judgment of experience is to give it a verbal reinterpretation as a definition. One would have to decide that the word *think* meant 'to conceive the actual as being in time'; this would enable one to say: Any philosopher who asserts—as for example Plato and Kant both did—that there is something actual which is not in time, is just *not thinking*. As a result the statement that the human mind is compelled to think of everything actual as in time becomes a purely verbal definition of the concept *think*. This device, however, lets us down when it comes to showing that philosophers who think otherwise are mistaken so to think.

A further effect of Beneke's basic psychological approach comes out in his definition of 'Being' as being known, and so—since on his view all knowledge is empirical in origin—as being perceived. He thus comes to the old proposition *esse est percipi* (to be is to be perceived)—though, having a certain feeling that this extreme empiricist standpoint cannot be carried through, he changes the proposition. He does not regard Being strictly as being actually perceived, but rather as being able to be perceived. This qualification is important for him. It also shows the inherent inadequacy of his theory.

Now if Being is supposed to consist of being perceived, or of being able to be perceived, in what does the Being of perception consist, for this is certainly essential to being perceived? Clearly, in perception being perceived or at least being able to be perceived. But the same would apply to this perception, in its turn. So this explanation again leads to an endless regress. The definition is obviously circular. Moreover, Beneke fails to provide any criterion for the possibility of being perceived. The test of whether something can be perceived cannot lie in its actually being perceived, so if we are to take this concept seriously, we shall clearly need some *a priori* criterion for the possibility of that process. Here we see how the metaphysical knowledge which was driven out of the front door creeps into the system again through the back door—as it must if that system is even to seem to gain a footing. There must be some metaphysical knowledge if Beneke's definition of Being is to acquire any meaning.

In this discussion I have followed Beneke's earlier works, which show clearly the origin of his ideas in his psychological misinterpretation of the Critique of Reason, and which develop the consequences of this misunderstanding in an extreme nominalist theory, a theory which must be regarded as a paradigm for modern Empiricism in its conventionalist and nominalist form. Beneke later qualified this extreme Nominalism. In his *Metaphysics*, which came out in 1840, he tried like the older and inconsistent Empiricism to derive the metaphysical concepts, for instance those of *substance* and *causality*, directly from sensible perception, and indeed from inner perception. In this he starts from the preconception, which we met earlier, that all knowledge of every sort is based on inner perception. Only inner perception is immediate knowledge. We come to assume that there are things outside us, and to apply metaphysical concepts to things outside us, only through an analogy, ascribing that which we perceive within us, by association, to affections of outer sense. As this shows, Beneke tries once more, in spite of his Empiricism, to avoid the sceptical conclusions of Hume and so inevitably makes another attempt at basing metaphysics on experience, in the manner of Hume's predecessors. This is obviously inconsistent. Nominalism alone, which he earlier worked out quite logically and from whose extreme consequences he later shrank, this extreme nominalism is the only consistent conclusion to be drawn, on the basic view of Empiricism. Anyone who cannot bring himself to accept this conclusion will have to drop the basic viewpoint of Empiricism itself.

Looking back over this whole development, it becomes quite clear that Beneke's Empiricism derives logically from the preconception which he inherited from Reinhold. This entire school of post-Kantian metaphysics can be explained, without remainder, as due to the basic mistake of method found in Reinhold's Basic Philosophy.

In his *Metaphysics* Beneke does set this science the task of investigating the relationship of knowledge to its object. His conception of the problem of metaphysics is unambiguously epistemological. This is in fact the key to the extreme Empiricism which his theory would force us to adopt. On its own, metaphysical Empiricism leaves room for *a priori* knowledge in the fields of logic and mathematics; but if one asks the epistemological question, quite in general, with regard to any and every item of knowledge, then, as every item of knowledge must find its basis in epistemology, it must also be of the same type as the knowledge which provides that basis. There can be no dissimilarity between items of knowledge at all. The only choice left to us is between extreme Rationalism and extreme Empiricism. As we saw earlier, the epistemological preconception which Reinhold presented in a systematic form led Fichte to extreme Rationalism, while the same preconception made Beneke revert to extreme Empiricism. Both views hold all items of knowledge to be similar in type and to form a closed system; on one view they are rational in origin, on the other empirical. So it is the fault of the epistemological misinterpretation of the Critique that post-Kantian philosophy revived the spectacle of the pre-Kantian battle of the schools between dogmatic Rationalism and dogmatic Empiricism.

II

Jakob Friedrich Fries

1

The Reasons for the Decline in Philosophy after Kant, and the Importance of Fries

How was it that in such an incredibly short time the affairs of philosophy, which Kant had put nicely in order, got completely tangled up again? Why were the fruits of his mental labours buried under a pile of rubbish and dust?

That may seem an odd question in view of the respect in which the person and the works of Kant were held throughout the nineteenth century. But only his name was really respected—he himself was little appreciated and his books have still not been understood.

How shall we explain this unhappy state of affairs? In my view an explanation from the scientific errors and dialectical mistakes which led philosophy astray in the nineteenth century is inadequate. There must be some further reason which gained these errors the support of public opinion and enabled them to achieve unchallenged rule. This further reason lies somewhat deeper in the history; in the weaknesses and onesidedness which we must admit even Kant to have shared, to some extent, with the spirit of his age. That age, the age of the Enlightenment, was justifiably proud of the great strides taken by the spirit of the Enlightenment. But it made excessive claims in this respect. It over-valued the contributions which had already been made or might yet be made by scientific thought. And combined with this justifiable pride was an unjustifiable disdain and contempt for the non-rational powers of the human mind and for the role and significance of those elements in human life and human history which cannot be derived conceptually; for the 'positive', as they used to say, in contrast to the 'natural' in religion, ethics, art, law and politics.

The exaggerated claims made for the Enlightenment also explain the general change, at this time, in people's interests, the new partiality of the educated for the irrational, the individual, even for the original and peculiar, the obscure, inexplicable, and miraculous. Educated opinion was concerned more and more with a purely historical and aesthetic position on the great problems of human life, both private and public, and even showed open and declared hostility towards everything related to reason and science.

This general change in thinking, marking the beginning of the age of Romanticism, did bring several genuine benefits. People achieved a much deeper understanding, a much more correct evaluation of the positive, the personal, the historical, and the individual, and there was a general revival if not of art and religion themselves, at least of the historical study of these phenomena of life.

Along with this change in the general mode of thought there was bound to be a movement of philosophical interest away from the strict type of thinking which Kant had required in philosophy. Serious love of truth was more and more undermined by a fancy for the clever, the witty, and the original.

Yet even this is not sufficient to explain fully that remarkable development in the history of philosophy. We must also discern the influence of an extraneous element on the progress of philosophy, an element which itself owed much to the spirit of the Enlightenment and which now reacted strongly on philosophy. That element was politics.

The aspirations of the age of the Enlightenment led to bold attempts at reforming society in accordance with the ideals of reason, but these bold attempts did not have the expected result. Or rather: they had not yet had the result anticipated too soon.

When the great revolution in France came to grief and reaction was seen to be victorious within States and in power-politics outside of them, this all produced a general weariness and disillusionment among the intellectuals. Hopes disappointed were closely followed by disillusionment and even by doubt of the ideals they had first blazoned on their arms—the ideals of humanity, of human rights, and of world citizenship.

When the fight for these ideals came to nothing, people did not seek the reason in their own inadequacy and unpreparedness, but were all too ready to blame those ideas themselves for whose sake the battle had been fought. The Enlightenment itself, and science, its pride, and especially in its strictest and clearest form, mathematical science of nature: these were branded as the real offenders, and war was declared against them.

The powers against which the Enlightenment had carried on its war of liberation thus lost their most dangerous enemy, indeed this enemy turned himself into an ally. This made it all the easier for the powers of the Establishment, of repression and authoritarianism, which had only been shaken, not destroyed, to re-establish themselves, to reconquer lost ground and to equip themselves for further conquest.

No real obstacle remained to such a conquest, once the resistance had been broken of the free spirit of philosophy, in which the ideals of the age of the Enlightenment had lived on. So it is not surprising that when reaction got on its feet again, its first stroke was aimed at a final suppression of this free spirit of philosophy. The only reason why that stroke could be so successful was that the prevailing trend of thought was so far removed from that free spirit of philosophy that no defence against the fatal blow was possible.

So we must first understand this radical change in the mode of thought and consider the general prostration of spirit resulting from the failure of all the hopes and efforts of the age of the Enlightenment. Only then shall we fully comprehend the deeper reasons for the reaction in philosophy after Kant.

There was *one* achievement of the mind, and really only one, which was not swept away in this reactionary development: the strict natural sciences. These were already so firmly established that—though practically outlawed from society—they could not be pulled into the general whirlpool; so in this area we can follow the line of progress a good deal further. We can also make out the fruitful results of science, expecially the amazing progress in engineering and so in industry and commerce generally—results whose obvious usefulness was bound to react further on the position of these sciences, preserving and indeed promoting them. But in the nineteenth century there is a remarkable contrast between this development and the way things went in other areas of life. The natural sciences went their own way, without regard to philosophy. The bonds by which Kant had bound them together so tightly broke, and the scientists, repelled by the fantasy and ignorance which they met in romantic philosophy, turned aside from all philosophy whatsoever—including the Critical philosophy, which escaped their notice, hidden and buried as it was in the rank growth of romantic philosophy.

It would be a major undertaking to follow this general historical development in detail through the nineteenth century and to study its symptoms and effects in the various departments of life. Its final outcome was that general anarchic dissolution of public life and that spiritual ruin, the fruits of which we reaped in the World War of 1914–1918, that war whose results threatened to destroy European civilization.

However, that study is not my task here. We must content ourselves with these general remarks and consider only whether this judgment says all that should be said about the scientific development of philosophy in the nineteenth century. Is it true that no one at all in the course of the nineteenth century took an interest in scientific philosophy and carried it on beyond the position taken up by Kant? Was there not even a beginning made anywhere which, if followed up, would lead us out of this general disintegration? It would really be astonishing if that were true.

The needed revision of the history of nineteenth-century philosophy would in fact bring to the foreground figures who had previously attracted little attention. So I must now discuss a philosopher whose name is little known in our time.

If one remarks how little Kant, or even Hume, whose theories are certainly much easier to understand, how little these thinkers have been understood so far, and how little—I will not say acceptance—but even knowledge there has been of their thoughts, then the situation which we now confront seems less astounding.

In the usual handbooks of the history of philosophy the name of Fries is hardly mentioned, or if it is, then with a scornful remark to the effect that he distorted Kant in a psychological direction. I for my part regard this man as the only one who really carried Kant's philosophy on further in the nineteenth century.

Justification for this statement requires a fuller discussion. But this much can be stated now, as established historical fact—and it will suffice for our present purposes—that Fries is the only philosopher of the past century who kept to the plan of a Critique of Reason and, moreover, worked at this science himself and applied the results thus obtained throughout the whole field. He is also the only philosopher in history since Plato to adopt Plato's basic idea, which had been banned from scientific philosophy since the arrival of Aristotle. These two distinguishing features of the philosophy of Fries—as we shall soon see, it is not by chance that they occur together, for there is a profound inner connection between them, a connection whose discovery was one of the most characteristic contributions of the Friesian philosophy—these features of his philosophy, which as historical facts are beyond dispute, are reason enough to take up the study of this philosophy in right earnest. For philosophy can progress beyond Kant only by further development of the Critique of Reason. That much is certain, from the results already obtained.

The combination of Kant's notion of the Critique of Reason with Plato's idea that philosophical knowledge is fundamentally obscure is characteristic of the philosophy of Fries. Indeed it combines two ideas which have as good a claim as any in the history of metaphysics to be regarded as classic.

Having said this, however, how are we to account for the fact that this philosopher has stayed in the shadows of philosophical and historical interest?

There are several reasons which could be adduced to account for this, each one of which would perhaps be sufficient explanation on its own.

For one thing, a strictly scientific development of Kant's Critique of Reason could not, for the general cultural and historical reasons already given, count on the good will of the age. That age had turned its whole interest away from these problems. People were tired of the school of strict logic. They pursued more attractive mental activities.

A second reason can be found in the political events of the time, as mentioned before, events which interrupted and prevented the progress of philosophical science. Fries took part in the festival at the Wartburg of the German students' union, and because of pressure from the reactionary regime of Metternich he was brought to court, with the result that he lost his position as a teacher. After this he was lost to the public eye, being overshadowed by his more influential contemporary, Hegel, who had shown himself more compliant to the reactionary rulers in Prussia so that his theories, as Fries remarked in his *History of Philosophy*, were guaranteed by the Altenstein ministry an exchange rate well above par.

There is, however, a third factor. Even if Fries' scientific career had not suffered this external interference, and if the interests of the age had been favourable to his efforts, so that the bitterness of romantic dilettantism against science had not spent its whole passion on his theory, even then the result might well have been much the same. New and pioneering thoughts in science share the fate of all genuine revolutionary achievements: they usually need a long time before they become common property or even familiar to a narrow circle of colleagues.

I mentioned in my *Preliminaries** the classic example of Newton's discovery of the principle of the calculus. This resolved a problem which in Newton's time was the centre of his colleagues' interest, and has occupied thinkers ever since. Even today the view still predominates among scholars that this problem was first solved in the course of the nineteenth century, although it was in fact completely and strictly resolved by Newton. Only when this solution was once more worked over in the nineteenth century did people discover—only then were they able to discover—that what had so long been sought, and seemed at least to have been found, had been taught by Newton

* Vol. I, p. 54.

with unrivalled clarity more than a century and a half earlier, and that people just had not had the sense to read it in his works.

Now if that can happen in mathematics where the mind has the double aid of strict proof and self-evident results, how much more is it to be expected in philosophy? There the results are not self-evident, everything depends on the reliability of the method of investigation, and everyone must tread the whole path of research from the beginning, step by step, and make each conquest for himself anew.

Profound and pioneering scientific thoughts always take a long time to become accepted in scientific circles, or even to arouse the interest of intellectuals sufficiently to take these ideas seriously. This is the case all the more with the ponderous Germans, of whom Alexander von Humboldt said: 'They need one century to forget the old, another to understand the new, and a third to apply it.'

Apart from all these reasons why the philosophy of Fries has never come to the centre of general interest, yet another is provided by his characteristic mode or 'style' of scientific work and exposition.

There are two different types of philosopher. Some, led mainly by a logical interest, concentrate on systematic construction. Others, unconcerned for the unity of the system, pile one discovery upon another, enjoying that gift which is popularly though misleadingly called intuition, but which is really a peculiar power and certainty of judgment, even when proof is not available.

Of course every genuine philosopher is interested in system. For only the systematic form can make his theories into a science. But how a particular philosopher comes by the theories which he then proceeds to clothe with the form of a system is another matter altogether. Closer enquiry shows that—contrary to what the layman would expect—important discoveries are never made along the route by which they are derived in a system. The logical construction of the system, and with it the real proof of those discoveries, always comes afterwards. This is, however, more noticeable in some philosophers than in others; this distinction of degree forms the contrast between the two types of philosopher to be met with in the history of philosophy, what I call the systematic type and the discovering type.

Even Kant owes his greatness as a discoverer to his belonging to the second type. Yet if we compare him with Fries he seems to revert to the series of purely systematic philosophers. That shows how far Fries embodies the discovering type. We could make this distinction in another way by pointing out that we can follow psychologically the development of Kant's theories with complete precision. We can make out in detail the particular steps of thought by which he gradually freed himself from the systematic metaphysics of the school of Wolff, under whose influence he grew up, right up to the completion of his *Critique of Pure Reason*. Following his development out like this considerably lightens the task of understanding the system which he eventually constructed.

Nothing remotely like that is possible in the case of Fries. We cannot trace the origin of his theory psychologically at all, for the whole theory is, in essentials, complete in his first treatise. He published this at the age of twenty-five, having by then dwelt for some considerable time on the ideas it contains and brought them to maturity. This is clear from the form of the treatise; the thoughts stand before us in classic perfection—like Minerva sprung from the head of Jupiter. To search into their origin is labour lost. That does make it rather more difficult to understand them; pedagogically, it is a hindrance to the study of Friesian philosophy. If one reads his books one has the impression that the writer omits the posing of the problem and simply propounds one solution after another.

The difficulties which thus arise for the reader of Fries' works are a further reason why they have been so little read and understood. For the intellectual of today, and even for the learned reader, they are written much too simply. One could say that they are written in much too difficult a manner, because they are written so easily: one reads past the problems.

The plan of my exposition is as follows. I shall divide it into three main sections, for reasons to be given shortly. I shall first discuss the development in philosophical method achieved by Fries. That will lead us into the field of logic. I shall then discuss the progress he made in the construction of the Critique of Reason itself. Thirdly and lastly I shall consider the contribution made to the world-view by this advance in dialectic, the properly systematic and metaphysical fruits of his work.

We cannot attack the real problems of metaphysics directly. It is characteristic of critical metaphysics that it does not attempt to solve these problems directly, but makes a detour—which is really the shortest route to the goal, as no other route gets there at all. This detour goes by way of the Critique of Reason. A preliminary inquiry, then, is required before tackling the real problems of metaphysics. Now in this preliminary inquiry the proper method is still a matter of dispute, and so is the mode of knowledge involved. So the first need is for a preliminary logical inquiry into the nature of this peculiar science, the Critique of Reason. My first section will be devoted to this logical task, to the theory of method.

M

2

The Doctrine of Method

In his very first publication Fries took up the problem of the critical method—the method introduced into metaphysics by Kant. This fact in itself is very significant; for it distinguishes Fries from the other followers of Kant in the nineteenth century; it marks him out from all of them. The others had all taken up the results of Kant's philosophy and concerned themselves with further construction, without bothering about the scientific foundation which Kant had given for these results, which was his real contribution to science.

Fries' concern with Kant's critical method can be seen in an article which came out in 1798 in Carl Christian Erhard Schmid's *Psychological Magazine*. (I mentioned C. Chr. E. Schmid earlier on as one of the first friends and followers of Kantian philosophy. He was the father of Heinrich Schmid, one of the first and most faithful disciples of Fries. This relation of father and son is a fine example of continuity in philosophical development.) The article, which like all pieces in that journal came out anonymously, is entitled *On the Relation of Empirical Psychology to Metaphysics*. As the title shows, this deals directly with an issue which is quite fundamental; for the decision reached on this issue will in the end determine the position to be adopted towards the whole of Kantian philosophy.

The ideas of this article are set out more fully in Fries' major polemical work: *Reinhold, Fichte and Schelling*. This was the first book that Fries ever published. This book, and this alone in the whole literature of philosophy, can be said not to teach philosophy but the art of philosophizing. I will go even further: if there is any book from which one can learn the art of arguing, this book is it. It is a masterpiece of scientific polemic on which it would be hard to find a more appropriate comment, even today, than that made at the time by Schleiden, the great botanist, one of Fries' most loyal disciples, in an essay which in any case is well worth reading: *Jacob Friedrich Fries, the Scientist's Philosopher*.

'His polemic is marked by a complete self-denial. His refutations always proceed from the other's viewpoint, not his own, showing an inadequate factual basis or an inner contradiction. Here one of his first books *Reinhold*

Fichte and Schelling is an unsurpassable model of philosophical polemic. No previous writer has ventured to attack his own criticisms of other philosophical theories, or to challenge as he does the foundations of his own mode of philosophizing. So no one can blame us, his disciples, if we continue to regard him as irrefutable, until an equally fundamental and thorough refutation is really attempted, and succeeds.'

I said that in *On the Relation of Empirical Psychology to Metaphysics* Fries deals directly with a fundamental issue, the verdict on which will determine one's position towards Kant's Critique of Reason. It gives a clear formulation of the decisive point, which Kant's other followers misunderstood, reverting in consequence to pre-Kantian Dogmatism.

This misunderstanding really concerned the relation of the Critique of Reason to the system of metaphysics, the principles of which the Critique is supposed to justify. Kant did not investigate this relationship very closely, but left the matter obscure. He set out the Critique of Reason and then established the consequences which it had for the system of metaphysics, but he did not inquire closely into the relation between these two sciences.

This relationship must be made clear if one is to find a methodical and reliable way for further development of Kantian philosophy. Fries' article puts this problem in the forefront; that is its importance for the history of philosophy. One could compare it in this respect with Kant's prize essay *On the Clarity of the Principles of Natural Theology and Morality*, in which Kant first set down his fundamental discovery of the critical method. That is where Fries takes up the discussion.

This work contains something of which its modest title conveys no hint, and that is a well-thought-out plan for a fundamental reform of logic, and especially of the logical theory about the justification of judgments. The judgments contained in the system of metaphysics are supposed to be justified by the Critique of Reason. At this point a logical question arises: what is special about this new method of justification? It is here that the ways diverge.

In order to understand Fries' answer to this question we must first give a more detailed account of the nature and significance of the problem itself.

2

The Critique of Reason was the new method introduced into philosophy by Kant in order at last to make metaphysics into a science. The results seemed at first to justify his attempts. No other philosopher had made such great advances along the road to science as Kant did in his Critique of Reason. But the real secret of Kant's progress still remained obscure, for no agreement was reached about the nature of the new method. Kant himself never expressly answered this question, indeed he never really raised it. He was far too much occupied expounding the extraordinary wealth of discoveries which had come his way in the Critique of Reason for him to give proper attention to the question of method. It was a different matter for his successors. They were bound to take this question up.

If one inquires what type of knowledge is to be found in the Critique of Reason, several alternative answers are available. One might suppose, first of all, that the Critique of Reason was itself knowledge of the metaphysical type. Now if that were the case, it would be impossible to see what contribution it could make. For the whole point of the new method was that before trying to construct metaphysics, one should first undertake a preliminary investigation as to whether there could be a metaphysics at all, and if so how? How then can the answer to this question itself be metaphysical? That seems quite absurd. If the new method is to offer us hope of escape from metaphysical Dogmatism, then clearly the Critique of Reason cannot itself belong to metaphysics. To what type of knowledge then does it belong?

Does it perhaps belong to logic? That seems equally absurd. For people had at last realized that formal logic alone is in no position to broaden the content of knowledge and thus to achieve genuine metaphysical knowledge. This had become perfectly clear when Kant discovered the distinction between analytic and synthetic judgments, for metaphysics is concerned with synthetic, and logic with analytic judgments. To construct metaphysics from mere logic is, in Kant's phrase, a hopeless undertaking.

The superstition that logic can do everything took a particularly severe beating from Kant in the field of mathematics. He really destroyed it here, and with it that will o' the wisp of the 'mathematical method', which was always enticing people to construct metaphysics on this same logicist model, since mathematics seemed to show it capable of realization. Kant showed that the security of mathematical knowledge is not based on its syllogistic mode of proof; on the contrary, that method can usefully be applied there only because mathematics possesses a guaranteed body of knowledge independent of any logic whatsoever. The discovery that there was in mathematics such a body of knowledge going beyond the competence of logic was the basis for the whole Kantian reform of philosophy.

This discovery was retained by Fries with all its fundamental significance. Indeed he was the first really to establish it firmly, thus guarding against the reversion to Logicism to which even Kant succumbed. Fries pointed out that this fact, which Kant had discovered, that mathematical knowledge is not analytic in character, proved the existence of an independent science, until then entirely unknown, which he called 'Philosophy of Mathematics'. He worked out a programme for this science, and indeed carried it out, developing the new science systematically by carrying over the critical method and applying it to all the branches of mathematics known at that time.

This science is concerned to determine the entire extent of that body of mathematical knowledge which goes beyond the bounds of logic, and to derive it systematically from first principles. To do this it is clearly necessary to make a sharp distinction inside each mathematical discipline between what can be proved logically and what is assumed in those proofs, and comes from perception. There is need, in short, for that method of abstraction which analyses the proofs of given judgments in order to discover their assumptions and to trace these back to their first principles. This task demands on the one hand that the number of axioms should be reduced to a minimum, that is to those suppositions which are essential for the logical construction of the theory in question, and that the others, which are provable, should really be proved. On the other hand, this task also requires us to increase the number of axioms—contrary to the usual procedure in mathematics—so that the whole body of axioms is sufficient, without the addition of further assumptions, to work out the entire theory by means of logic alone.

Clearly this 'Critical Mathematics' or 'Philosophy of Mathematics' is that same axiomatics with which modern mathematicians are so familiar. Fries, then, is the real founder of modern axiomatics; for he was the first not only to pose the problem of this science in general terms, but to work at it systematically.

A third alternative remained: to regard the Critique of Reason as a form of empirical knowledge. That would make it an empirical science. But this seems as impractical as the previous suggestions. For metaphysical knowledge must be established independently of all experience. How then can experience enable us to justify metaphysics?

The usual answer to this dilemma is to say that the Critique of Reason is an 'epistemological' enquiry; that it belongs to neither of the types of knowledge so far mentioned, since it is the critique of knowledge itself which makes it possible for there to be objectively valid knowledge.

There is something surprising and indeed disconcerting about this answer. We should, however, not be misled by the imposing sound of the word 'epistemology', but should ask instead what this explanation really means. We then find that it really says nothing at all. For epistemology also, if it is to be a science, would have to consist of knowledge and so could not refuse to say of what type that knowledge was, and whence it came. That would take us back to the dilemma from which we just tried to escape. And we actually find that the various directions in which this enigmatic science called epistemology was developed after Kant all end up once more in one of the two earlier types of Dogmatism, and so bring us no nearer the goal of justifying metaphysics as a science, but take us much further away from it.

Is there any way out of this dilemma? Can we find in the history of philosophy in the nineteenth century a philosopher who will show us the way out of it?

There is in fact one way of regarding the Critique of Reason which affords an escape. That is the one I have called genuinely critical, as opposed to epistemological, because it really retains the basic and decisive ideas of the Critique of Reason.

As I said earlier, it was Fries who showed us this way out. This discovery was first set down in 1798 in his article *On the Relation of Empirical Psychology to Metaphysics.*

Let me recapitulate and explain the essential ideas developed there, at the same time surveying the relevant logical discoveries, some of which were first set out in detail in other works of Fries—in particular in his *System of Logic.*

3

We here find a sharper distinction between the two tasks which Kant had set himself in the Critique of Reason. He had already distinguished there a *quaestio facti* (matter of fact) and a *quaestio iuris* (question of justification). The first of these is the question whether our knowledge does in fact contain metaphysical principles. The other is the question whether these principles are justified. One must first show that there are in fact such principles, for only then can one properly comprehend the question how they are to be justified.

It is clear that even if Kant gave a complete answer to the *quaestio facti*, still some inquiry was needed about the method of his solution. Kant set himself to work backwards from particular items in our knowledge to a general principle. This involved pointing out which metaphysical principles in our knowledge are most general and isolating them from the rest of our knowledge. This can be done, as Kant shows, by starting from particular statements which are known as certain and working back from them to their general presuppositions, and so on until the most universal principles are reached.

There are, however, two quite different methods of regress. For the term 'regressive' is applied to any method which works back from the particular to the general, from the conclusions to the premisses. The distinction between the two modes of regress is that one is based on real reasons, the other on merely epistemological reasons. The transition from conclusions to real reasons is achieved by the method of induction; that from conclusions to epistemological reasons by the method of abstraction, as Fries called it; more precisely, by the method of speculation.

The difference between these two regressive methods—that of induction and that of abstraction—was never recognized in the history of logic until Fries. Ever since Aristotle introduced the concept of ἐπαγωγή (induction, lit. leading-on) these two methods had been regularly confused by logicians, and Leibniz and Kant were the first even to feel that they were different. According to Aristotle, ἐπαγωγή is the method of discovering principles, and he therefore contrasts it with συλλογισμός (syllogism, reasoning). But he identifies it with induction.

Now induction is clearly a mode of proof. It concludes from observed particular instances to a general law. Its results are therefore theorems, not principles, though these results could be used as principles in a new theory. They are reached by induction from facts of observation. So induction does not lead us to the real principles; indeed no method of proof can ever do that, only abstraction can. This is not really a method of proof, but is concerned with analysing a train of thought. It starts from particular judgments recognized as true and analyses their presuppositions, in order to ascend to the principles.

So the contrast between the two methods is this; in induction we draw a conclusion from given premises, but abstraction works the other way, discovering the premises of given judgments. The results of induction, therefore, are in every case statements of experience; for they are concluded from facts of observation. The results of abstraction, on the contrary, hold good—in so far as they hold good at all—independently of experience. For they are general presuppositions for the possibility of experience, and it is in this role that abstraction points to them. Their validity does not depend, as does that of the results of induction, on the particular judgments from which the regressive process began. Quite the reverse, for abstraction shows that the judgments from which it began depend for their validity on the general presuppositions which it is to reveal. Such an abstraction cannot, then, justify these presuppositions on the basis of the judgments from which the abstraction began. This also shows that a single example may be adequate for discovering a law by means of abstraction, whereas induction requires the comparison of a number of instances.

That general truths can be discovered by means of abstraction and that abstraction is the only way to discover principles, is far from self-evident. Indeed it shows a very remarkable characteristic of our knowledge: that we are aware of the particular, of the application in an individual case, before being aware of the general principle, although the latter is logically prior to judgment on the individual case.

4

What about the other task of the Critique of Reason, the answering of the *quaestio iuris* for the metaphysical principles which have been revealed? All abstraction does is to point them out as in fact presupposed by our judgments; it does not justify them. The question whether they are justified must be decided independently. This question is supposed to be answered by the process Kant called deduction. How do affairs stand here?

Deduction is intended to derive these principles from their epistemic ground. What sort of derivation is this?

Must it be, as Kant assumed, an objective deduction, i.e. one concerned not with the subjective ground which makes those metaphysical principles possible, but with their objective validity?

To answer this question we shall have to take a wider sweep and become familiar with the nature and point of the justification of judgments, quite in general. The demand that judgments be justified rests on the logical 'Law of (Sufficient) Reason'. To understand this law correctly and avoid mistakes about its area of application, one must first conceive *judgment* correctly, distinguishing it properly from the notion of *knowledge*. What is the relation between these two concepts?

Every true judgment clearly contains knowledge; but it does not follow that every item of knowledge is in the form of a judgment. What is a judgment, then? In itself, it is not an item of knowledge. Judgment depends on a combination, in itself quite arbitrary, of concepts, which we can make this way or that as we please and which is therefore inherently problematic. So the first question is always *why* a particular combination should be singled out; for it is singled out in the assertion which the judgment adds to an inherently problematic collocation of ideas. Hence the need to justify each judgment, i.e. to derive each such assertion from some other item of knowledge. For a judgment becomes an item of knowledge only when it is based on some other item of knowledge, which the judgment simply recapitulates. The agreement of the judgment with this item of knowledge on which it is based is the test of its truth, and to demonstrate this agreement is what is called justifying the judgment.

Now that is not to say that every item of knowledge requires justification. Such a notion is absurd as can be seen from the fact that it would lead to an endless regress of justifications. For each item of knowledge to which we get back in justifying another item of knowledge would in its turn require further justification. So we should never have a starting point from which to begin the process of justification. Taken to its logical conclusion, this idea would make the justification of judgments quite impossible.

Every judgment requires justification, because a judgment is only mediate knowledge and can never itself be immediate knowledge. For in the judgment an assertion is added to a collection of ideas inherently problematic, and this assertion needs to be derived from some knowledge which is not added as assertion to an inherently problematic collection of ideas, but is itself an inherently assertoric collection of ideas. This item of immediate knowledge yields the criterion we sought for singling out that particular combination of concepts which can be regarded as a correct judgment; in brief, for the truth of the judgment.

5

It is commonly supposed that a proof is the only fully valid justification. To prove a judgment means to derive it from another judgment which contains its logical ground. So the main difficulty in justification clearly arises when we come to judgments which are not provable, to 'basic judgments'. A basic judgment is one that cannot be derived from any further judgments. There must be such basic judgments, if we are to be able to speak of truth at all.

What about these basic judgments? They also, being judgments, are merely mediate items of knowledge and so require justification, i.e. they need to be traced back to some other item of knowledge. So if they are to be justifiable they must be based on items of knowledge which are not judgments, that means on 'immediate knowledge'.

The business of justification is complete only when judgments are traced back to some such immediate knowledge.

The question of justifying immediate knowledge does not arise. It ought not even to be asked. For it would lead to an impossible comparison of knowledge with its object. It is impossible to justify knowledge by comparing it with its object, because we know the object only by means of our knowledge and so cannot produce it independently for purposes of comparison. The validity of immediate knowledge would thus have to be presupposed for the sake of such a supposedly objective justification. Such a justification is therefore impossible. This so-called 'task of epistemology', as we can now see, only arises through a misinterpretation of the Law of Sufficient Reason, through the confusion of knowledge with judgment; and even to propound this task involves assuming that every item of knowledge is a judgment. Once we are clear what a justification of an item of knowledge is and what it can provide, viz. the derivation of one piece of knowledge from another, we shall see that the programme of justifying immediate knowledge is self-contradictory.

The requirement of justification does not apply, then, to immediate knowledge. What does apply is the fundamental principle, established by Fries, of the self-reliance of our reason. This principle brings out the fact that our reason relies on its immediate knowledge, the psychological datum that immediate knowledge has an inherent and original certainty of objective validity, independent of any justification, since immediate knowledge simply is that originally given certainty. The principle simply expounds what is implied in the concept of *immediate knowledge*, just as the requirement of justification for all judgments simply expounds what is implied in the concept of *judgment*. For it is the essence of what we call knowledge to contain the certainty of objective validity, an immediate relation to its object. One cannot without contradicting oneself question whether what one knows to be true really is true. All that the basic principle of the self-reliance of reason really says is that we do have knowledge. Once we grasp properly the factual character of knowledge, we can get past the misleading questioning of epistemology. For this insight shows us that to justify the objective validity of our knowledge is as unnecessary as it is impossible.

It would therefore be a mistake to take the agreed impossibility of justifying immediate knowledge as a sceptical renunciation, as an admission that we must leave the truth of immediate knowledge up in the air because we are unable to justify it. Quite the opposite! Immediate knowledge requires no such justification, for the simple reason that it already contains as immediate fact just what such a justification would be meant to gain for us. This fact must be accepted as such. It is not a problem for us. It is our situation. All we need is to grasp it and recognize it.

Fries once put paid to epistemological grousing by remarking that the task of philosophy is 'to guard us against error in our judgments, not to transform a houseful of nitwits into an Academy of Sciences'.

In his discovery of the relation of judgment to immediate knowledge Fries was the first philosopher to get free of the epistemological problem without thereby falling back into the error of Dogmatism. As Apelt neatly put it, he tuned thinkers to another pitch, replacing Jacobi's sentimental yearning for certainty by that certainty itself, demonstrated as immediate, original and first.

6

This demonstration leads at once to a proper reduction in the field of error in our knowledge. It would really have been wiser to inquire into the possibility of error, instead of into the possibility of knowledge. That knowledge is possible is a fact. Once we recognize this fact, the problem arises how on earth error can enter our knowledge. The answer is that error can only occur in the field of mediate knowledge, since it concerns the agreement of mediate with immediate knowledge, and that our knowledge is therefore liable to error only so far as it consists of judgments. Error is only possible in our knowledge at all because we have something of the nature of mediate knowledge, where certainty is added indirectly to ideas in themselves problematic. Error is thus at home in this field of ideas inherently problematic, of mediate knowledge; in the field of the judgment. Immediate knowledge, with its certainty, is an original fact, and is not open to doubt. But knowledge through judgments is not an original fact of that sort.

The truth which is contrasted with error, and which consists in the agreement of mediate with immediate knowledge, Fries calls 'intellectual truth'. It presupposes, for anyone concerned with it, reliance on the possession through immediate knowledge of that other truth which concerns the relation to the object and which, as it is not contrasted with error, but simply with irrationality, Fries calls 'rational truth' (*Vernunft-Wahrheit*, as opposed to Verstandes-Wahrheit).

7

Once it is granted that error is restricted to reflection, to the field of judgments, and cannot touch immediate knowledge, Kant's problem of an objective deduction disappears. The justification of basic judgments cannot take the form of a proof, tracing them back objectively to logically superior grounds, but only of a subjective tracing back to some immediate knowledge.

The basic principles of metaphysics are therefore logically the highest principles in their field, and no further logical reduction or objective justification can be given for them. But they can be justified by tracing them back to the immediate knowledge on which they are based. The line which divides judgment from immediate knowledge divides that part of our knowledge which requires justification from that which requires none.

Fries thus settles the dispute between Dogmatism, which starts by postulating unjustifiable items of knowledge, and epistemology, which starts by postulating that all judgments require justification.

In this dispute the original starting point on both sides is entirely correct. There are in fact items of knowledge which require no justification. There must be some such items if the justification of judgments is to be possible. That is taught by Dogmatism, and it is quite correct. On the other hand, all judgments must be justified if they lay claim to truth. That is taught by epistemology, and it is equally correct. So far, no dispute arises between the two.

The dispute arises from the false assumption, made on both sides, that all knowledge must consist of judgments. Only when one makes this extra and false assumption does one reach a contradiction between the postulate that all judgments be justified and the postulate of unjustifiable items of knowledge. For one then gets the false postulate of unjustifiable judgments and, in contrast with it, the equally false postulate that all items of knowledge require justification.

This dispute loses its point once the postulate of justification is restricted to judgments, and the postulate of an unjustifiable knowledge is restricted to immediate knowledge.

To make this point completely clear, let us set out the inferences on both sides in a diagram (Diagram VIII).

To summarize this discussion from the point of view of method: not every justification takes the form of a proof. Proof, as a means of justification, applies only so long as the judgments that require justification can be derived from other judgments. This series must come to an end. This end is reached with basic judgments which do, as judgments, require justification. So there must be some other method of justification besides proof. It thus appears that the method of justification available to us in the form of proof is not adequate on its own.

(VIII) Knowledge and Judgments, and their Justification

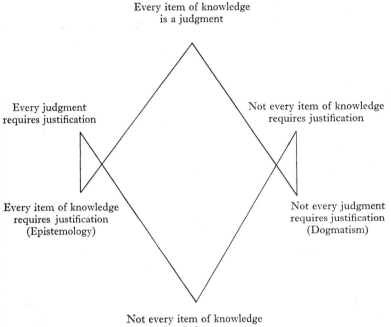

Every item of knowledge
is a judgment

Every judgment
requires justification

Not every item of knowledge
requires justification

Every item of knowledge
requires justification
(Epistemology)

Not every judgment
requires justification
(Dogmatism)

Not every item of knowledge
is a judgment

We can now readily conclude that the method of justification, other than proof, which we are seeking must consist of tracing basic judgments back to immediate knowledge.

This must also apply to the justification of basic judgments of metaphysics

The question now arises, what sort of immediate knowledge could possibly serve as justification for the basic judgments of metaphysics.

This much is clear. The knowledge on which metaphysics is based—if such there be at all—cannot be like perpetual knowledge. For the principles of metaphysics are not evident, as they would ceatainly be if they were based on perception. Their truth becomes apparent only on reflection.

Where the justification of a basic judgment consists of tracing it back to perception, Fries calls it demonstration; in other cases he calls it deduction, following Kant's usage.

'Deduction' thus means the justification of a judgment by tracing it back to some immediate knowledge which is not perceptual. So the justification of the basic judgments of metaphysics, if it is possible at all, must take the form of a deduction.

Now this distinction between demonstration and deduction is so far based only on a merely verbal definition, and we must ask what the real significance of this distinction is. Does it correspond to a genuine difference between methods of justification? According to the verbal explanations just given, the distinction between them is simply that the judgments they are meant to justify are traced back to different sorts of immediate knowledge. But to what extent does this mark a difference in the methods of justification in each case? In demonstration, one justifies judgments by pointing out the perception from which knowledge of them derives, and it appears that in deducing a judgment one likewise has only to point out some corresponding immediate though not perceptual knowledge. The distinction between demonstration and deduction would not in that case have any further significance for method. It would be mere logical hair-splitting, rather like distinguishing different types of proof by the sort of premises from which it begins. In that case we could make do with the distinction between proof and demonstration. The distinction between demonstration and deduction would have no further significance. But this is not the actual situation. It was in fact this lack of a distinction of method between demonstration and deduction—which amounts to the assumption that all basic judgments are open to demonstration, an assumption made throughout logic until Fries' time—it was this that was ultimately responsible for the repeated re-introduction of Mysticism into philosophy. It was this assumption that all judgments which cannot be justified by means of proof can be demonstrated, which meant that Scholasticism in metaphysics could be overcome only by reverting to Neo-Platonism.

9

If we wish to criticize this basic conception of traditional logic—the assumption that all basic judgments can be demonstrated, an assumption which does not of course appear in this conscious and explicit form, though it really underlay everything else—we must first get rid of two mistakes.

The first mistake is due to a lack of conceptual clarity with regard to the concept of *perception*. As long as one is affected by this lack of clarity it does seem as though the entire problem has no point at all, so that one cannot even approach this genuine and profound problem. For it seems in that case absurd even to ask for knowledge which is immediate and yet not perceptual, which is the basic problem of deduction. For this very concept of a non-perceptual and yet immediate knowledge seems contradictory. Is not immediacy the very mark of perception? So what on earth do we mean by a non-perceptual and yet immediate knowledge?

The discussion of this question brings out a characteristic feature of Fries' style of philosophizing, one which can be found throughout his writing. I refer to the remarkable security he obtained by conforming to linguistic usage undistorted by philosophy. This enabled Fries to make the wealth and grace of language scientifically fertile and to guard himself against sources of error to which other philosophers were defencelessly exposed, because they disregarded the signs and warnings which language itself provides and so gave arbitrary verbal definitions—an abuse of language which took its own revenge on them, barring their way not only to a solution but even to the problem itself.

We have already come across a remarkable example of this in Fries' distinction between knowledge and judgment. The situation here is similar.

There is in fact nothing to prevent our so defining the concept of perception that it coincides with that of immediate knowledge. Only one runs the risk of fallacious inference, due to confusing the object which comes under the one concept (owing to its connection with the word in common usage) with the object which according to usage comes under the other concept. One is thus liable to take it as self-evident and requiring no further proof that every item of immediate knowledge is a perception in the usual sense of the word, and not merely in the sense introduced by that arbitrary definition. To avoid such fallacious inference, the best thing is to stick to the natural usage of words, which has much more delicate and reliable distinctions than any philosophers' hair-splitting. The fact is that if we analyse the meaning which the word 'perception' (*Anschauung*) really has in ordinary, philosophically unsophisticated usage, we can no longer assert in this meaning of the word that every item of immediate knowledge must be a perception. For—and here we come to one of Fries' most profound discoveries—there are two quite different things: immediacy of knowledge and immediacy of our consciousness of the knowledge, which is the essence of perception. 'Perception' in the ordinary sense goes with what we call 'immediate clarity' or 'self-evidence'—a property not contained in the concept of *immediate knowledge*. It is this immediate clarity or self-evidence that one has in mind when one tries to justify a judgment by demonstration, i.e. simply by pointing to some other item of knowledge, the immediate clarity or self-evidence of which ensures that mere reference to it is enough for a complete justification of the judgment; enough, that is, to ensure that we perceive the agreement of the judgment with the content of the immediate knowledge. Where this immediacy of consciousness regarding the knowledge is lacking such a reference is not adequate to assure us of the agreement of the judgment with the immediate knowledge. For in that case the immediate knowledge itself is still quite obscure, so that even its existence, let alone its content, is far from self-evident.

10

The other mistake which Fries had to eliminate in order to gain the clarity essential for decision of this profound question concerns the nature of the feeling-for-truth. There is a psychological illusion here to which one easily falls prey. It does seem as though in justifying the judgments of metaphysics we could appeal to a non-reflective 'immediate consciousness' as their ground. Now there really is a consciousness of truth of that sort. It occurs in a non-conceptual form, even and especially in the field of metaphysical knowledge. It guides us in the application of metaphysical knowledge to particular given instances, which we safely decide 'by instinct', without being able to give any account of the basis of our decision. Fries calls this consciousness the 'feeling-for-truth'.

He did not make up this word; it belongs to the general fund of language. But he was the first psychologist to give a proper account and correct interpretation of the nature of this feeling-for-truth. People previously had either treated the feeling-for-truth as a type of pleasurable feeling, which is certainly encouraged by its ambiguous name, or had confused it with a type of perception (*Anschauung*), led by the equally common and misleading expression 'intuition' (*Intuition*). Fries showed that both interpretations are wrong. To start with, the feeling-for-truth has nothing to do with feelings of pleasure or dislike. It is an act of knowing, not of interest. It is, however, an act of knowledge of a particular sort. It contains an obscure consciousness of truth, not one that is already clear, so we must not mix it up with perception, as is easily done by using the expression 'intuition'. This mode of expression may be harmless in popular usage, but science requires a stricter definition of concepts. Perception involves an immediate clarity in consciousness of the truth perceived.

But the feeling-for-truth, however certain and definite it may be, is a consciousness of truth whose content becomes clear only when it is resolved, i.e. brought into conceptual form in a judgment—which shows that this judgment is not a basic judgment of metaphysics, but only the application of such a judgment to a particular instance given in perception. The metaphysical principle on which such a judging is based is not present to our mind at the time. Abstraction is required in order to bring it to consciousness, abstraction from the particular case of application in judging which we are guided by the feeling-for-truth—abstraction, therefore, from the perceptual element contained in the judgment. If we analyse this instinctive judgment, that is, if we abstract from its perceptual content and inquire into the general presuppositions on which the judgment is based, this reflection makes us conscious of the metaphysical principle involved.

The feeling-for-truth, then, does not belong to perception but to the faculty of judgment. It is an obscure act of the faculty of judgment, and for this very reason the feeling is to be distinguished from that conception of truth which we call conceiving.

This shows that it is the feeling-for-truth which embodies that paradoxical aspect of our knowledge which I pointed out earlier: that the particular case of application comes to mind before the general principle, which in logic is admittedly prior to that application. In other words, what is logically composite and posterior is prior and simple for our consciousness, and what is logically simpler and more general is later for our consciousness, as we have to follow the way of abstraction to get from the one to the other.

That is all the more reason why this feeling-for-truth should not be alleged as the basis for our knowledge of metaphysical principles. It is the feeling which must be traced back to the principles, for it is in the application of those principles that this feeling has its place.

II

The peculiar character of the feeling-for-truth comes out in the fact that the particular case of application of a general principle comes to mind before the general principle which, logically, precedes that application. This very fact is responsible for the failure of Dogmatism in metaphysics. Metaphysical Dogmatism is the attempt to start directly by establishing a general principle, so as to erect the required system of science upon it, whereas it is in fact the general principle that our mind approaches last, since we must first make our way to it by means of an artificial abstraction, which must start from what is immediately given, from the instance in which it is applied. In this

N

abstraction errors and mistakes in plenty can occur. The history of philosophy is indeed a unique and eloquent witness that errors do arise from this source. For the history of philosophy is mainly concerned with the attempt, always being renewed, to perform this abstraction in an unambiguous and compelling manner—even where people thought they could establish the principles directly. The continuing dispute between philosophers is an unintentional but none the less convincing experimental proof that in metaphysical questions nothing is immediately evident. One could say that their efforts, by failing to produce results, have produced a result all the more reliable: that it is a mistake to expect such self-evidence. Unless for the sake of a preconceived doctrine we are to do violence to the psychological facts, we must be content to admit that the basic judgments of metaphysics are not open to demonstration. We must therefore seek some other means of justifying them.

This other method of justification must consist of tracing the basic judgments of metaphysics back to some immediate knowledge. Of that we are already sufficiently convinced. But if there is immediate knowledge of the basic truths of metaphysics, at any rate it is not there in front of us so that we could simply point to it, as we do with perception. If someone doubts a metaphysical judgment, it would be futile simply to refer him to this immediate knowledge, and to demand (as Beck does) that he adopt the standpoint of original representation, as though that could be done straight off simply by applying one's mind to it. For we have no immediate consciousness of immediate metaphysical knowledge. Metaphysical truth becomes clear to us only by means of reflection, in the form of judgment, and not apart from judgment. But we want justification of the judgment, i.e. to find its basis, as contained in immediate knowledge, apart from reflection. Now we cannot take up this justification, as we do in the case of demonstration, by comparing the judgment with the immediate knowledge on which it is based; for we have no separate consciousness of this as distinct from the judgment, which we could set beside the mediate element of the judgment to justify it.

In fact, to say that the basic judgments of metaphysics are not based on any perception is simply another way of saying that we have no consciousness of the truth expressed in them, apart from those judgments. The case is different for a judgment which can be demonstrated. Demonstration is possible precisely because we possess a consciousness of that which the judgment asserts, which is independent of that judgment; so we can set this independent consciousness of the truth beside the judgment in order to compare the two and thus justify the judgment. This is the situation for all basic judgments of experience; this is the situation—despite all the other differences—also in the case of the basic judgments or axioms of mathematics. The case of the basic judgments of metaphysics is quite different. If we form judgments about God or the world, about causality or substance, about duty, goodness, freedom and beauty, we have no consciousness of that which we are judging, apart from that judgment itself. Judgments of this sort are never open to demonstration. If they are to be justified at all, then it must be possible to compare them in some way with the immediate knowledge on which they are based. But how is this undertaking to be carried out?

12

The answer lies in the most artificial and difficult of all the methods of justification: deduction. This consists in tracing the basic judgments of metaphysics back to an immediate and non-intuitive metaphysical knowledge. But this immediate knowledge does not come to us independently of the judgment. So our only way to carry out this comparison is to make an artificial detour, and first to inquire separately into immediate metaphysical knowledge, to make sure that it does exist, and what it contains—thus acquiring a knowledge of it which is distinct from the judgments of metaphysics and which allows us to justify them.

It follows that in order to carry out a deduction, we must first undertake a preparatory task of an entirely different sort. We must first come by a Theory of Reason from which we can work out the actual stock of the immediate metaphysical knowledge which our reason holds. For immediate metaphysical knowledge is by nature rational knowledge, a priori knowledge; so if immediate metaphysical knowledge, or anything like it, exists at all, our stock of it must be determined, independently of all experience, by the nature of the rational mind itself. So it should be derivable on the basis of a sufficiently sophisticated Theory of Reason.

This Theory of Reason can only be developed by means of a psychological enquiry. For we are here dealing with facts about our knowledge. We are not enquiring into its objective validity, into the relation of knowledge to its object, but into the relation of one item of knowledge to another, namely into the existence of an item of knowledge which the other item simply recapitulates in the form of a judgment. Now reflection and speculation are powerless to decide questions of fact; these are to be settled simply and solely by experience—and in the case of facts about knowledge, only by inner experience, i.e. psychology.

This empirical and psychological knowledge is, however, not possible for us in the form of immediate observation; for the non-intuitive immediate knowledge, which is here to be the object of another knowledge, does not lie directly under observation; we do not know it directly through inner perception, but only indirectly, by inferences from that perception. So we cannot proceed to discuss it in a purely descriptive manner, but are forced to undertake a theoretical enquiry.

A psychological Theory of Reason, then, is to lead to a deduction of the basic laws of metaphysics. This deduction is not a proof of the metaphysical judgments which require justification; let me say that once again, in express terms. It is, rather, the psychological proof of the existence of a non-intuitive and immediate knowledge which underlies these judgments.

This is the method for answering the *quaestio iuris* in the Critique of Reason.

13

This process involves a number of difficulties which I will discuss in detail, in order to safeguard the basic ideas of the new method against possible objections and show its necessity in an even clearer light.

One can raise several distinct but related questions at this point.

Firstly: would not the psychological procedure just described obliterate once more the distinction between *quaestio facti* and *quaestio iuris*? Would it not involve returning a purely factual answer to the *quaestio iuris*, thus leading us back once again to the *quaestio facti*? The question whether an item of knowledge is justified can clearly not be settled simply by referring to the fact of this knowledge. We wanted to decide the *quaestio iuris* apart from the *quaestio facti*, but where is that decision now?

Secondly, a very closely related question: would not the empirical process of justification here undertaken throw doubt on the rational character of the judgments being justified? Would we not revert unavoidably to Empiricism and Psychologism?

Thirdly: how on earth can an empirical process ever guarantee apodeictic certainty? Instead of guaranteeing apodeictic truths for metaphysics, would not this method abandon metaphysics to all the possibilities of error to which judgments of an empirical nature are exposed?

Fourthly and finally: does not inner experience, to which we here appeal, presuppose, like all experience, metaphysical principles as conditions on which it is possible? But we are supposed to be justifying those principles. Would not the proposed empirical critique involve us unavoidably in a circular argument? I shall consider in turn these objections to the psychological method of deducing metaphysical principles.

1. Is it true that our empirical procedure in pointing out that we do in fact have certain knowledge obliterates the distinction between the *quaestio facti* and the *quaestio iuris*, and limits us simply to dealing with the factual situation, instead of enquiring into the matter of justification?

There is an ambiguity in this way of putting the question. Once it is uncovered the whole matter becomes clear. Certainly the *quaestio iuris* is here traced back to a *quaestio facti*. Our tests for the judgments we are justifying is whether they agree with an immediate knowledge which we point out as a fact. But there are two different facts here which must be sharply distinguished. The fact to which we here refer is not once again the fact that we do really make the judgments which we are to justify, but the other fact that our knowledge does contain a basis for those judgments.

So we are really dealing with a question of fact. This method does infer from facts of experience. It does not, however, infer the validity of the principles of metaphysics, it infers instead another fact, namely the existence of an immediate knowledge on which those principles are based. The validity of this knowledge does not come into question at all. For we have rejected any such question as insoluble and inadmissible. There is for us no *quaestio iuris* for immediate knowledge. For the certainty thus supposed to be sought for is already there in the very nature of immediate knowledge, and if we prove the existence of an item of immediate knowledge, that already settles the question of its certainty. For what we do here is precisely to point out that certainty as a fact in us.

Any further question about objective validity is meaningless in this context. Here and here alone we can properly appeal to what Fries called the basic principle of the self-reliance of reason, which asserts that certainty is *de facto* inherent in immediate knowledge and needs only to be pointed out as a fact.

The distinction between the *quaestio facti* about these judgments and the *quaestio iuris* for them is thus preserved. For the fact reached as a conclusion of the deduction is not the judgment which was being deduced, but the existence of a justification for it: namely, an item of immediate metaphysical knowledge. There is no contradiction in deciding the *quaestio iuris* by reference to a fact so long as the fact contains, as here it does contain, a justification for the judgments in question.

2. This discussion makes clear what the second and third questions are about, namely whether pointing out the basis of metaphysical judgments psychologically puts their apodeictic character at risk.

The Critique certainly contains a proof. Not, however, a proof of the principles of metaphysics, but of empirical and psychological statements about the existence of an immediate knowledge underlying the principles of metaphysics. The judgments contained in the Critique are therefore different in modality from those which they justify. Here again there is no contradiction. The judgments of the Critique can perfectly well have a different modality from those of metaphysics, because the metaphysical judgments do not stand in any relation of logical dependence on them. The principles of metaphysics do not depend logically on any other further principles whatever; they are themselves the highest logical principles in their field.

It is also true that the epistemological basis of *a priori* judgments must itself consist of *a priori* knowledge. But from this entirely correct postulate of modal similarity between knowledge and its epistemological basis one cannot infer the incorrectness of an empirical justification of metaphysical judgments. For this justification does not contain, though it does concern, the epistemological basis of metaphysical judgments. One must distinguish the content of critical knowledge, by means of which the deduction is carried out, from its object. In other words, one must distinguish the basis of metaphysical judgments from their justification. The judgments in question can be based only on *a priori* knowledge, yet their justification properly proceeds by means of empirical knowledge. There is no contradiction in this.

The peculiarity of the Critique of Reason, as practised by Fries, lies in this: the knowledge contained in the system of metaphysics forms the object of the knowledge contained in the Critique of Reason. This single idea solves all the difficulties which have been raised again and again against Fries' method in the Critique of Reason. The axiomatic method is familiar to every mathematician today. But what does it do, if not to take the statements contained in the system of mathematics as objects of the statements contained in the axiomatic or critique of mathematics? Consider for example the axiom of parallels. Here we have the statement—which we may call *A*:

A. For any straight line through a point in a plane there is only one other straight line in that plane and through that point which does not cut the given line.

This is a statement from the system of geometry. Now this statement A becomes the object of a statement which we may call A', in the geometrical critique:

A'. A is unprovable.

This statement in the geometrical critique has the statement in the geometrical system as object, as one can straight away see from the way it is put. It has nothing to do with the validity of that geometrical statement. The validity of that statement is not in question here at all, but only whether it is open to proof. And this question is settled by proving the statement A'. It is not the statement A that is here proved, but the statement A'. The critique cannot be concerned with the proof of the axiom, as is immediately obvious in this case, since it is the *un*provability of A that is asserted by A'.

The case of metaphysics and of the critique of its principles in deduction is exactly similar. Let us take as example the metaphysical statement we may call B:

B. Every change has a cause.

This statement is the principle of causality. In the Critique of Reason it becomes the object of the statement B':

B'. B recapitulates some item of immediate knowledge.

This statement B' is then proved, and the proof of B' is the deduction of B.

Modern axiomatics thus present us with a relationship entirely analogous to that between Fries' Critique of Reason and the system of metaphysics. The principles of the system are the object of the Critique, and the aim of the Critique, and particularly of the 'deduction', is not at all to prove the principles in question; and finally the statement which has as its object the statements of the system is itself proved—and that by means of a psychological theory.

3. Connected with this is the answer to the third question, concerning the liability to error of an empirical Critique. Does this not put at risk the apodeictic certainty of the statements to be justified?

The fact is that the judgments of metaphysics are supposed to be apodeictic in character. So if the deduction does not guarantee their apodeictic certainty, it fails entirely in its aim. Does it follow that this aim of the Critique is irreconcilable with its empirical character?

Anyone who draws this conclusion is confusing the modal distinction between empirical and apodeictic knowledge with a distinction of degrees of certainty. All empirical knowledge is of course merely assertoric, not apodeictic. But assertoric knowledge is not for that reason any less certain.

On closer inspection it appears that the argument from the liability to error of an empirical critique proves too much. For one would not say that a rational science is immune to error and that therefore a rational critique is better protected against the danger of error than an empirical one. Errors occur in mathematical and logical enquiries just as much as in those belonging to empirical science. Indeed, experience teaches us that philosophy, which as a rational science can here be contrasted with the empirical critique, is more exposed to the dangers of error than is any science of experience.

The sceptical attacks on this method are therefore entirely inappropriate, in so far as they are based on its empirical character. Any one who brings forward these sceptical arguments in order to evade the empirical method has failed to recognize that, in Fries' striking phrase, to question facts is a proof of ignorance.

Let us, however, assume that a rational critique would be possible, i.e. that a deduction of the principles of metaphysics could be conducted along the lines of *a priori* knowledge, and let us ask what advantage there would really be in this.

The Critique, which is supposed to decide whether metaphysics can exist as a science, would then itself be a metaphysical science—a meta-metaphysic. So its own principles would for the same reason require a critique, from which our own Critique would then originate—a critique of a higher order, and so a meta-meta-metaphysic. This, however, being a rational science, would for the same reason require a critique of a yet higher order; and so on indefinitely. Our task would thus be an impossible one. Indeed one must say more. Apart from the fact that this task could never be completed, we should all the time be getting further away from our aim, not nearer to it, the aim for whose sake we first undertook the Critique. For the further we progress in this series of critiques, the more abstract do the principles become to which we ascend, and so the greater becomes the danger from that source of error which we intended our critical labours to render harmless. For it is the abstract character of metaphysical principles, and that alone, which accounts for their lack of self-evidence, their obscurity, and is thus the source of the unreliability and dispute from which we were trying to escape.

A rational critique would thus be in no way superior to an empirical one, as it would quite frustrate the purpose for which we undertook the Critique in the first place. Far from freeing metaphysics from its state of confusion, it would immeasurably increase that confusion— a general assertion, this, for which the history of so-called 'German Idealism' after Kant, which followed this route, provides unintentional and empirical, but none the less convincing evidence.

4. It is now easy to answer the last objection that a deduction from inner experience involves us in circular argument, because inner experience itself presupposes metaphysical principles, without which it could not take place at all.

This objection rests on a confusion between deduction and proof. The deduction would be circular only if it was intended to prove the metaphysical principles which, like every empirical method, it does presuppose. The statements which it proves—genuinely proves—are statements of experience, statements which as I showed have a metaphysical knowledge only as their object. So there is no circular argument here.

The question could still be raised why one should use this method at all. The deduction does not, it is true, involve any circular argument, nevertheless one is bound to presuppose the principles being deduced—at least in part—in order to make a beginning on the process of deduction. This procedure, though not open to logical objection, does in consequence appear superfluous and unnecessary, as its end-result must be already presupposed, separately and independently of these labours.

The Critique of Reason is not for us an end in itself, but is meant to help us in construction of the system of metaphysics. Now if we cannot undertake the Critique without some *other*, and previous, guarantee of the basic truths of metaphysics, then the Critique itself does seem an unnecessary detour. Should we not do better to start simply by a direct statement of the basic propositions of metaphysics?

Put in this way the objection is somewhat more profound. But it is still erroneous, for it quite mistakes the meaning and purpose of critical labour and loses sight of the real task of the Critique of Reason. Moreover this objection makes sense only from the standpoint of Dogmatism—the logical standpoint of a system which has no place for the Critique—and it disappears as soon as one adopts the critical way of posing the problem. For our purpose in the Critique of Reason is not to guarantee metaphysical knowledge as valid, nor to obtain it in the first place. Metaphysical knowledge, if there be any such at all, is something we just discover we possess, without any action on our part. The point is simply this: metaphysical knowledge, though we do possess it, is something intrinsically obscure in our reason. This does not matter in the ordinary concrete use of the intellect in experience, but it does mean that the abstract use of metaphysical principles is not easily successful, but lies exposed to all those errors and confusions of which the history of the dogmatic systems provides so many warning examples. To avoid this danger we require the Critique of Reason. And the Critique really does achieve this aim for us, for in it we make only a concrete use of metaphysical principles, obtaining at the end criteria which enable us to handle and decide on the deepest metaphysical abstractions with safety.

The Critique is not meant to guarantee metaphysical knowledge, but only the abstract form of metaphysical principles. In the Critique itself, however, we do not need to make abstract use of these principles; the concrete use suffices. And the fact should be recognized that this concrete use really is free of those difficulties which our critical undertaking was intended to avoid. The concrete use of metaphysical principles, which alone is required here—we could also call it the implicit use—is in fact much easier and simpler. The difficulty begins only when one moves on from the concrete and implicit use of metaphysical principles to expounding them *in abstracto* and using them explicitly. This difficulty does not arise in the Critique of Reason, any more than in any other science of experience. Far from hindering us, the empirical nature of the Critique is really helpful, enabling us to resolve our problem— the problem not of guaranteeing metaphysical knowledge but only of guaranteeing the abstract system of metaphysical principles.

In this connection, finally, there is a striking and noteworthy parallel between the Critique of Reason and modern research into the foundations of mathematics. The device which Hilbert used to attack the profound problem of consistency in arithmetic presents a close analogy to the deduction of Fries. It consists in replacing the problems of transfinite numbers, which are too abstract to think about, by corresponding problems in elementary number theory, which is based on perception, thus resolving the former problems without really posing them—just as Fries' deduction, which raises only psychological questions, nevertheless leads to the solution of the main question of metaphysics, without ever posing that question on its own. The analogy is exact. The statements and modes of inference of transfinite arithmetic are here made the object of a mathematical critique, which Hilbert calls 'metamathematics'. To put it more precisely: the object of critical enquiry here is not so much the judgments and inferences of transfinite number theory, but rather

the signs by which these judgments and inferences are denoted—
the mere signs, without regard for their significance. These signs are
simply finite and perceptually comprehensible figures and can
therefore be the objects of a concrete mode of knowledge, involving
demonstration. The result of this procedure is not a logical derivation
of the statements of transfinite number theory from those of elementary number theory, but what in modern mathematics and logic is
called a 'modelling' of the statements of the one system on those of
the other, i.e. each statement in one system is linked to one in the
other in such a way that if a contradiction were to arise in the one
system a corresponding relationship, which can be precisely defined,
would appear in the other system and would be open to demonstration. A contradiction is not itself open to demonstration—one can
only think it; but demonstration can be applied to certain combinations of signs which are the expression for such a contradictory
relationship, for example to this set of signs:

$$O \neq O$$

The occurrence of such a set of signs is a matter that perception can
decide.

Fries' deduction, similarly, instead of dealing with general metaphysical truths, which are the objects of abstract judgments, enquires
into the concrete facts of our knowledge of metaphysical truths,
disregarding the objective significance of this knowledge and so
disregarding what they allow us to know of their object, and con-
centrating entirely on their place of origin in the human reason. They
thus become the object of a knowledge which, although it is not, like
Hilbert's, directly demonstrable, is nevertheless empirical, a knowledge whose content consists not of abstract but of concrete judgments; which is therefore free of the difficulties to which we are
helplessly exposed if we attempt direct construction of a system of
abstract metaphysical judgments. Thus the analogy is really exact, as
far as the logical relationship at issue is concerned. Here let me only
remark in passing on the astonishing fact that in Fries' deduction
operating with signs in place of the intended metaphysical concep-
tualization does play a limited but fruitful role.

There remains of course a difference between the two procedures.
This is clear from the fact that Fries' deduction does not operate with
items of knowledge belonging to pure intuition, as Hilbert's metamathematics does, but with empirical, i.e. psychological items of
knowledge. This difference is, however, due to the nature of the case
and is not accidental. It is due to the difference in aim of the two en-

quiries. While metamathematics is concerned with a proof of consistency (absence of contradiction), Fries' deduction is concerned with a genuine justification. One would expect a logical problem such as that of consistency to require different methods of solution from the psychological problem of proving the existence of an immediate knowledge.

14

Fries' reform of philosophy was in fact a reinstatement of the old ideas of Socrates and Plato, which Aristotle had dismissed and which had never been revived again in all the history of philosophy. The method of the Critique of Reason consists, in practice, simply in carrying out and making more scientific the basic idea in the old 'Socratic method' and of pure Platonism in general, as opposed to Aristotle's misinterpretations of it. Fries' tribute to Kant in his *History of Philosophy*, which praised Kant as the first to remove the mistakes of Aristotle without falling back into those of Plato, can really be applied to Fries himself. It was his own contribution, which he modestly ascribed to his teacher.

Fries was able to take this great step forward because of the corrections he made in the traditional logic, in the theory of the justification of judgments. As Fries himself put it, securing general recognition for this simple theory of the justification of judgments was enough to make philosophy as simple a school subject as geometry and arithmetic had been for thousands of years. There were two profound mistakes, which had propagated themselves through the whole history of philosophy and were entirely responsible for holding up this great step forward for so long. They explain sufficiently why even today Fries' theory still meets so much opposition. First there is the prejudice that logic is almighty, which lies at the basis of all logical Dogmatism and Scholasticism. Here it is correctly perceived that we require reflection in order to become conscious of philosophical truths; but people think this means that one must first discover some art of dialectic, which can then beget philosophical knowledge for us. This effort runs right through the history of philosophy. Ever since Aristotle founded logic people have thought they could rely on it for this great service. Secondly those who realized the barrenness of all such efforts tried to work in the opposite direction, and as proof was useless for justifying philosophical truths they tried to give a demonstration of them. They were thus compelled to rely on a faculty of metaphysical intuition in order to base metaphysical truths upon it. While the first party failed to see that logic is empty and that all reflective knowledge is merely indirect, the latter party overlooked the basic obscurity of metaphysical knowledge, the necessity, in other words, of employing reflection in order to get one's metaphysical knowledge clear. These two contesting parties started from the same point, and that starting point contained the whole riddle of the history of philosophy. Plato has a hint of the correct solution to this riddle in his theory of reminiscence, which was only a further development of the Socratic theory that a philosopher does not so much need to acquire philosophical knowledge as to realize that which he already has.

The secret of Plato's dialectic was not a device for producing philosophical knowledge so much as one for clarifying the philosophical knowledge which is already there and bringing it into the form of a science.

The misunderstanding which runs through the whole history of philosophy and is bound to lead over and over again to the old mistake is simply due to the basic obscurity of metaphysical knowledge. The result of this obscurity in metaphysical knowledge is that one can be mistaken not only about the content of that knowledge, but even about its existence, thus giving rise to the idea that the gaining of metaphysical knowledge is due to the labours of the understanding. It is now clear why these labours are condemned always to come to nothing: they come to grief on the simple fact that all reflective knowledge is mediate and originally empty.

Reflective knowledge consists of the judgment. But the judgment is knowledge only in so far as it recapitulates some knowledge which is independent of thought, putting into the form of a judgment some knowledge which does not of itself possess that form. To try to extract a new content of knowledge from the mere form of the judgment will always be labour lost. If we abide by the mere form of the judgment, we are left with nothing except the empty analytic principles of logic, and no logical inference however sophisticated can extract new content for our knowledge from them.

Here we find a direct link with the efforts of Socrates and Plato. The profound thought which they had prophetically adumbrated is at last established scientifically and made fruitful. None of the thinkers who came in between could make anything of this thought, as they either abandoned philosophy to Empiricism or wasted their mental powers in the futile dispute between Scholasticism and Neo-Platonism. For Scholasticism reduces to the hopeless attempt to squeeze metaphysical information out of the mere form of thought, and Neo-Platonism reduces to the equally hopeless attempt to achieve at last a demonstration of metaphysical truths. The former goes wrong by failing to see that reflection is originally empty, and the latter by failing to see that metaphysical knowledge is originally obscure.

It is now clear that Scholasticism and Neo-Platonism of every sort are mere self-deception and tomfoolery. We can also see the profound significance of the Socratic idea that it is not for a philosopher to increase his knowledge, but only to realize what he does know already and what he does not know.

The history of philosophy, seen from this point of view, is like a spectacle in which captured animals run to and fro in their cage, racing from one set of bars to the other in the desperate hope that in this way they might yet find the way out to freedom. The basic obscurity of metaphysical knowledge is one set of bars, and the basic emptiness of reflection is the other set.

15

So much for the revival of the Socratic method and of pure Platonism. But for a proper assessment of Fries' place in the history of philosophy one must add something further, and that is the final reconciliation of this pure Platonism in metaphysics with the achievements of Aristotelian logic on one side and those of modern natural science on the other. To bring about this reconciliation with both parties was a major task.

The first part of it, the reconciliation of pure Platonism with the achievements of Aristotelian logic, took place when Fries set the Aristotelian logic free of the logicist misinterpretation, which trapped even Aristotle himself, with regard to his own discoveries.

The other part, the reconciliation of pure Platonism with the achievements of modern natural science, came about when Fries released the methods of the science of experience from Empiricism, in which most of the modern scientists had become involved; from the empiricist misinterpretation of their own way of work, which had trapped them just as Aristotle was trapped by the logicist misinterpretation of his logic.

The first, the reconciliation of pure Platonism with Aristotelian logic, was achieved by freeing logic from the preconception that logic is almighty, which would make logic into a source for widening our knowledge; in other words, by showing that the Aristotelian laws of identity and contradiction are principles only for our analytic judgment, and that for the system of metaphysics we must find synthetic principles independent of the principles of identity and of contradiction, as Kant had already done. Only the question of justifying these synthetic basic principles, which are required for all metaphysics, had been left unresolved by Kant. The reason was that he had a faulty view about the justification of judgments, having never revised the traditional teaching on the subject. Even Kant retained the preconceived idea that judgments which do not rest directly on perception and so cannot be demonstrated must be proved. This assumption that the principles of metaphysics could and should be guaranteed by a process of proof was the reason why his revolutionary undertaking of the Critique of Reason issued in a restoration of that scholastic prejudice. The only way forward here was that of Fries' logic, with its theory of deduction as the mode of justification for metaphysical principles.

16

The other part of Fries' achievement was the reconciliation of Platonism, correctly understood, with modern natural science. This major accomplishment depended on freeing the method of the empirical sciences from the prejudice of Empiricism—the prejudice that experience can do everything—in which philosophizing modern scientists had become involved. To put it another way, this accomplishment depended on building up a correct theory of induction. Fries provided a correct theory of induction by developing further what Kant called 'the theory of the principles on which experience is possible'. Kant had discovered that experience can take place at all only on the assumption of certain synthetic, and not merely logical principles, which are set over all experience *a priori* and are thus the basis on which experience is possible at all. Fries called them the guiding maxims of any rational induction. A rational induction is one which implies a scientifically based mode of inference, as opposed to a merely habitual generalization due to the expectation of similar cases. Empiricism, from which the methods of empirical science require to be freed, consists in trying to base induction simply on inferences from observations. This is an old mistake, due simply to an erroneous presentation of logic by Aristotle himself. This false theory of induction goes right back to him. The mistake is basically that of confusing induction and abstraction, the two types of regressive method. A method is regressive if it goes from the particular to the general. But there are two different ways of going from the particular to the general in our knowledge. Induction is one method of inference; it consists in inferring from the particular to the general, from individual cases to the law. So it cannot, as Aristotle and all the logicians who followed him supposed, be the method for discovering principles. If that were the case, if induction were the method for finding principles, the principles of our knowledge could be discovered by inferences from particular to general and so could be based on inferences from experience. But that comes down to saying that they could be based on probable inferences. For one can never infer with certainty from particular cases of observation to a general law. In experience we can never infer with certainty from the particular direct to the law; for the law includes infinitely many possible cases. This is the problem that has for so long occupied those great scientists and mathematicians of modern times who gave thought to the principles of their science, and which in particular led the French mathematicians Condorcet, Laplace and Lagrange to attempt to justify induction by the aid of the calculus of probability.

This attempt proceeds on the empiricist assumption that all induction is originally empirical induction, i.e. that our inferences from particular to general are guided by the expectation of similar cases, and that to make these empirical inductions rational one must come to their aid with the calculus of probabilities.

It was this that led Fries to rethink the theory of probable inference.

The first point he had to establish was that probability arises only where an inference is drawn on insufficient grounds. From this there follows at once the important statement that probability only has meaning in the field of derived judgments, not in that of basic judgments. Demonstrable or deducible judgments cannot be held to be more or less probable, but are established as completely certain when they are demonstrated or deduced. Uncertainty has a place in our judgments only when we do not possess completely adequate premises for the inference.

The second important discovery in this revision of the theory of probable inference was Fries' distinction between philosophical and mathematical probability.

Every probable inference is based on a major premiss concerning a general rule, the sphere of which falls into parts. Now there is an important difference here, depending on whether this partition of the sphere of the major premiss is based on our knowing that the statement does not hold for one part of the sphere, or on our not knowing whether it holds for all parts.

In the first case, where we know that we are dealing with an objectively divided sphere, i.e. that the rule in question holds for one part but not for the other, then if we can determine the ratio of the parts by calculation we can from this ratio infer the probability of a particular case coming into the one or other part of the sphere. All probable inferences in mathematics are of this nature. But in this case 'calculus of probability' is an imprecise expression: it is not the unknown, but the known that is calculated, namely the partition of the major premiss.

In the other case we infer from the known part of this sphere to the whole sphere, from the plurality of cases to the general law. Fries calls this the inference of philosophical probability. In the justification of induction this inference alone is relevant.

There is, however, a third point. This inference from the plurality of cases to a general law is intrinsically meaningless unless universal truths are presupposed already quite apart from it—strictly universal, not just probable—truths which authorize us to move from part of the sphere to the whole sphere. But if such authorization is available in a universal truth, that relieves us of amassing observations of similar cases in order to guarantee the general statement. This is the decisive point. If we were reduced to amassing similar observations in order to move on to the general law, the number of observed similar cases would always be infinitely small in relation to the possible cases, and there could be no probable inference to the general rule.

What often happens in practice is that a single experiment or a single observation decides that a general law obtains. The certainty of a law never depends on the number of cases observed. Why, for example, was the Copernican theory superior to the earlier theory of epicycles? Not because it amassed new observations. These cannot decide such questions. Nor was it, as people often assume, because of its supposedly greater simplicity in calculation. The reason was that it brought the movement of the heavenly bodies under the laws of mechanics, which the theory of epicycles did not attempt to do. To take another example: in order to show that there cannot be a *perpetuum mobile* (instance of perpetual motion) one is not reduced to counting the cases in which attempts at constructing one have failed. If one wanted by this method to infer with probability the impossibility of a *perpetuum mobile*, one would never achieve one's aim; for the number of cases tried would always remain infinitely small in comparison to the number of all possible cases. It was bringing this problem under the Law of the Conservation of Energy that gave a sufficient reason for the strict assertion that there cannot be a *perpetuum mobile*.

The compulsive nature of induction never depends on the amassing of similar observations or trials, but always and only on the

o

firmness with which the area of experience in question is brought under general principles; and as the highest of these principles cannot depend in its turn on induction, they must be established independently of all experience and therefore purely *a priori*.

Fourthly and finally: it is evidently a mistake to suppose that even empirical induction, which simply results from the habitual expectation of similar cases, would be possible on empiricist presuppositions. Even empirical induction can take place only if *a priori* knowledge is assumed. Had we no such *a priori* knowledge, then even the blindly habitual expectation of similar cases would be impossible. This assertion admittedly takes us into the field of psychology. We shall soon see how the Theory of Reason, worked out psychologically, got rid of the sensualist preconception that a merely empirical induction, the expectation of similar cases, can take place without *a priori* knowledge.

3

The Doctrine of Reason

I

Kant knows only the name 'deduction', not the thing. What he called deduction is really a form of proof. This had the effect of limiting his Critique of Reason to the method of logical Dogmatism, with the result that the fruitful beginnings he made on a Critique of Reason were never properly developed in his own work. Fries completely destroyed this whole logico-dogmatic framework, thus allowing those fruitful beginnings room and freedom for further development. Freed for development, this science took on an entirely new appearance. The Critique of Reason was transformed, one could say, into a Theory of Reason. Our present business is with the basic ideas of this Theory of Reason.

The first point to pay attention to if we are not to misunderstand Fries' Theory of Reason is that the original Humean problem comes to the fore once more, and that the mistaken epistemological way of posing that problem disappears once and for all. So the Theory of Reason must not be judged by whether or not it has answered that mistaken epistemological question; that would be to misunderstand the theory completely, both in its general significance and in all its details. Properly understood the *quaestio iuris* of the Critique of Reason is nothing but Hume's problem over again—Hume's problem correctly understood and generalized to the greatest possible extent. Hume was right to try to solve this problem psychologically.

We must make clear precisely what is implied in demanding that the method of deduction be strictly psychological. Such a procedure (as set out in our discussion of the Theory of Method) will not, of course, serve to indicate a foundation for the principles of meta-physics, but only the condition laid down by logic for the possibility of metaphysical judgments. Not that this logical requirement itself provides a justification for metaphysical judgments. Far from it. What it really does is to demand that such judgments be justified. But we are not here dealing with this question of the condition on which metaphysical judgments are justifiable, a condition which can be determined on purely logical grounds, but with a question of fact; do we, or do we not really possess some such immediate metaphysical knowledge, as basis for our metaphysical judgments? Our deduction cannot start from the validity of metaphysical judgments, but only from the fact that they lay claim to validity.

2

How can this claim be made?

Universal judgments, whose claim to validity is in question here, are not self-evident. Their truth is not immediately clear to us. Instead, they are in an obscure way taken for granted, under the influence of that feeling-for-truth which guides us in deciding the particular cases we come across in perception. We realize the truth of the universal judgments only by abstraction from the perceptual content of the judgments of experience. We reach the universal judgments of metaphysics only when we ask what assumptions (*apart* from any perceptual content) are involved in the judging to which that feeling-for-truth guided us. These assumptions cannot, therefore, arise from any perception.

Nor can they arise from reflection. For it is synthetic judgments that are at issue here, judgments which increase the content of knowledge; and such judgments cannot derive from reflection alone. All reflection can do is to recapitulate, in the form of the judgment, knowledge derived from elsewhere. That is what abstraction does here, for abstraction is simply reflection on the universal assumptions which, owing to the feeling-for-truth, do in fact find application in some particular judgment. Abstraction simply isolates these assumptions from the perceptual content of the particular judgment by casting them in the form of a properly universal judgment, which is free of that perceptual content.

Fries gives another turn to the underlying problem here, thereby making it even clearer. He puts it like this: how can the arbitrary combination of concepts lead to knowledge of necessary truths?

This is really just another way of expressing Kant's problem—how can synthetic judgments be made *a priori*?—but it puts it in a way which shows better what the psychological Theory of Reason is for, just as Kant's way of putting the question shows the object of this theory in its scientifically purest form; a form which we cannot observe as a psychological fact in us so readily as that arbitrary combination of concepts which actually takes place in every judgment. Kant's synthetic *a priori* judgments are just the most abstract principles of any and every synthesis that takes place in our judgments.

From the point of view of logic they are the bases on which synthetic judgments can be made at all, bases reached, however, only through an extremely artificial process of abstraction, and not directly present to us as facts of consciousness.

Fries moreover formulates the problem in what is basically its oldest form, in which it troubled the thinkers of antiquity and particularly the Sophists of Greece. It was this problem that drove the Sophists to their scepticism—and also drives their modern disciples that way. It seems impossible that we should come to a knowledge of necessary truths by means of an arbitrary combination of concepts, and for this reason the sceptics declared that there could be no knowledge of necessary truths.

This ancient theory can be found in various modern clothes, and particularly in the conventionalist form of metaphysical Scepticism adopted by many empiricists. Those assumptions are here explained as conventional contributions of thought to the content of observations, as arbitrary creations of our understanding, which may be admitted for the convenience of their application but not as necessary truths. For some extraordinary reason people do not notice that this explanation is circular. For a decision on grounds of suitability, on which reliance is here placed, is itself just another form of application of metaphysical presuppositions. Suitability is a particular form of causality; for an 'end' or 'aim' is just an effect, the idea of which causes that effect to be produced. It is moreover clear that we can judge as suitable for use only those ideas that we already possess apart from this decision. So the question of where they come from can certainly not be resolved in this way.

3

The rule for that combination of concepts whose necessity we assert in a judgment can be found neither in perception nor in the mere form of reflection. That is the result established by Hume, with his remarkable acuity, and it provides the Theory of Reason with a firm starting point. The only question, for someone who has followed Hume thus far, is how we are to intepret this result, and what we should conclude from it. So we must first examine the conclusion Hume drew from this result—that the judgments in question have no basis in knowledge at all and are really just combinations of ideas arising by association, the ideas in their turn all deriving from perception. If this conclusion is drawn, it is impossible to justify metaphysical judgments. But we should at least be able to give a psychological explanation why they should seem to claim validity.

Now the Critique which Fries directed at empiricist association-psychology should not be misunderstood at this point. His Critique was not concerned with association-psychology as such—as far as that goes, we are still in Hume's position—but only with the empiricist interpretation which Hume gave to association-psychology. This interpretation is such an easy and obvious one, of course, that not only Hume but every other psychologist without exception up till Fries regarded it as the only possible one, and as self-evidently correct; so that the step that led from the theory itself to this interpretation was not noticed at all and for this reason was not put to the test. The defenders of association-psychology took it as a sufficient justification for Empiricism, just as the opponents of Empiricism regarded their denial of Empiricism as sufficient reason for denying association-psychology.

The difficulty which leads to misunderstandings at this point concerns the application of association-psychology to the facts of reflection or of thought in the proper sense of the word. We must first get clear on this preliminary point if we are to attack our main problem with any hope of success.

Fries' theory of reflection is based on the distinction between what he calls the higher and lower thought-processes. The lower thought-process consists of the involuntary play of ideas, while the higher thought-process is directed by the intervention of the will in that play of ideas, guiding it for its own poetic or, maybe, scientific purposes. So the problem of the Theory of Reflection can be put in this simple question: how is it possible to have ideas at will (*willkürlich vorzustellen*)?

When we look into this we find that the distinction between the lower and higher thought-processes does not consist, as might at first appear, in the authority of the laws of association being restricted to the former, as though these laws did not apply to reflection. A more precise inquiry into the laws of the process of arbitrary choice (*Willkür*) will show that this is no more exempted from the laws of association than is the play of ideas of the lower thought-processes. Reflection is of course possible only if the will takes the initiative of intervening in the play of ideas. But this intervention of arbitrary choice in the play of ideas does not involve any breaking of the associations, but itself depends entirely on the laws of association holding good. Willing (*Das Wollen*) is a psychic phenomenon, and like other psychic phenomena it must take its place in the series of psychic appearances with their associative interconnections. Having ideas at will is possible because of the associative connection of willing with the ideas conditioned by willing, on the principle that an idea on which the will is directed is thereby increased in clarity and thus by the intervention of the will is reproduced in the play of ideas, just as in the lower thought process one idea is reproduced by means of another. Fries thus manages to explain—and this is the peculiar contribution of his Theory of Reflection—the distinction between the lower and higher thought-processes, without setting any limits to the application to the laws of association. The distinguishing of the higher and lower thought-processes is here combined with an explanation of the higher (as well as the lower) thought-process along thoroughly association-psychological lines.

4

The limits of association-psychology lie elsewhere. We do not reach them by way of the general problem of how one can decide to have ideas, but by way of the particular problem of how by deciding to have ideas one can gain knowledge of necessary truths. Fries showed that Hume's attempt at an association-psychological explanation of our judgments of necessary connection is inadequate. This attempt consists of deriving these judgments about connections from the phenomenon of the habitual expectation of similar cases. The remarkable turn which leads Fries to his solution is his proof that this habitual expectation of similar cases is not itself explicable on mere laws of association. So in order to show the inadequacy of empiricist psychology we need not enter on the complicated logical problem about rational induction. It is sufficient to inquire closely into the phenomenon of habitual expectation of similar cases, a phenomenon which itself belongs entirely to the lower thought-process. Even here an item of *a priori* knowledge is found to be at work.

All Hume can really explain by the application of his laws of association is the increase in intensity and clarity of ideas which are already present, not the origination of qualitatively new ideas. Metaphysical ideas which require explanation (including even the problematic ideas of unity and necessity in the Being of things) are qualitatively new ideas as compared with those which derive from mere perception—though it is to these perceptual ideas that empiricist theory tries to trace them back. What this theory fails to recognize is the distinction between a merely subjective combination of ideas and the idea of an objective combination of objects. Once we grasp this distinction, the way to a solution is clear. For association explains the subjective combination of ideas, but can never explain the idea of objective combination. To say this is not to destroy the authority of the laws of association. Objective combination is not really the business of association-psychology. From ideas which do not include that of an objective combination we cannot derive that idea. Where it seems as if we might be able to, this is in every case due to our confusing the combination of ideas with the idea of a combination. The mere subjective presence of the idea of objective connection, whether justified or not, cannot be explained by laws of association, though of course in empirical inductions not governed by scientific maxims the ideas of unity which we are trying to explain are often applied merely by habit.

This discussion shows that there must be a third source in our knowledge, in addition to perception and reflection, a mode of representation which itself is neither perception nor reflection: an immediate, though originally obscure knowledge. Only from this could our ideas of objective unity and necessity in the Being of things arise.

5

The concept thus introduced of *a knowledge immediate yet not perceptual* does contain certain difficulties. These difficulties provide an unusually plausible explanation for the misunderstandings to which Fries' psychology is still exposed.

It seems paradoxical to speak of a knowledge which is not perceptual yet is immediate. A non-perceptual immediate knowledge is one which, although as knowledge it is immediate (not mediated by reflection), yet it comes to consciousness only mediately (by means of reflection). This seems contradictory; but only because the immediacy of the knowledge is confused with immediacy in the consciousness of the knowledge. This shows how important and useful is Fries' distinction between these concepts. We must not infer directly from immediacy of knowledge to immediacy in the consciousness of knowledge, and equally we must not infer from mediacy in the consciousness of the knowledge to mediacy of knowledge.

The fact is that consciousness of the metaphysical knowledge in question is mediated to us only by reflection. But the fact that we become conscious of it only by means of reflection does not allow us to infer that it derives from reflection. If we are to achieve a tenable psychological theory, everything depends on our reconciling two facts: the fact that metaphysical knowledge does not derive from reflection, and the fact that we become conscious of it only by means of reflection. These two facts can be combined without contradiction by positing a non-perceptual immediate knowledge, and that is the only way to combine them without contradiction. These two facts thus clearly compel us to assume an immediate, non-perceptual metaphysical knowledge.

It was perhaps Fries' greatest service to psychology—it was certainly his greatest service to the Theory of Reason—to have made this distinction between immediacy of knowledge and immediacy in our consciousness of that knowledge.

The confusion of immediacy of knowledge with immediacy in our consciousness of it explains the illusion that the disjunction between perceptual and reflective knowledge is exhaustive. This confusion stands revealed as the profound psychological error underlying the false logical theory that all judgments which cannot be proved can be demonstrated, or that all judgments which cannot be demonstrated can be proved. So this universal and basic psychological mistake also explains the basic mistake in logic which prior to Fries had led so many astray in the history of philosophy.

6

The Theory of Reason which avoids this basic psychological mistake starts from the fact that all the particular items of knowledge which may be present in the mind at any one moment can be dealt with separately only by an artificial abstraction. In the real life of the mind knowing does not take place on its own, apart from other distinct mental activities. Our mind never has knowledge apart from expressions of its practical faculties such as pleasure, desire or decision. These expressions all combine in the intensive unity of our living activity (*Lebenstätigkeit*) and can be thought of as separate from it only by an artificial abstraction.

This general law provides the deeper reason why association is both possible and psychologically necessary. All the expressions of mental life* which are present at any one time must be part of one and the same intensive unity of consciousness, which has a particular degree at any given moment. It follows that one of them can be strengthened only if the others are correspondingly weakened. The laws of association are simply laws of the reciprocal weakening and strengthening of the expressions of mental life.

We shall, however, find it convenient to abstract for the moment from this relation of knowledge to the expressions of the practical faculties and to concentrate solely on the theory of knowledge.

The next point is that knowledge is not an activity undertaken by our reason entirely on its own initiative, i.e. it is not solely responsible for its manifestations, but comes under the law of sensibility. This

* *Lebensäusserungen unseres Geistes.*

law implies that mental manifestations depend on conditions not provided by reason but by an external stimulation which is quite contingent as far as reason is concerned.

In so far as reason does not determine its own activity, but comes under a law, foreign to itself, of external stimulation, it may be called 'sensible reason'. It is (to use a phrase coined by Fries) a faculty of stimulable activity. And this openness to stimulation, i.e. the fact that the manifestations of mental life depend on stimulations which are contingent and foreign to the mind, is called its sensibility. Sensibility, then, is not a distinct active faculty alongside the self-activating reason, it is the openness of the reason itself to stimulation, the dependence of its own proper activity upon external stimulation.

This law that human reason is sensible means that reason does not itself provide the content of its knowledge of individual real things, but receives it from outside, in a relationship which for it is essentially contingent—so that all it can on its own prescribe to any determinate item of knowledge are certain conditions which may be necessary but are by no means sufficient and which do not appear as something isolated, but would have to appear in any real knowledge which was sensibly stimulated.

I said: conditions 'which may be necessary' for determining the content of genuine knowledge. For whether reason achieves even this on its own initiative, and whether it provides anything at all extra to sensible stimulation, is a matter that the law of sensibility does not decide. This law simply says that our reason is not enough on its own for the knowledge of individual real things: if it is sufficient on its own for any knowledge whatever, it certainly does not suffice for knowledge of individual real things.

Whether it is sufficient on its own for any knowledge whatever is decided by a third law. This makes us aware of the fact that the reason is not a merely sensible faculty, i.e. not just a capacity for being stimulated, but also, as pure reason, a capacity for entirely independent activity, by which it determines the basic and identical form of any activity of knowing that may be stimulated sensibly, and the only form in which that activity is possible.

Hence this law, which I shall for brevity call the 'law of spontaneity', asserts that there is a quite autonomous activity of knowledge, and thus what for brevity we call *a priori* knowledge. We must now make this notion of *a priori* knowledge more precise, and this in two respects. The first and for this law the decisive point is this: the term '*a priori*' is applied to an item of knowledge in respect of its origin, not its content. So '*a priori* knowledge' must not be defined by the qualities of universality and necessity or, in short, of being apodeictic. It may be a property of *a priori* knowledge to be apodeictic, i.e. to be universal and necessary in form, but it does not follow that this is its defining characteristic. The move from describing an item of knowledge as apodeictic to asserting that it is *a priori* involves a separate inference, so if we are to avoid psychological sleight-of-hand we must not straight away treat these two concepts as interchangeable, but must ask ourselves: how do we come to infer at all from the one to the other? This is properly a problem of psychology.

The second point is this: how are we to distinguish the *a priori* nature of the knowledge not only from the marks of objective universality and necessity but also from the psychological marks of subjective universality and necessity?

There are in fact two distinct concepts involved: the objective universality of an item of knowledge, which is concerned with its relation to its object, and its subjective universality, i.e. its being possessed by everyone and, in the case of the individual, its being possessed at every time and under all circumstances.

To call an item of knowledge *a priori* is, first of all, to give only a negative description of its origin: to say that it is independent of sensibility and so of external stimulation. It is not a positive description, like calling it subjectively universal and necessary. Our present law is concerned only with the first relationship, i.e., it gives us only a negative description of apodeictic knowledge: that it is possible only as knowledge independent of sensible stimulation.

By clarifying the relation between describing knowledge as apodeictic and as *a priori* we have really provided that extra precision which was still needed for the Theory of Reason, for we have shown that it is subjectively possible for knowledge to be apodeictic only if some knowledge is *a priori*, if, therefore, there is a faculty for a purely autonomous activity of knowledge*—from which result it then automatically follows, in combination with the previous law, that apodeictic knowledge must be purely formal in character.

Wherever necessity and universality themselves are recognized, there the knowledge can be apodeictic, appearing as that of a 'universal consciousness', only if it is due to a purely autonomous activity of the mind and independent of circumstances. This purely autonomous activity in knowledge is therefore not merely a law of knowledge, but is itself a distinct knowing activity, independent of sensible stimulation. It is this we can call '*a priori* knowledge' in a strictly psychological sense. For this term does not denote some law of knowing where

* *Vermögen einer reinen Selbsttätigkeit des Erkennens*

the knowing itself could be sensible, but a real item of knowledge distinct from sensible knowledge.

In this sense we can make the empirical statement that apodeictic knowledge can occur only as *a priori* knowledge, i.e. only as one belonging to the purely autonomous activity of the mind. Apodeictic knowledge originates in a purely autonomous activity of the mind. What is still lacking is an explanation of the relationship of this purely autonomous activity to the phenomenon of arbitrary choice, which also expresses independence of circumstances. The clarification of this relationship requires a new law, the law that reflection is originally empty.

The autonomous activity of thought or reflection is an activity of arbitrary choice. That is what the Theory of Reflection teaches. The faculty of reflection, the intellect (*Verstand*) is seen to be the faculty of guiding the sequence of ideas where one will. Pure reason (Vernunft) as a faculty of knowledge is to be sharply distinguished from the intellect. For pure reason is the faculty for the purely autonomous activity of knowing. The intellect, by contrast, is not really a faculty of knowing, but of choice. Having ideas at will, which is the proper activity of the intellect, is something quite different from the proper activity of knowing, which is the peculiarity of the reason. The ideas which in combination make up the lower thought-process, and therefore the higher also, must already be provided from elsewhere, before they can be combined at all either in the lower or the higher thought-process—which differs from the lower only in the intervention of the will. The thought-process thus depends on that law of the combination of ideas in the intensive unity of every activity of life, though the possibility of these ideas must itself be independent of their combination. Arbitrary choice in the combination of ideas can therefore never provide a basis on which one could creatively increase the stock of ideas. To put it another way, the arbitrariness of reflection can never be a source for an autonomous activity of knowing.

This is the law of the original emptiness of reflection, or of the mediate nature of all reflective knowledge. It follows from this that pure reason, as the source for all apodeictic knowledge, is independent both of sensibility and of reflection. There follows what we could in the narrower psychological sense call the law of pure reason, that the purely autonomous activity to which apodeictic knowledge is traced can occur only as an autonomous activity of knowledge which belongs to the mind originally, and therefore permanently. To put it another way, it follows—what was undecided before—that just as the objectively contingent knowledge which we call assertoric is also subjectively contingent and varies with the circumstances, so also objectively valid and necessary knowledge, which we call apodeictic, can occur only if it is subjectively universal and necessary as well. This establishes that there is in fact a pure reason independent both of sense and of intellect, an autonomous faculty of knowing which is native to the mind and a permanent characteristic of it, and which unites all individual items of immediate knowledge into a whole. Now the question arises: what is the peculiar content of this native autonomous activity of pure reason?

The answer to this is found in the next law. What is peculiar to this native autonomous activity of our reason, which alone and permanently determines the form in which it may be stimulated, is simply the basic notion of the objective synthetic unity of all the manifold given in sense: formal apperception. This not only brings the plurality of individual items of knowledge sensibly stimulated in the mind together psychologically into one whole of immediate knowledge; it also transforms all sensitive knowledge, in respect of the determination of its object, into a mere determination of content for one and the same basic notion of an objective form of combination. This all-embracing whole of immediate knowledge is therefore called transcendental apperception.

This law is the mainstay of the whole theory. It is (not any more than the other laws which I discussed earlier) a principle erected dogmatically, as a mere hypothesis on which to base the Theory of Reason, but is a law derived by induction from inner experience. What it really asserts is that all particular notions of objective unity and necessity which may occur in our mind are simply modifications or partial representations of a single idea of objective synthetic unity, which underlies and comprehends them all.

There is another important law which comes in at this point. This states that the mind is not only tied to the law of sensibility in respect of its immediate knowledge, but is bound by a corresponding law in respect of its consciousness of this knowledge, the law that we can become conscious of immediate knowledge only step by step. Immediate knowledge, as the whole which it really is and which is therefore called transcendental apperception, is not present to the mind. We become conscious of it only in bits, realizing only those of the ideas in it that we possess at a given moment as clear ideas. Only of sensible content are we immediately conscious. Linked with this is a mediate consciousness of the formal ideas which properly belong to pure reason. It is only reflection that enables us to become fully conscious of formal apperception. Just as the form of stimulability, as the property of the purely autonomous nature of reason, has to be distinguished from sensibility, to which the expressions of its activity are bound, so here we must recognize the division for the mind between that in our knowledge which, simply because we possess the knowledge, is immediately clear, i.e. perceptual, and that which becomes clear only indirectly, by means of the logical form of reflection. We thus reach the law that metaphysical knowledge is by nature obscure.

The decisive point in understanding this law is that the distinction between perceptual and non-perceptual knowledge is not so much a matter of the knowledge itself but rather of its relation to consciousness. Not every item of knowledge carries with it immediately the possibility that we should become conscious of it. This alone provides the basis for distinguishing between perceptual and non-perceptual knowledge. As knowledge, the one has the same immediate certainty as the other, though I may be immediately conscious of this certainty in the one case and not in the other.

This relation between knowledge which though immediate is originally obscure and knowledge which merely recapitulates it in thought explains why doubt is possible. Doubt, as we know, is possible only because the assertion which a judgment contains is added to an idea arbitrarily constructed, abstract, and therefore intrinsically problematic. But this also explains why it is possible to resolve doubt in the field of metaphysical knowledge. Doubt is resolved by showing that the assertion which in a judgment is added to a problematic idea is just a recapitulation of some immediate knowledge.

The law that one becomes conscious of immediate knowledge only gradually has its own application to formal apperception. The basic idea of objective synthetic unity, which we call formal apperception, is realized by us partly in the form of perception, that is in space and time, the pure forms of intuition or perception, in which it becomes possible to combine the content given in sensibility. This pure-intuitive basic form must be distinguished from what Apelt called the speculative basic form of our knowledge, that is formal apperception, as this is realized only through thought. But again this distinction between a pure-intuitive knowledge of figurative unity and the originally obscure knowledge of intellectual unity is a matter of the relation of either sort of knowledge to consciousness, and not of their certainty or objective validity, their relation to the object. The speculative basic form, as the originally obscure part of formal apperception, is therefore as reliable a background for all metaphysical certainty as the perception of space is for the axioms of geometry. This metaphysical basic form of our knowledge is (to use Apelt's phrase again) like an obscure space with which all our metaphysical knowledge is concerned, just as the propositions of geometry are concerned with perceptual space. This analogy is very appropriate, as it reveals the objectivity which belongs as much to the speculative basic form of our knowledge as to the pure-intuitive basic form of our knowledge. The objectivity of the speculative basic form is easily overlooked, simply because it is entirely withdrawn from perception.

The metaphysical basic concepts or Categories belong, as concepts, entirely to reflection; they are artificial constructions of abstraction. So they are not innate concepts at all. They enable us to think of the simplest relationships of that basic speculative form and to describe these in detail, just as the axioms of geometry describe the simplest basic relationships of space. But just as space is not itself a geometrical figure, but only that which makes such figures possible, so also the speculative basic form is what makes Categories possible. Metaphysics therefore possesses, in this speculative basic form, an unassailable foundation like that possessed by geometry in the perception of space.

I hope I have now made the general basis of Fries' Theory of Reason sufficiently clear to show that its hypotheses are not arbitrarily set up, but can be derived by induction from inner experience.

What does this theory do for us?

First, we have now found a complete answer to the question of psychology with which we began, the question of how the combining of concepts at will can lead to knowledge of necessary truths.

The combination of concepts at will can lead to knowledge of necessary truths only because the knowledge of necessary truths which appears to be newly acquired thereby is seen to be the recapitulation of a knowledge which is immediate and independent of all arbitrary or deliberate (*willkürlich*) reflection, a recapitulation needed so that what was already in us obscurely may be brought into the clear light of consciousness.

The first thing, for consciousness, is the perception of particular realities. The idea of a necessary connection between these particular realities is for consciousness the artificial result of reflection, that is of applying the logical forms of concept, judgment, inference, and finally of science. It is thus the result of a deliberate activity. In the case of immediate knowledge, however, things are just the other way about. The primary and original point here is the idea of combination itself. Any determination of content of particular reality, by contrast, is added on afterwards to this basic idea of objective synthetic unity, so that the whole of immediate knowledge is continuously enriched by the influx of sense-perception, by new determinations of content flowing into the identical basic idea of objective synthetic unity. Now as only these sensible determinations of content come directly to mind, the mind's first task is artificially to recombine this and that perceptual reality by the forms of reflection, using abstractly conceived forms of combination. The distinction between the sensibly determined content of our perception of particular real things and their form of combination does not apply to immediate knowledge but arises in the differing relationships of immediate knowledge to consciousness; for the ideas of combination can only be conceived by means of the analytic forms of reflection, separately from the matter, from the particular content of perception, in universal and, in themselves, problematic ideas.

Everything here depends on distinguishing between the deliberateness of reflection and the original spontaneity of pure reason.

The spontaneity of pure reason, as we have come to see, does not signify arbitrary choice, but rather independence of external stimulation. Our mind is independent of external stimulation, in so far as it can itself determine its content of apodeictic knowledge. This is precisely what is meant by the term 'a priori knowledge'.

7

Before going on to a detailed derivation of the items of so-called a priori knowledge, and in particular of the metaphysical ones, it will be a good thing to see what philosophically important consequences we have already obtained, apart from the solution of this particular problem, on the basis of the general part of the theory; consequences, I mean, which have a direct significance for the Critique of Reason and so will also be important as assumptions for the deduction.

We are in fact already in a position to set certain general limits to a priori knowledge and to the principles of metaphysics in particular, without consideration of their content.

One such limitation results from the relation of the knowledge in question to perception. No knowledge of what is actually present can come from thought alone, all knowledge of particular realities originates ultimately in perception. This is the first law that we can derive at this point. It is a simple consequence of the law that reflection is originally empty, or that all knowledge gained by thought is mediate. One could of course consider the possibility of there being some immediate knowledge of particular realities independent of thought which yet did not derive from perception. That would be an originally obscure assertoric knowledge. But even this would be bound to the forms of reflection, so that we could become conscious of it. This would conflict with its assertoric nature, according to which it relates to particular reality. For the abstract forms of reflection, in which alone it could come to consciousness, do not make it possible to move on to determination of particular realities. This, then, must depend on perception: apart from perception, knowledge of individual realities is impossible.

A second and similar limitation can be established with regard to the relation of the knowledge in question to sensibility. All knowledge of particular realities is sensible in origin. Its ultimate derivation, in short, is from experience. This can be put as a law for *a priori* knowledge: that all *a priori* knowledge is purely formal in character. Which simply means that it cannot determine the nature of particular reality.

By combining the limitation due to perception with that due to sensibility we obtain the law that all knowledge of particular realities derives in the end from sensible perception. Kant called this the law of the immanence of all human knowledge.

8

This also provides us with quite clear confirmation and justification for certain statements already made in the Theory of Method, which are of decisive significance for the Critique of Reason.

The first of these is the statement that an objective justification for knowledge is impossible. All justification is in the end subjective in character, i.e. it cannot concern the relation between knowledge and its object. The only candidate, as an objective method of justification, would be proof, which does derive one truth objectively from another. But that would not suffice here, for it would simply postpone the question of objective validity. All it does is to derive one assertion which requires justification from another assertion which equally requires justification, one judgment from another, a provable one from an unprovable one, from a judgment which, in view of the original emptiness of reflection, needs some basis independent of all reflection and which therefore cannot be justified by means of proofs, but which does need justification, if it is to be distinguished from a mere arbitrary fiat. At this point justification can only be subjective, comparing the judgment in question with the immediate knowledge which alone enables us to know the object.

P

This applies with special force to justification by means of demonstration. The fact that a judgment can be demonstrated does not make it an exception to the rule. It is a mere prejudice, though a very common one, that being demonstrable makes a judgment objectively superior to one which is not demonstrable. But the self-evident character of perception cannot give such superiority. For the self-evident character of intuitive knowledge, as we saw, is simply immediacy of consciousness of the knowledge and so does not make one item of knowledge objectively superior to another. It is not an objective matter concerning the relation to the object, but a subjective matter of its relation to consciousness. It simply means that for consciousness of the knowledge reflection is dispensable. Demonstrability is therefore relevant to justification only if immediate knowledge, quite apart from any self-evidence it may possess, is in itself a sufficient ground for the validity of judgments.

In view of the law of the unity of reason, such validity, to which immediate knowledge does lay claim, is a property of the whole of immediate knowledge, of what Fries called 'transcendental apperception', and does not apply to individual items of knowledge, which can be considered only by abstraction. The validity of individual items of knowledge can therefore be decided only by reference to their relation to this whole of immediate knowledge.

Validity can properly be ascribed to an idea only if it is assertoric in character. (Assertoric is not to be taken as contrasted with apodeictic, but generally as opposed to what is problematic, as certainty.) Otherwise our decision that the idea is valid would be baseless, that is to say we should have no reason for regarding this decision itself as valid. But this assertoric character is not attached to any individual idea on its own—for in separation from the one whole of genuine immediate knowledge it is an abstract and therefore problematic idea—but only to the one genuine immediate knowledge which consists in the unity of transcendental apperception.

To this transcendental apperception therefore applies that law of the self-reliance of reason, which following Fries we could put like this: everyone relies on his rational mind in his belief that he can receive and participate in truth.

This law is the essential counterpart to the earlier law that an objective justification for knowledge is impossible. For it guards us against drawing a false and sceptical conclusion from that law. From the impossibility of an objective justification for immediate knowledge it does not follow that this knowledge is doubtful, uncertain, or invalid. Nor is the assertion of this law to be thought of as a hypothesis, a sort of *ultima ratio* (final argument) to which we cling for good or ill for lack of objective justifiability of our knowledge. It simply expresses the factual character of knowing—knowing which carries with it the certainty of its own validity just because it does in fact exist as the one whole of transcendental apperception; knowledge which as it carries its own certainty with it need not receive that certainty from outside by means of any artificial argument or justification. All that such a justification could or should attempt we already possess independently of all such labour and antecedent to it, in the fact of the self-reliance of our reason on the truth of its immediate knowledge.

So while the earlier law says that there cannot be any further justification for the certainty of our immediate knowledge, this one informs us that any such justification, if it were possible, would be superfluous. One could call it the basic law of the superfluity of an objective justification of knowledge.

The basic principle of the self-reliance of reason must not, then, be thought of as a universal axiom which could or should serve as an epistemological criterion, so that by applying it to this or that particular item of knowledge we could infer its objective validity. That is not the position; for it would lead instead to a new attempt at proving the objective validity of the items of knowledge in question—a proof obviously circular, as its major premiss (our basic principle), from which the objective validity of some item of knowledge would have to be inferred, itself expresses a particular item of knowledge, a psychological item, which as far as its validity goes is no better than the other which it is supposed to justify.

Our thesis does not say that objective validity belongs originally to our knowledge. That would be a universal statement, to justify which we should first have to show in some other way that it applied in each particular case—and therefore to the case in question. The meaning of our thesis is quite different. It asserts that (not objective validity but) reliance on the objective validity of its knowledge is native to the mind, so far as that mind does in fact possess knowledge and is a knowing mind. For knowledge is simply immediate representation. It has an assertoric character and does not, like problematic representation, require an assertion of its objective validity to be added as a separate statement. If we point out that the knowledge really is there, that makes any further justification of its validity superfluous.

It is this point—that no further justification is needed once some immediate knowledge has been shown actually to exist in us—which

is expressed in the law of the self-reliance of reason. This makes the
deduction of the principles of metaphysics—which in fact consists
simply in pointing out some immediate knowledge which does
actually underlie these principles—a complete and adequate justification for them. The justification consists in showing that doubt of the
validity of the principle whose deduction is required conflicts with
our actual certainty of its validity as an item of immediate knowledge;
i.e. in showing that to entertain such a doubt is literally 'against our
better knowledge'. That it can be entertained at all is due to the fact
that the doubter, owing to the original obscurity of immediate metaphysical knowledge, deceives himself about the fact of his better
knowledge. It comes down to this: we do not claim self-evidence for
the immediate knowledge here said to obtain in fact. This lack of
self-evidence explains how people can deceive themselves about the
certainty which they do in fact possess.

This law therefore gives us, as Fries said, 'a criterion which accords
completely with experience and is free of any suspicion of speculative
mistakes', a firm footing on which to settle all disputes and uncertainty in metaphysical matters on a method as strict as that used in the
sciences of experience and in mathematics. This is achieved by the
subjective application of the method of justification of the Critique
of Reason, in deduction. On the subject-matter of the philosophers'
disputes we postpone judgment altogether and inquire instead into
the knowledge which is in us originally and discover what verdict
is reached through the fact of this knowledge, in advance of all
artificial reflection; for it is to this verdict that our judgment must
ultimately conform. To ensure recognition of this verdict just as it
is in us, obscure, but independent of all arbitrary decision and undis-
turbed by any of the errors of reflection: this is the task and the
meaning of the psychological deduction. We must now discuss in
greater detail how that deduction is performed.

9

Our preliminary discussion of this has been entirely general in
character and enables us to make only one very general point about
the knowledge in question: that there is an original spontaneous
activity (*Selbsttätigkeit*) of knowing, as formal apperception, i.e.
as the basic idea of objective synthetic unity.

We have indeed drawn this conclusion from the mere fact that the
knowledge claims to be apodeictic in character. However, we did not
conclude that the assertion for which this claim is made is of purely
rational origin, and that there must therefore be some *a priori*

knowledge underlying this particular assertion; but rather, that for knowledge to be apodeictic in form at all is something purely rational in origin, and that there must therefore be an immediate apodeictic knowledge, and so an immediate *a priori* knowledge, i.e. formal apperception. All we have shown, in other words, is that for a merely sensible reason the idea of necessary unity would be an impossibility. A reason of that sort could not locate within itself the occurrence of this idea, as we do locate it in ourselves in fact, namely in that idea, problematic though it might be or even quite mistaken, which comes out in the characterizing of knowledge as apodeictic. So there is in our reason, as *a priori* knowledge, a basic idea of necessary unity, and it is only through this that we come by all the particular individual ideas of unity and necessity in our knowledge.

This general demonstration does nothing to determine the content of particular items of *a priori* knowledge for our reason; that is the business of the deduction. From the mere fact that formal apperception is present in our knowledge nothing follows about the actual forms of *a priori* knowledge which occur in our reason, such as those of Space, of Time, of the particular Categories and of Ideas.

Yet even without embarking on the solution of this profound problem we can, simply on the basis of what has already been said, make one point of decisive positive significance for the main business of our theory and so of the Critique of Reason.

The main philosophical aim of the general Theory of Reason was to solve Hume's problem by proving the existence of some immediate knowledge which underlies metaphysical principles. It is now clear that this is precisely what our theory does. By proving the existence of some non-perceptual immediate knowledge it finally solves Hume's problem and destroys the basis of Hume's metaphysical scepticism. At the same time it also refutes that other form of metaphysical scepticism which we meet in Kant: Formal Idealism. For Kant's Formal Idealism really results from the same line of thought which led Hume to his metaphysical Scepticism. One is bound to arrive at Formal Idealism if one cannot admit that metaphysical judgments have any objective validity; and one cannot admit this unless one can point out the basis on which these could be known. But this one cannot do as long as one is enslaved by the assumption that there is a complete disjunction between perception and reflection as possible modes of knowledge. Kant took over this assumption from Hume, and indeed from all his predecessors, without examining it. He never enquired whether this disjunction is complete—clearly because he saw and could see no problem here, as the concepts of *reflective* and *perceptual knowledge* seemed to him to form a logically complete disjunction. That is how it appeared to all philosophers and psychologists until Fries, with the sole exception of Plato. Fries showed that this disjunction is not logically complete, and that if one wishes to assert its completeness, one can do so only after investigating the facts of inner experience. But such an investigation shows that the disjunction in question is not only logically, but also factually incomplete. Not only is there no contradiction in the concept of a non-perceptual and yet non-reflective knowledge, but we actually possess such knowledge—knowledge which though not originally obvious is yet immediately certain.

By showing that this disjunction of perceptual and reflective knowledge is incomplete, and by pointing out the basis on which metaphysical judgments can in fact properly be known in non-perceptual immediate knowledge, Fries refuted Formal Idealism in metaphysics.

The Deduction of the Categories

Kant made a decisive discovery which enabled him to demonstrate the system of metaphysical principles as actually present in our knowledge. He called it Schematism of the Categories. The Categories in themselves, as basic metaphysical concepts, do not give us any knowledge. How then do they enable us to know objects? For this we must apply them to phenomena, to the objects of sensible perception. If one asks how it is possible to apply the Categories to phenomena, then a difficult problem appears. For the Categories, as basic metaphysical concepts, and phenomena, as objects of sense-perception, are intrinsically quite heterogeneous. So it is far from clear why we should apply a particular Category to one particular phenomenon and not to another, and why to a particular phenomenon we should apply one particular Category rather than another. Nothing in sense-perception has any resemblance to the Categories or could suggest to us which Category to apply to an observed phenomenon.

The criteria which Kant sought for applying the Categories, the so-called 'Schemata' of the Categories, are pure-intuitive ideas (*rein anschauliche Vorstellungen*). And at this point, where we are concerned with the principles on which experience in general is possible, and not just with outer experience, only ideas of Time can provide general Schemata of the Categories.

On this profound thought is based Kant's discovery of the metaphysical principles of our scientific knowledge. He gave a complete and correct enumeration of the metaphysical principles which result from combining the basic concepts of metaphysics with the corresponding pure-intuitive Schemata, but he was not able to show the reason for this combination.

Fries' Theory of Reason enabled him to provide the backing for this discovery. The reason why the Categories are schematized, as Kant had shown they were in fact, is simply that the pure-intuitive basic form is originally bound up with the speculative basic form in the unity of formal apperception. Consciousness introduces into our knowledge a quite artificial division, which is not in it by nature, when we distinguish the intuitive from the non-intuitive parts of formal apperception in our knowledge. This distinction only concerns the different relationships of immediate knowledge to consciousness, following the principle that the whole of immediate knowledge can come to consciousness only step by step. This identity of original formal apperception provides the reason for combining Category and Schema into particular metaphysical principles; so once the basic concepts of metaphysics have been deduced, the deduction of the principles of metaphysics follows automatically from the law of the unity of formal apperception.

The further development of the Theory of Reason therefore depends entirely on whether it enables us to achieve a satisfactory deduction of the Categories.

The Theory of Reason is supposed to provide a deduction of all the principles of metaphysics. This deduction can be achieved only by a progressive application of the general laws already derived concerning the structure of our reason.

The main result contained in these laws can be formulated as follows: our reason is the faculty of stimulable self-activity (*Selbsttätigkeit*), but this activity contributes only the empty form of unity and necessity to the content of knowledge determined by external stimulation and is subject to the law of the unity or identity of all actual self-activity of knowledge, so that each individual item of knowledge can occur only as a determination of content for this original, identical, formal apperception (as Fries called it): and in view of the principle of grades of consciousness (the principle of reflection), only the particular item of knowledge which was sensibly stimulated comes immediately to consciousness, and we can become aware only step by step of the whole of our immediate knowledge (called by Fries 'transcendental apperception'): by means, that is, of the forms of reflection.

Now as each particular item of knowledge is, on this view, simply one determination of content for formal apperception, items of what is called *a priori* knowledge must also be such determinations of content, but with this difference that these determinations of content do not depend on sensible stimulation, but as original determinations of content for formal apperception derive from the nature of reason itself. The particular forms of *a priori* knowledge can therefore be derived by pointing out their origin. For in the nature of our reason there are only certain possible reciprocal determinations of the elements to which the general Theory of Reason traces back the peculiar structure of our particular sort of mind: a mind subject to the laws of sensibility and reflection and therefore limited in two respects, in respect of content of knowledge by its dependence on external and essentially contingent stimulation (as stated in the law of sensibility), and limited also for consciousness by its dependence on reflection (as stated in the law of grades of consciousness).

Following up these relationships Fries works out his own combinatorial method of deduction.

The basic elements on which the structure of the knowing mind depends—for the present we neglect the practical faculties—are the following:

A. For immediate knowledge:
  (a) the content (material apperception),
  (b) the original form of unity for all the content which material apperception will provide (formal apperception).
B. For consciousness:
  (a) immediate consciousness in perception,
  (b) mediate consciousness through thought.

We thus obtain for combination the following basic forms of determination of an object through our knowledge:

1. Determination of the object through perception is the 'what' of knowledge, the given element of the object:—*G*

2. Determination of the object through thought is the relation of the given to formal apperception and so is not the 'what' but the 'how' of knowledge, not the given as such, but the mode of being given. It is this that first determines objective validity of the knowledge and makes the *what* of knowledge into something actual, the Being of the object:—*B*

3. Determination of the object through material apperception is Variety:—*V*

4. Determination of the object through formal apperception is Unity:—*U*

The combination of these basic elements can be undertaken in a diagrammatic form and is most easily done with the aid of a table (IX). We thus combine the two divisions.

(IX) Combinations of Basic Elements in Knowledge

	G	B
V	G V Quality	B V Modality
U	G U Quantity	B U Relation

This table has four parts. But that only settles the positions and gives them signs. What do these signs mean?

All content of knowledge is immediately determined through sensible stimulation, and only to that extent does it occur in perception. So sense-perception, or perceptual knowledge of content, is the first moment; we call it the moment of Quality.

All sensible content, however, comes immediately into the original unity of rational activity. Even perceptual consciousness must therefore contain some knowledge of objective unity, as a formal determination of the object perceived. This is the moment of pure intuition, the moment of Quantity.

Moreover, the complete relation of the content of knowledge to the form of objective unity occurs through thought, when through the forms of reflection we conceive in consciousness any content of knowledge as a material determination of formal apperception. This is the moment of analytic unity, the moment of Modality.

Finally, by means of these forms we become aware in thought of the formal synthetic determination of all content in immediate knowledge. This is the moment of intellectual synthetic unity, the moment of Relation. (Intellectual, as opposed to the moment of Quantity, synthetic, as opposed to that of Modality.)

We must now consider the principle that we become fully aware of the unity of the whole of immediate knowledge only in thought, so that we must first re-think the content of perceptual knowledge in order to combine it in consciousness into the necessary form of intellectual unity.

In knowledge which is thought there thus appears:
the moment of *sensible perception*
                in the scientific form of *observation* (*Empirie*),
the moment of pure *intuition*
                in the scientific form of *mathematics*,
the moment of *analytic unity*
                in the scientific form of *logic*,
the moment of *intellectual synthetic unity*
                in the scientific form of *metaphysics*.

The artificial detour via the construction of all these sciences is essential in order to realize our knowledge as a single whole. This is achieved by the method of induction. Induction is simply the method of thought which combines those distinct and separate sciences into the unity of a science of experience, not concerned, like mere observation (*Empirie*), simply with the description of what is given in perception, but with the connection of the Variety of perception under necessary laws. For only in the abstract form of a law does the thinking consciousness realize the intellectual synthetic unity in the Being of things.

(X) Division of our Knowledge as a Whole

immediate knowledge	intuitive	empirical ... sensible intuition	...	Observation (*Empirie*)
		non-empirical ... pure intuition	...	Mathematics
	non-intuitive	.... pure reason	...	Metaphysics
mediate knowledge	.... reflection		...	Logic

It is the aim of all these enquiries to provide a deduction for the principles of metaphysics. In themselves, these concern only the moment of Relation; for this was the moment of intellectual synthetic unity. But, as we saw just now, they can be applied only if each individual perceptual consciousness is first raised to a universal consciousness and each perceptually given thing first conceived in thought. We therefore need special metaphysical concepts for the other moments also, so that the intrinsically non-metaphysical content of our knowledge may be conceived in thought and combined in consciousness with its proper metaphysical content, the basic concepts of Relation. For this reason a complete table of basic concepts of metaphysics must include all four moments.

Within these four moments, moreover, conception in thought can be achieved only step by step. Our consciousness has to start by conceiving in thought a particular individual content given in perception, then to proceed in thought to comprehend this conceived content in the form of synthetic unity, and finally to rise to consciousness of the unity of the whole, filling and completing that form. The basic relationship of our knowledge in general is therefore repeated within the various moments in the three stages: content or filling, form, form fulfilled, corresponding to the relation between material apperception, formal apperception, and transcendental apperception. We thus obtain in each moment:

1. a notion of the conception in thought of a given content or filling, by which we are led from empirical consciousness to consciousness in general;
2. a notion of the conception together in thought of a varied content or filling, in formal apperception;
3. a notion of the necessary determination of what is thus comprehended in a whole of transcendental apperception.

Combining that division into four moments with the threefold division within each moment we get a twelvefold division, the complete table of the Categories:

(XI) The Categories*

	Quantity	Quality	Relation	Modality
1.	Unity	Reality	Substance	Actuality
2.	Plurality	Negation	Causality	Possibility
3.	Totality	Limitation	Reciprocation	Necessity

I have here put the four moments alongside each other on purpose. For if we now draw the horizontal line connecting the first members of each moment together, then that connecting the second members, and finally that connecting together the third members, the derived law becomes immediately apparent. In this we can and indeed must disregard completely the objective content of the terms contained in the table, and therefore their metaphysical significance. We employ these words simply to convince ourselves that the deduction has really achieved its aim, which is to show that all the basic concepts to which the discussion led, and only these, have their origin in the structure of the mind.

Quantity, as determination of an object through pure intuition, is really the form of a whole so far as this is composed of similar parts. Here unity is the concept by which a particular given thing is conceived in thought as mass (i.e. as a unit of comparison), plurality is

* cp. Vol. I, p. 149.

the concept by which the particular similar parts are conceived in thought, and totality is the concept by which a whole of similar parts is thought.

Quality is the determination of an object through sense-perception. Here reality is the concept through which a perceptual quality is conceived in thought, negation (or contrast) is that for determining one by comparison with another, and limitation is the concept for combining a reality and its opposite into one whole.

Relation, as the determination of an object through intellectual synthetic unity, is the form of connection of a given Variety. Here substantiality is the concept by which the individual given thing is conceived in thought, causality that by which two given things are conceived together in thought, and reciprocation that by which a given Variety is knit together into unity in the form of a whole.

Modality is the mediate determination of an object with respect to the knowledge by which it is known. Here actuality is the concept by which an object given in sense-perception is thought of as such, possibility that by which an object is thought of in relation to the purely rational form of knowledge, and necessity that by which we think of the whole of a given object as determined through the purely-rational form of knowledge.

This, however, by no means completes the task of the Critique of Reason. We have so far deduced the most general principles of metaphysics, the Categories. With the aid of the Law of Schematism, we can move from the table of the Categories to the table of the metaphysical principles of our knowledge of nature.

The knowledge to which these principles lead is restricted to the form of nature; that is to say its synthetic unity takes the form of lawlikeness, of a knitting together of a Variety of sense-perceptions according to general laws in space and time, the Variety itself being of course subject to these laws but not determined by them and therefore intrinsically contingent. In place of the totality of the real and its necessity, which are beyond perception, our thought has only the abstract form of universality, which though not itself actual and real, does condition everything actual and so can become the object of our knowledge, thus giving our knowledge the impress of the form of nature.

For the same reason the metaphysical principles of scientific knowledge are not constitutive principles of a theory of nature. No definite scientific knowledge can be logically derived from them; they can only be used as criteria for the induction by which the constitutive principles of all natural science must first be found. They are just guiding maxims of rational inductions and are not themselves the constitutive principles of scientific theories.

Our knowledge is subject to this abstract form of nature because we are quite unable to determine the perceptually given in thought in any other way than by the intrinsically empty intellectual forms of connection, according to the rules of the mathematical Schematism.

In all this Fries' theory provides the requisite supplement, in the way of a deduction, to the perfectly correct exposition given by Kant. This shows that Kant's discussion, with its apparently peculiar dependence on the table of Categories, is not along arbitrary lines at all, but that its guideline is itself firmly based and necessitated by pure reason.

THE DEDUCTION OF THE SPECULATIVE IDEAS

One major problem remained unsolved in Kant's *Critique of Pure Reason*. There is a gap in it, at the point where the critique of the metaphysical principles of science should have been supplemented by a critique of the corresponding principles of the Theory of Ideas. I am referring to Kant's Transcendental Dialectic. His enquiry was less successful here, and the weaknesses of his method also affected his results. The exposition itself was defective. So it is at this point that Fries' improved method of the Critique of Reason will face its decisive test. We are here concerned with the most profound and difficult problem for the Critique of Speculative Reason. A scientifically satisfactory, strict and clear solution of this problem would in Fries' own words be 'the masterpiece of all philosophy.'

The reason for Kant's mistake, here again, was that he conceived all relationships only as they appear in the forms of reflection, without going on to the basis of these principles in pure reason itself. What Kant calls 'pure reason' is not what Fries means by that term, but comes entirely under the faculty of reflection. Kant does describe the Ideas as concepts of reason, in contrast to the Categories which he calls concepts of the understanding. But this distinction between understanding and reason, as made by Kant, remains entirely within the limits of what Fries calls understanding, or the faculty of reflection. Kant sees pure reason, the faculty of Ideas, as the faculty of inferring, when it is used transcendentally and not just logically. But one must ask how the mere ability to infer can acquire its own set of principles. Kant here follows the unfortunate notion that the Ideas can be enumerated by taking the forms of inference as a guideline, in the way that he was able to enumerate the Categories by the guideline of the forms of judgment.

Fries shows up his mistake here. Inference, as Fries shows, is just a particular form of judgment. It consists in deriving one judgment logically from another, and this derivation is itself just an analytic hypothetical judgment. The table of forms of inference will not, therefore, enable us to discover fresh metaphysical principles not already discovered in the system of the Categories.

This shows the mistake in Kant's exposition. The deduction also is faulty, and here the fault affects the whole structure of his theory. Kant had tried to justify the Categories by what he called the transcendental proof, that is by showing that they are principles which make experience possible. He saw that it would be impossible to provide a similar justification for the principles of the Theory of Ideas. This led him to conclude that the assertion of objective validity of Ideas for our reason depends on a transcendental illusion. As no transcendental proof can be given for the Ideas, they must—so he argues—be rejected by the Critique of Speculative Reason as unjustifiable, though the illusion of their reality is transcendental, i.e. an illusion not dependent on a merely logical fallacy, but originating in pure reason itself, which is the faculty of Ideas.

There is a clear contradiction, not indeed with this theory of transcendental illusion, but with the basic theory of Formal Idealism, when Kant tries subsequently to give a proof for the reality of Ideas in the field of practical reason by showing them to be postulates of practical reason, i.e. conditions for the validity of the moral law, just as he had shown the Categories to be conditions on which experience is possible. Fries points out the mistake in this theory also. It consists in treating all relationships in our knowledge, other than perception, as given in the forms of reflection—with the result that Kant feels compelled to decide all questions about the validity or invalidity of metaphysical principles in a logicist manner; for he limits himself, within reflection, to showing that one item of knowledge is the condition on which another item is possible, thus leaving the transcendental reality of the whole open to question.

As against this, Fries shows that even the ultimate question of all speculation, the question about absolute reality, can be decided only by the subjective method of the Critique of Reason, by reference to ideas present in our own immediate knowledge. This gives us a quite different perspective on Transcendental Idealism and on the method by which it is justified. Even the demonstration that we have no knowledge of things-as-they-really-are can only be based on a subjective comparison between items of our knowledge, without our having to step outside our knowledge and compare it with the object.

If, then, we do decide that our knowledge is limited to knowledge of phenomena, this must be due to what Fries calls the self-knowledge of our reason in respect of its limits. What is the position here? Is our reason aware of its own limits, in this way?

Fries shows that our reason does in fact recognize its own limitations, and that in two ways. It is limited firstly by the law of sensibility and its unavoidable result, the lack of congruence between the form and the content of its knowledge. It is also limited by the law of reflection and its unavoidable result, the distinction between immediate knowledge and consciousness. Our reason, being a pure reason, is not perceptual. It is not a faculty of intellectual intuition. It cannot itself determine the content of its knowledge, but must await external stimulation which, for it, is quite contingent. And it is not immediately conscious of the knowledge which it does itself possess, but reaches complete consciousness of its knowledge only step by step, through the forms of reflection. The second limitation only concerns consciousness, but the first concerns immediate knowledge itself.

Fries here shows that a reason which is bound up with sense, as ours is, will inevitably conceive the content of sense-perception in an incompletable form. For a reason of this sort can never be said to be acquainted with the totality of all actual things. Its knowledge can never carry with it the impress of completion. For precisely because it depends on contingent external stimulation for knowledge of the actual, that knowledge must always be open to progressive increase. But this means that the form in which it conceives the content of its knowledge must necessarily and essentially bear the stamp of incompletability.

This is the basis, from the subjective point of view taken in the deduction, for the infinity of the forms of pure intuition: Space and Time. A reason not bound up with sense, which could therefore provide itself with the content of its knowledge, for which, in other words, there was no distinction between *a priori* and *a posteriori* knowledge, since as an intellectual intuition it would itself know reality directly—such a reason would not come up against any limits in its conception of reality. It would not have the possibility of progressively widening the content of its knowledge. So it would not know itself as a limited reason.

The infinity of Space and Time give objective expression to the limited nature of immediate knowledge itself: a limitation which is not only gradual in character, so that we can think of removing it by an increase in quantity, but is also qualitative, applying to that knowledge which we do actually possess and applying of necessity, for it is a limitation which our reason is unable to overcome;—for that could be done only by changing the structure of our reason itself. This limitation means that complete unity and necessity, though an immediate requirement of pure reason for the Being of things, can never be realized in our knowledge. The clearest indication of this is given by the fact that the original contingency of every Variety that can be given to us in sense is retained in our knowledge, however much this may develop in quantity. All unity and necessity, in so far as we can know them, remain merely relative. We become aware of absolute unity and necessity only by thinking of the limits to our knowledge as negated, that is only through the Ideas. Necessity and unity make a positive appearance in our knowledge only in the abstract form of universality. We can only express them hypothetically, by asserting a lawlike connection between one contingent given thing and another equally contingent given thing, by saying that if ever the one is given, then the other is always given also.

This insuperable contingency in the givenness of the objects of our knowledge shows very clearly that the existence of the objects of our knowledge is dependent on their being known. For we are compelled by an unavoidable notion of our own pure reason to assume that nothing can be really real unless it is also determined as necessary. On this assumption contingency cannot be a quality of reality, but can only express some defect in our knowledge of reality, namely lack of knowledge of its necessity. So the insuperable contingency of the objects of our knowledge is the clearest proof of the fact that our knowledge is necessarily limited in quality, the fact that we do not know things as-they-really-are.

We can rise to consciousness of complete unity and necessity, as demanded by pure reason, only by the aid of the Ideas. Ideas are, in general, representations of objects of which no definite knowledge can ever be obtained. Definiteness of knowledge involves two elements, perception and concept. Perception on its own leaves a certain ambiguity with respect to the object which it is to determine. Suppose that on a nocturnal stroll we perceive a moving source of light, perception will not alone determine the object which appears to our eyes. We do not know if the appearance is due to a shooting star or to the glowing ash of a cigar or to a fire-fly or to something else. So perception does not determine the object completely. But concepts are equally insufficient to determine the object itself. Concepts in themselves determine only classes of objects; the individuality of the actual object cannot be reached by conceptual determinations, however far they go. Perception is needed as well, so that we can move from the idea of a class of objects to that of the individual object itself. In brief, definiteness of knowledge involves a combination of perception and concept.

Now if Ideas are representations of objects which cannot be given in any definite item of knowledge, there will be two sorts of Idea, firstly concepts of objects which cannot be represented in any possible perception, and secondly perceptions which cannot be brought under any concept. The former, concepts of objects which cannot be determined through perception, Fries calls 'logical Ideas'. The latter, forms of perception which escape conceptual determination, he calls 'aesthetic Ideas'. I shall discuss the logical Ideas first.

Logical Ideas are simply concepts we are forced to construct in order to recognize the limits of our knowledge as limits of *knowledge* and not as applying to the Being of things. Logical Ideas are concepts of the negating of the limits of our knowledge, concepts of an unlimited unity and necessity in the Being of things.

This single statement resolves all the difficulties left unresolved by Kant's Theory of Ideas. The first point here is a matter of exposition. In the logical Ideas we conceive absence of limits, yet the pure forms of intuition are incompletable. This contrast leads to the Antinomies which Kant discovered. Fries in fact traces them all back to this one contrast between the incompletability of the forms of intuition and the Idea of the lack of limits, of the Absolute. The theses in Kant's Antinomies are those assertions which arise immediately from the demand, contained in the Idea, for an absolute unity of reality. The antitheses are corresponding assertions deriving from the incompletability, determined in pure intuition, of Space and Time. The conflict between these two arises only because people apply the Ideas to the objects of perception in Space and Time. The Antinomies are therefore resolved by showing that the Ideas do not apply to the objects of perception, as they conflict with the conditions on which perception is possible, namely with the law of incompletability which applies to the objects of any possible perception.

This theory, to which the resolution of the Antinomies leads, is Transcendental Idealism: the theory that we do not know things-as-they-really-are. We can rise to the recognition of the objective synthetic unity of what is really real* only by supposing the limits set by the conditions of perception to be once more removed. We thus achieve a strict justification for Transcendental Idealism, and one free of all epistemological assumptions. We do not compare our know-

* *des an sich Wirklichen*

Q

ledge with its object in order to see if the two coincide, but only compare items of knowledge with each other, viz. the ideas which we
have of the objects experienced with the ideas we have of things-as-
they-really-are, and we find that the two conflict, the former ideas
being inapplicable to the latter. From this the theorem of Transcendental Idealism follows directly. So even in this most speculative
of problems we still remain true to the critical method.

Fries was thus able to give a correct exposition of the Ideas, a point
on which Kant had fallen down. This shows that the contrast from
which Kant had started, between Categories on the one side and
Ideas on the other, is untenable. For this reason alone the Ideas
cannot be traced by means of some sort of transcendental guideline
and co-ordinated with the Categories. For the Ideas are concepts
which can properly be contrasted not with the Categories as such,
but only with the schematized Categories. The Categories themselves are by no means negated in the Ideas. What the Ideas negate
are just the limits set to empirical employment of the Categories, i.e.
the incompletability of the mathematical Schematism of the Categories. We should really contrast concepts of nature with Ideas, i.e.
mathematically schematized Categories with Categories thought of as
absolute.

Indeed, just as the concepts of nature, as principles on which
experience is possible, can be constructed by the mathematical
Schematism of the Categories, so the Ideas also can be similarly
constructed by their own, ideal Schematism of the Categories. This
ideal Schematism of the Categories is negative. It presupposes the
positive and mathematical Schematism of the Categories. It is
developed from this and would not be possible without it. It does not
result from the forms of pure intuition, but, in direct contrast, by
negation of the limits which apply to them. So we do not need any
new guideline, in addition to that of the forms of judgment, to help
us discover the system of Ideas. We shall reach the Ideas, rather, by
starting from the table of the mathematically schematized Categories
and negating the limits these involve. Just as the pure intuition of
Time was the principle for the mathematical Schematism of the
Categories, so for the ideal Schematism of the Categories the principle is provided by what Fries calls the principle of completion,
which is really the same as Kant's principle of the impossibility of an
endless regress, his principle of totality. This expresses the general
basic idea of the Absolute, the idea of negating the limits to the empirical use of the Categories. Categories, schematized in accordance with
this basic law of completion and so thought of as unlimited, are Ideas.

This demonstration of the negative origin of the Ideas shows that they have no basis of their own in pure reason apart from the Categories. But it also shows that they do not need any such basis. This discovery is really responsible for that 'masterpiece of all philosophy', which is a masterpiece precisely because it is so surprisingly simple.

The Ideas are concepts which we construct arbitrarily, through reflection, by thinking of the limits to the empirical use of the Categories as removed. In themselves, the Ideas are merely problematic and arbitrarily constructed concepts. How then can we ascribe any objective validity to them? How can we assert that anything real corresponds to them? To put it another way: why, once we have through recognition of our own mental limitations realized that we have no knowledge of things-as-they-really-are, do we not reject our knowledge as mere illusion, but assert that nevertheless something really real does correspond to it?

The answer to this question is provided by the deduction of the speculative Ideas. We are led to it by the simple thought that what we negate in the Idea is simply the limiting of the Categories to empirical use, which is itself only a negation of the validity of the Categories in our knowledge. So what we negate in the Idea is itself only a negation, and by negating this negation we realize the most fundamental notion of pure reason itself. So the Ideas are by no means arbitrary products of reflection. What we realize through them is, after all, something necessary and positive. For we need this artificial detour *via* double negation in order to become fully aware of the original positive basic notion of our pure reason.

Our pure reason contains, as we were able to show empirically, a notion of objective synthetic unity and absolute necessity, without any limitation. But in their application by means of the mathematical Schematism to the content of experience this unity and necessity do not appear in their original form, but only in the abstract form of a concept of nature. So if we are to realize them in their original basic content we must first think away the limitations involved in the concept of nature; so it is only by a double negation that we come to realize the most originally positive thing in our knowledge. This originally obscure positive basic conviction of pure reason, which contains the basis of the Ideas, Fries calls 'pure faith of reason'. Faith is here contrasted with knowledge not as a different degree of certainty, but rather as a different type of certainty. 'Knowledge' is applied to a conviction whose object can be known perceptually, but 'faith' to one whose object cannot be known in that way—not that the latter conviction is for that reason of lower grade than the former.

Faith is thus an immediate property of speculative reason, indeed its most original property, coming before all knowledge, and so does not require any guarantee by means of practical reason, such as Kant tried to provide for it. The pure faith of reason, though it lacks the direct self-evidence of perception, is nevertheless equally certain. Its certainty is immediately present, as a fact in immediate knowledge itself, on the principle of the self-reliance of reason, so that if we could not rely on it we ought not to rely either on that certainty which we call knowledge. For knowledge has no independence as against the certainty of faith, but presupposes it and would be impossible without it.

The Deduction of the Aesthetic Ideas

The critique of the logical Ideas leads to this proposition of method: no theory can be based upon Ideas. Logical Ideas, because of their negative origin, their contrast with the limits which unavoidably belong to the forms of perception, admit of no scientific development. The Ideas can be said to apply to the objects of sense-perception only so far as we recognize these objects as subject to the conditions of absolute synthetic unity, but without being able to know this unity itself scientifically. But for this very reason all objects of sense-perception do stand related in our knowledge to the Idea, contained in our reason, of absolute synthetic unity, even though this relation cannot be set out in a theory. This relation can come to consciousness, but only as a mere feeling, since the objects of perception are not theoretically subsumed under the Ideas. This feeling is one of recognition that these same objects which we come to know in sense-perception stand under the condition of an absolute synthetic unity, so that what appear to us as objects of our sense-perception are things-as-they-really-are.

This is a quite ineffable feeling, i.e. one whose content can never be positively conceptualized, because of the original and irremovable limitation on our knowledge. It is this ineffable feeling which leads us on from the logical to the aesthetic Ideas. The aesthetic Ideas are forms of perception or intuition which cannot be conceptualized. To judge an object of perception aesthetically means to relate it by an ineffable feeling directly to the Idea of the Absolute. The necessity of this relation results, as we now see, from the basic law of our Theory of Reason, from the unity of reason itself, whereby the original and basic idea of its immediate knowledge must relate to the content of its sensible perception, as this relation alone can confer reality on any ideas of our reason.

This deduction enables us for the first time to eliminate completely the mistaken speculative consequences of Kant's prejudice of Formal Idealism. This prejudice prevented Kant from recognizing the objective significance of aesthetic judgments. In his aesthetics, Formal Idealism appears as what he called 'Aesthetic Idealism'. In his aesthetics Kant had recognized the correct principle of aesthetic Rationalism, i.e. the principle that aesthetic judgment is based on certain *a priori* principles. This discovery made it possible for the first time to give a critical justification for aesthetics. But Kant thought that this discovery of aesthetic Rationalism compelled him immediately to adopt Aesthetic Idealism—the view that aesthetic judgments have no objective significance and that their universal validity is a merely subjective one. As against this, we have here an aesthetic Realism, in contrast to Kant's Aesthetic Idealism.

Schiller had already taken exception to this defect in Kant's aesthetics. He found that it lacked what he appropriately called an objective principle of taste. Such an objective principle of taste, in view of Kant's preconceived Formal Idealism, which he held to apply in aesthetics also, was bound to seem a contradictory idea. For the attempt to establish such a principle would to all appearances lead to the resolution of aesthetic feelings, i.e. to conceptualizing them, thus reducing judgments of taste to theoretical judgments, which is really to suppress them altogether as judgments of taste. Correctly understood, the objective principle of taste can make no such claim. This principle relates appearances to Ideas, but in a relation which by its very nature admits of no theoretical formulation. So there is an objective principle of taste—as stated in the principle of aesthetic Realism—but it cannot be positively conceptualized and so admits of no theoretical development. It can be hinted at conceptually only through the logical Ideas, in a negative way. Aesthetic judgments can never be changed into theoretical ones. Yet they do have objective validity just as theoretical judgments have.

That aesthetic judgments could thus have objective validity, that therefore there is room in our knowledge alongside the theoretical judgment for an aesthetic judging of things (a latitude which is not merely a gap in the knowledge we have of nature so far, but is necessary and can therefore not be suppressed by any progress in our scientific insight), this circumstance is due to what Fries called the law of the contingency of mathematical combination. The combination of objects of sense-perception or intuition in the pure-intuitive forms of Space and Time is originally contingent and so does not admit of any further scientific explanation. The coincidence of certain phenomena at a certain time can be known as necessarily conditioned only if thought of as resulting from a corresponding coincidence at another time, and so we could go on tracing the conditions of a given set of circumstances further and further back, without ever reaching a conclusion in an unconditionally necessary circumstance.

Scientific explanation yields only relative necessity; for each member in this series is only relatively necessary. The original contingency—since we cannot eliminate it from the series altogether, and since it would be arbitrary to give preference to any one member in this series—really applies to every member equally. This contingency in the mathematical combination of phenomena in Space and Time is what makes it possible to judge phenomena aesthetically. Phenomena are not exhausted by what we know of them theoretically. The theoretical reduction to conditions is only relative; for all its lawlikeness, the content of this series of phenomena is contingent, and this is left untouched. A law of nature makes the hypothetical statement that if at a given time a certain circumstance occurs, then at another time another circumstance is combined with it. But which circumstance does in fact occur at a given time is a contingent matter as far as the law of nature goes. It is not determined by any law of nature.

To recognize that the combination of objects of perception is contingent is at the same time to recognize that they could be judged by another principle than that of natural lawlikeness, judged not by concepts of nature but by Ideas. That which remains contingent for knowledge is not thereby recognized by our reason as absolutely contingent. Rather, if reason recognizes any reality there at all, it must represent that reality as necessarily determined in some other respect, even though contingent for laws of nature, for only so can it be regarded even as the appearance of something really real. Such a judging is aesthetic.

In aesthetic judging we do not know the object of perception as a natural object. We ascribe a certain independence to it, an inner necessity which it could not have as a natural object. In judging theoretically we recognize phenomena as conditioned by other phenomena, i.e. we insert them in a general mechanism, in which the individual phenomenon has no independence; but when judging aesthetically we ascribe to objects of perception an absolute significance, an individuality. We relate them to Ideas, by recognizing them as appearances of things-as-they-really-are.

This recognition of the reality of Ideas in sense-perception shows the religious significance of the aesthetic judging of nature. We shall be able to explain this relationship fully only when we have introduced the Theory of Practical Reason. But we are already in a position to assess the great step forward made in the discovery, due to Fries' theory of the origin of aesthetic Ideas, of the profound connection between religion and aesthetics. Kant had already spoken in his Aesthetic of an intellectual, as distinct from an empirical, interest in the beautiful. While the empirical interest in the beautiful derives from the subjective desire to behold beauty, the intellectual interest is satisfaction at the existence of the beautiful object. There is no doubt that such an intellectual interest in the beautiful does exist. But Kant's Aesthetic Idealism compelled him to view this correctly observed fact as of non-aesthetic origin, and the only alternative origin he could find was a moral one.

This interpretation of the intellectual interest in the beautiful as moral in origin, which was imposed on Kant by the one-sidedness of his system, is incorrect, as Fries' deduction shows. The intellectual interest in the beautiful is really based on our recognition in the beautiful phenomenon of the reality of the Ideas in nature. This interest is thus not so much moral as religious. For religion, if we are not to limit it to the merely negative concept of faith, is really the recognition of the reality of the Ideas in nature; a recognition which comes to life only in the feelings for beauty and for the sublime. Religious feelings do not, therefore, depend on moral principles, as in Kant they appear to do. Fries called this recognition of the reality of the Ideas in nature 'intimation' (*Ahndung*), thus distinguishing it both from knowledge and from faith. 'Knowledge' is the name for a form of conviction whose object can be known in perception; 'faith' by contrast describes a form of conviction for which this is not possible, although this like the other can be expressed in definite conceptual form, even if in the case of faith this can be done only in negative concepts, in logical Ideas. 'Intimation' however, consists in subordinating the objects of knowledge to those of faith and thus represents a third form of conviction, as it can neither claim the self-evidence of knowledge nor even (as faith can) become clear in the logical form of definite concepts. Yet it is not inferior in its degree of certainty and in the reliability of its conviction. Only through the ineffable feeling of intimation is the unity of nature and Idea achieved in our knowledge, the unity of knowledge and faith, which cannot be realized theoretically.

This theory of intimation enabled Fries to open up for strict philosophical investigation a field of convictions which until then had been left to mystics and dreamers, and to provide scientific justification for its well-founded claims. He was particularly successful in doing justice to the true significance of religion, in a manner quite different from that of Kant, who held totally inadequate ideas about the nature and origin of religion. Kant finds in religion nothing but the recognition of our duties as divine commands, and thus bases it entirely on morality. That is why he tried to interpret the positive teaching of the Christian religion according to the theories of his own moral philosophy. As Fries showed clearly, everything positive in religion is significant only as an aesthetic symbol. But we are dependent on such symbols, because faith can apart from them be expressed only in the negative concept of the denial of limits. Everything that in the field of religious convictions can conceivably lay claim to truth is negative in origin. It reduces to the logical Ideas and must therefore, if correctly understood, underlie all religions equally. But there is also, as Fries so profoundly and justly says, a truth of beauty. And this, as he goes on to say, is the truest truth of our spirit. On this depends the true meaning of what is positive in religion. But for this very reason the choice of symbols is not to be made by science, but by good taste.

Once this truth is recognized, all disputes between positive religions are undermined. They continue only so long as the symbols are not recognized as symbols, but are held as dogmas, i.e. are confused with supposed truths of faith, which could not possibly exist. It is only because of this confusion that the different symbols come into conflict at all. For one and the same truth of faith can be symbolized in very different ways, and this difference in the symbols is solely responsible for the distinction between the various individual religions.

In addition to his justification of aesthetic Realism and the connected recognition of the religious significance of beauty, Fries was responsible for an important broadening of the field of aesthetics, for he not only brought intellectual beauty within its scope, but made it the centre-point of aesthetics, showing that all other beauty is in the last analysis judged only by analogy with intellectual beauty. By introducing this concept of intellectual beauty, here again following in Schiller's footsteps, Fries also provided an entirely new foundation for ethics. To follow his line of thought here, we must first make the acquaintance of his Theory of Practical Reason.

THE THEORY OF PRACTICAL REASON

In his *Critique of Practical Reason* Kant confuses under the term 'faculty of desire' two things which should not be ascribed to the same basic faculty. He failed to distinguish between desire as a mere motive force (*Antrieb*) and desire as a decision (*Entschluss*).

Here Fries comes in with his improvement. He shows that desire is an expression of interest, i.e. of the faculty of ascribing to things a value or lack of value. It is this faculty which makes us strive for the one and avoid the other. So the faculty of desire, as faculty of motive, is just a special form of interest, in so far as this acts upon the will and so becomes a motive force.

From this it follows firstly that desire and the capacity to feel pleasure and displeasure both belong to the same basic faculty, the faculty of interesting oneself or, as Fries also puts it, the faculty of impulse. It follows secondly that for action to take place yet another faculty must take part, in addition to the faculty of interest, namely that of the will, in the sense of the capacity to take decisions. The basic faculties of the mind are therefore those of knowledge, interest and decision.

This shows that the various forms of decision must be sharply distinguished from the various types of motive. Decision, as Fries appropriately puts it, is either impulsive or intellectual; it is determined either by the immediate impulse of a motive or, mediately, through reflection on an assessment of values. Motive, however, is either sensible or purely-rational. It arises either from sensible stimulation or from pure reason.

If we compare this double distinction with Kant's theory of the possible determination of the will, it becomes clear that the elements in the Kantian division, sense and intellect, really belong to two different divisions. One element of his division denotes a particular form of motive, while the other denotes a particular form of decision, so that no useful contrast results. Equating the possible forms of determination of the will with the possible types of ground of determination of the will, Kant wrongly supposes that the relation between the origin of such a ground and a form of determination can be decided by logic alone. This suggests that two points are established *a priori*: firstly, that an impulsive decision must be a sensible one, and secondly, that in an intellectual decision the mere form of intelligence takes the place of the ground of determination.

By the first inference Kant anticipates the result of an empirical psychological enquiry. Conceptually we can only claim that in an impulsive decision the motive of the will must be determined apart from reflection, so that, in Kant's phrase, the motive which determines the will must here be a pleasure; for this is a motive of which we are conscious apart from reflection and which can determine the will directly. But that every pleasure is of sensible origin could be established only as a fact of inner experience. We have in fact no intellectual pleasure that can determine the will by an impulsive decision. But that is a synthetic statement, based on inner experience, and cannot be derived by purely logical means from concepts or their definitions.

The second consequence of Kant's mistake does not so much anticipate an intrinsically correct result of experience as falsify the result of the enquiry. For Kant, apart from the form of rational decision, the only other possible ground that could determine the will is pleasure, so it is quite consistent of him to infer that as all pleasure is sensible in origin, the pure will, being independent of sensible motives, must be able to act without any motive of its own, on the basis of the mere form of intelligence in willing. This form of intelligence is the empty form of reflection, which can provide no proper motive. This fits in with Kant's actual inference that all motives are sensible in origin, and that the pure will therefore provides a decision which has no motive at all.

Fries also, like Kant, discusses the question of how a pure will is possible. Fries formulates the question more precisely, asking how a moral decision is possible. A moral decision is one determined by consciousness of duty, apart from all inclination and so apart from sensible motives. It could therefore occur only as a purely-rational decision, i.e. as a decision from a purely-rational motive. Pure reason must here be practical, it must determine the will. That can happen only if pure reason is a possible ground for the determination of the will and so is a motive faculty. It is only by pointing out some such purely-rational motive that we can resolve Kant's problem of how pure reason can be practical.

Whether there is a separate motive of this kind in addition to the sensible one, cannot be decided simply from the fact that an intellectual decision is possible. The principle that pure reason does not determine the will impulsively does not settle this point. Whether there could be a purely-rational decision depends in the first place on whether pure reason is a genuine and distinct motive faculty, in addition to pleasure. Only the existence of a motive independent of the understanding, and yet not determining the will impulsively, would explain how pure reason can determine the will.

Alongside Kant's axiom of the impossibility of intellectual pleasure we therefore set the other equally justified axiom that reflection is originally empty. The theoretical task now is to combine these two axioms, which on Kant's assumptions cannot be combined without contradiction.

To make these premisses even clearer, thus showing up the basic outline of the theory, we shall once more present in diagrammatic form the logical relationship between our statements and their possible consequences.

(XII) Inferences on the Grounds of Decision

The forms of determination of the will are the same as the possible grounds of determination. The disjunction between pleasure and understanding as grounds of determination is complete.

The will cannot be determined by intellectual pleasure. Determination of the will depends on reflection.

P_1

The will cannot be determined by the understanding alone. The ground of determination is independent of reflection.

P_2

C_3
There cannot be a pure will

There can be a pure will

P_3

C_2

The will can be determined by the understanding alone. The ground of determination depends on reflection.

C_1

The will can be determined by intellectual pleasure. Determination of the will is independent of reflection.

The disjunction between pleasure and understanding as grounds of determination is incomplete. There is a pure practical reason, a motive independent of reflection which determines the will, but only in the form of reflection. The possible forms of determination of the will are distinct from the possible grounds of determination.

We have on the one side the premiss (P_1) which asserts that the will cannot be determined by intellectual pleasure, and on the other side the premiss (P_2) which asserts that the will cannot be determined by the understanding alone. These are our two major premisses. They seem to be mutually exclusive; for the first says in effect that determination of the will (more precisely, determination of the pure will) depends on reflection, while the other says in effect that the ground of determination (of the pure will) is independent of reflection. And Kant does in fact infer from the one to the falsity of the other.

But is this conclusion logically compelling? On closer inspection it appears that this conclusion does not follow directly. The inference becomes unavoidable only if one confuses the forms of determination of the will with the possible grounds of determination, the forms of decision with the types of motive. That is really what is happening here. So these inferences are based on an implicit assertion concerning the connection of the members of the one division with those of the other. This same point is prejudged in both inferences. It is assumed without any justification, appearing as it does to be logically self-evident; for one sees the connection of concepts it contains as an identity, in which case no further justification is needed for the transition from one to the other. We can express this implicit assumption in the form in which we met it earlier* as a decisive presupposition of Kant's theory, as the assumption that the disjunction between pleasure and understanding as possible grounds for determining the will is complete.

The premisses we actually have thus require a complement. Taken strictly, the one implies the exclusion of pleasure and the other of understanding as ground of determination of the pure will. We may infer from our premisses that this ground of determination must have some other origin—meaning that *if* there really is something like a pure will, *then* its ground of determination will have this other origin. Unless we assume that there can be a pure will, our two premisses can be combined (though still strictly alternative) by drawing the precisely opposite conclusion that a pure will is impossible. In order to exclude this interpretation of our premisses and move from that merely hypothetical assertion to the assertion that there is in fact such a ground of determination we require a further and factual premiss, and one which we do find given in Kant's theory, in his very statement 'that there can be a pure will'. This is the third premiss (P_3), and for completeness we ought to insert it in our diagram.

* Vol. I, p. 228.

Only with this addition can we properly infer from the two negative premises to our positive conclusion.

We can now further improve our diagram by adding a third conclusion (C_3) as counterpart to this third premiss. For by combining the other two premises we reach the conclusion of the empiricist theory that there cannot be a pure will.

What is the real significance of this third premiss?

One point must be made quite clear. The concept of *a pure will*, as here employed, must not in its turn be defined by the origin of the ground of determination as the concept of *a will whose motive is purely-rational*. That would be to anticipate the solution of the problem. At this point a pure will cannot be described by reference to its origin, but only by the content of its maxims. Its content, viz. a maxim for moral decision, is determined by the moral law, as Kant indicated when he described the pure will as one deriving simply from reverence for the law.

At this point we encounter a profound difficulty. For the pure will, thus described, is just a moral postulate, not a fact that could be discovered psychologically. The possibility of a pure will can be asserted if we presuppose the moral law. For if there is a moral law, it must be possible to fulfil it, so it must be possible for a will to be pure. The assertion that there can be a pure will thus finally reduces to that same metaphysical assertion whose deduction is our main concern at this point. Whether or not there is a moral law is a purely metaphysical question, which we neither can nor should enter on in our psychological theory. So a decision on this point must not be made the starting point of our theory.

How are we to get out of this difficulty?

The way of escape must be the same in this case as the one we adopted in the Theory of Speculative Reason. Refraining from an objective statement as to whether a pure will is possible and confining ourselves to the psychological fact that we do have the concept of *a pure will*, we ask: how does this come about?

The concept of *a pure will* is something which our reason does in fact have, as can be established psychologically, even if it is quite imaginary. Even if there is no moral law, still we have in us the idea of *a moral law*, and with it the concept of *a pure will*. For the idea of such a law directly involves the claim that the will is determined through this idea. For it is the idea of *what ought to be* and therefore *can be*. This idea is given to us directly in the consciousness of duty evinced in the various phenomena of conscience. This gives us a reliable starting point for the psychological enquiry.

Consciousness of duty involves consciousness of a practical necessity. How can this be? On looking into this question we are led to a deduction of the moral law. For it then appears that the idea of practical necessity is a psychological possibility only if there is a pure practical reason as a distinct faculty of motive, and this is the necessary and sufficient condition of there being a pure will—which proves all that we require, without recourse to that awkward metaphysical assumption.

Now we can conclude that consciousness of practical necessity, as we actually come across it in ourselves in consciousness of duty, could not be based either upon pleasure—for the idea of *duty* comes to consciousness only through reflection; nor on mere reflection—for this is empty. The only remaining alternative is to assume that there is a pure practical reason, as an independent faculty of moral motive and so as a possible ground of determination of the pure will, in order to account for the fact of consciousness of duty.

The consciousness of duty, the fact from which we begin, in the only form in which it is open to observation, appears as a mere feeling. To interpret this fact correctly we shall need a correct theory of feeling. For as the fact which we are investigating is available to us only as a feeling, it would be very easy to give a mistaken psychological interpretation to this feeling, thus arriving at the mystical theory that we are here dealing with something like an intellectual pleasure. This mistake would prevent any further enquiry. We are preserved from it by Fries' theory of feeling.

Feeling, as we saw in the case of the feeling-for-truth, is not the expression of a practical faculty of the mind, but is really an act of the judgment (*Urteilskraft*). It is the judging of an object by a universal rule, though we are not aware of the rule with conceptual clarity, but only presuppose it obscurely. A judgment is thus said to be 'in accord with feeling', as contrasted with one made abstractly, by logical inference based on some mediating concept, which we do not have here. We distinguish between feelings which can be expressed and those which cannot, by whether such a mediating concept can be subsequently formed or not, i.e. by whether the judgment can be justified logically as an inference or not.

That is just the position here. The feeling in question, such as we find it for example in the feeling of *duty*, is one which passes judgment not on the existence but on the value of the object. The feeling of *value* also is essentially an act of the judgment, and so of reflection, and is not itself the expression of a practical faculty of the mind. But the rule in accordance with which the feeling here judges is concerned not with the existence but with the value of things. This shows that it is only in this presupposed rule that the practical faculty properly appears, and not in the feeling itself, which judges the given object according to that presupposed rule. In the presupposing of this rule of value the practical faculty of the mind shows up as a faculty for the assessment of values: as interest or the faculty of impulse or drive (*Trieb*). Feeling itself is indifferent with regard to this distinction of possible major premises for its judgment—i.e. whether these are speculative or practical. It is just the faculty for subsuming given objects under such a major premiss. So the distinction between speculative and practical does not apply to supposedly different sorts of feeling, but only to the origin of the presupposed rule in accordance with which the feeling judges, which derives sometimes from the faculty of knowledge and sometimes from that of drives. So in an enquiry into the practical faculty as such, even if we are compelled to start from feeling, as the only thing open to observation, we must not rest content with that, but must look also into the origin of the various rules of value on which the feeling is based. This will supplement the theory of feeling with a theory of drives.

Let us look more closely into this. Kant had only recognized the sharp contrast between the impulse of inclination, which tends towards happiness, and the moral impulse—though the structure of his theory was too restrictive even for this. Fries shows that this contrast is insufficient and supplements it by introducing a third impulse, which he calls 'reflected'. The evaluation due to this impulse is not concerned, as is that due to the sensible impulse, with the particular situation in life of the subject, but rests—hence the name 'reflected impulse'—on the comparison of the particular situations in life of the subject in their relation to the whole of life. The demands of this impulse are therefore quite different from those of the sensible impulse. They are not directed towards enjoyment, but involve the judging of enjoyment. That there really is a separate impulse here, in addition to the sensible impulse, can easily be established by noting that this evaluation of enjoyment is not simply by strength or duration—for that would be to evaluate it on the basis of the sensible impulse itself—but by an independent standard, that of the object enjoyed. We prefer the one form of enjoyment to the other irrespective of the strength and duration of the enjoyment. We distinguish between cruder and finer forms of satisfaction, more and less noble enjoyments—a qualitative distinction involving a standard of value quite different from enjoyment itself, and so presupposing some impulse other than the sensible. This gradation in the evaluation of enjoyment is itself sufficient evidence for the existence of an impulse different from the sensible. But it goes further than this; for we also evaluate each particular part or aspect of life by the rule of this reflected impulse. We evaluate them in relation to the whole of our life by a rule concerned with perfection or culture. That is why Fries also calls this impulse the impulse for perfection. But the demands of this impulse are not the same for everyone, following a rule which holds equally for all, but depend on the individuality of particular people. Perfection requires one thing from one man, and something else from another, according to the difference in their abilities.

Evaluation of this impulse has also to be distinguished from moral evaluation. For while moral evaluation always appears as limiting, i.e. in itself requires only omissions, we are here concerned with a positive demand. The reflected impulse gives us positive goals for our life. It actually sets us aims, while moral judgment puts limits on these. So it is this impulse that is ultimately responsible for every effort at the development of individuals and towards the culture of society. Fries gives it another name, to distinguish it from the impulse of sensible inclination. He calls it the impulse of pure love.

We must also distinguish it from the moral impulse. The existence of a moral impulse independent in origin from those just referred to is evidenced by the consciousness of duty, as met with in the manifold phenomena of conscience. Consciousness of *duty* is consciousness of a practical necessity. Its object is for us an object of respect, quite apart from either inclination or love. What we must do is to determine the content of the rule of value which this moral impulse provides in addition to the demands of inclination and to those of pure love. This is in the first place a task of exposition, i.e. of giving a proper account of the conceptual resolution of the moral feeling, but it is also a task of deduction; for the deduction so far performed only shows the existence of pure practical reason as the faculty of an independent motive (*Antrieb*) and does not determine the content of the rule which this motive employs.

In discharging the first task and so giving an exposition of the principles of morality, Fries gives the much disputed formalism of Kant's ethics the critique it deserves as well as the credit which is its due. For only when the mistakes and misinterpretations in the Kantian version of this formalism have been eliminated can its correct kernel be seen in a clear light.

The defect in this formalism, which really made it impossible to determine the content for the rule of the moral motive, was that in the absence of a moral law we have no usable criterion by which to distinguish actions in accordance with duty from those which conflict with it. The criteria given by Kant are not altogether subject to this defect. They do provide a genuine content, but this has been imported into the system surreptitiously. For the strictly logical conclusion of his theory is that we have only the mere concept of *a law*, not any content of the law itself, as a supposed criterion of duty. This concept does not provide any basis on which to decide whether a particular action is our duty or not.

Kant did have in mind the proper content for the moral law, but he could not reconcile it satisfactorily with his psychological theory. He saw that the content of the moral law and so of the criterion of duty was determined by the command to respect human dignity. This determination of content, which remains without justification in Kant, was taken up by Fries with only minor amendments. This led him to his great discovery that the content of the moral law is really the same as that of the law of right—which also occurs in Kant's practical philosophy, though it has no justification there—the law that every person is of equal worth.

This law is the true Categorical Imperative and provides the basic principle not only for the Theory of Rights, but also for the Theory of Duties. But as a rule for moral decision this Categorical Imperative provides only the major premiss. It is only a law of motive. Now this motive does not lead to a decision as a matter of necessity. For it is not the objective necessity of the law, but only the relatively subjective vigour of the motive that in nature determines the will. So the law does not apply in nature simply by its own validity, but only by establishing a sufficient force of moral motive to overcome the simultaneous non-moral motives. So a rational being in nature has another law in addition to the law of the moral motive, a law which is properly one of decision. This proper law of moral decision brings out for us the correct kernel contained in the formalism of Kantian ethics. For it is in fact the Kantian law of acting from duty or from respect for the law, the Categorical law, which is the major premiss for a moral decision. Fries calls it the Imperative of virtue, in contrast to the Categorical law of right. He also calls it the command to have the courage of one's moral convictions. It tells us to make the moral motive superior in strength. It is only through this law that human beings can apply the Categorical Imperative of right in the Theory of Virtue.

Now in deduction of the basic laws of practical philosophy we must once more start from the general Theory of Practical Reason,

R

whose laws we have already come across. We found that the practical reason, like the speculative, is a receptive spontaneity, a self-activity not absolute but dependent on external stimulation. So like the knowing reason it comes under the law of sensibility. Practical reason can no more provide the content of its particular determinations of value than can the knowing reason provide the content of its knowledge of particular reality.

Yet it is not a merely sensible, but a pure reason, i.e. in addition to sensibility it also has the permanent form of stimulability met with in each actual (and externally stimulated) manifestation of life. As a pure self-activity it provides an apodeictic determination of every possible sensible content—a determination which of course, owing to its formal character, is super-imposed on the sensible content merely as a limiting condition.

Now we found the law of reflection also holding in the organization of the practical reason. This came out in the following fact. The will cannot be determined directly through pure reason. Pure reason does not of itself determine the will, but requires for this the form of an intellectual decision. Only sensible interest can determine the will directly and on its own, in an impulsive decision. The purely-rational motive, by contrast, does not determine the will directly. One could put it like this. The degree of value is not decisive in determining the will. Nor does practical necessity bring the will to a decision as if by a law of nature. The purely-rational interest must also lead to a development of reflection itself, establishing a force of inner self-control in the struggle with contrary motives. For it is only by overcoming these—in the form of an intellectual decision—that a will can be pure. It was in this fact that we recognized the law of the original obscurity of pure reason, the law of the dependence of consciousness on reflection.

We thus see that the practical reason also is limited in two respects: firstly, by its dependence on sensibility, which is directly concerned with the actual content of the determination of value; secondly, in respect of the determination of the will, which is restricted to the form of an intellectual decision for all purely rational resolutions. The first limitation is objectively expressed in the merely formal and limiting character of all apodeictic determinations of value, and the second in the compulsion (whether of inner or external pressure) which is needed, in addition to practical necessity, for our action to conform to it.

Now for the purpose of our deduction we must make use of the fact that because of the unity of reason the determination of value, which is additional to mere knowledge, carries with it an original material determination of formal apperception. The Idea of necessary value or of worth is here combined with the speculative Idea of a necessary unity in the Being of things. That yields the Idea of *laying down objective laws of value*; not that this has any positive application, in view of the limitation of our reason to the senses, but which quite apart from its application or lack of it within our knowledge is related as Idea in its absolute significance to the whole of reality, thought of through speculative Ideas as the Being of things-as-they-really-are. But there is another side to this. In its significance for the Being of things-as-they-really-are, this Idea of practical necessity or of worth cannot be thought of simply as a task, as it is in its application to nature, where the law of practical necessity appears alongside the law of nature as a law of *what ought to be* or of *duty*. In application to nature, laws for the Being of things and for their value diverge, so that the second type of law is only a task, an Idea of what our action ought to bring about, which in nature must be regarded as still in the stage of Becoming. Such a division cannot apply to the Idea, for here necessity does not, as it does in the restricted knowledge of nature, take on the abstract form of lawlikeness, of a merely relative necessity unable positively to determine the existence of the phenomena and leaving this as something essentially contingent. For Absolute Reality, where this divergence between necessary and actual is eliminated, there cannot be laws of Value distinct from the laws of Being. The separating of these two types of law, laws for the Being of things and those for the value of things, is just the expression of the subjectively limited nature of our reason. If we are to rise in thought above this limitation, we can do so only by recognizing—absolutely, in Idea—that very same necessity in this Being of things-as-they-really-are, so that necessary unity and necessary value or worth are thought of as one and the same. If, guided by the original unity of our reason, we try, prior to reflection, to state fully its basic immediate idea, we can do so only by asserting the objective identity of that necessity in the Being of things which is conceived in both the speculative and the practical Ideas.

We thus come to the principle that for the Being of things-as-they-really-are the necessity of value is directly determinative of their existence. To put it another way, Absolute Being is necessarily an absolutely good being. In short, we come to the idea of the highest good, the religious principle of optimism.

This shows that it is the practical determination of Ideas that provides the complete principle for the Theory of Ideas, which thus becomes a practical Theory of Ideas, or a philosophy of religion properly understood. The principles of the philosophy of religion therefore have their origin in this practical determination of speculative Ideas. The principle of method for constructing the basic propositions of the philosophy of religion is the moral Schematism of the speculative Ideas. Just as the speculative Ideas are constructed through the ideal Schematism of the Categories, i.e. through an Idea of the Absolute which negates limitations, so also the basic laws of the philosophy of religion are fixed through a further practical or moral Schematism of the speculative Ideas, by combining the speculative Ideas with the Idea of absolute value. This combination is expressed in certain principles of metaphysics, which as articles of faith recapitulate the most profound and original convictions of reason. However in consequence these principles allow of no theoretical development, being purely ideal principles, but only of aesthetic subsumption (*Unterordnung*) through ineffable feelings of intimation.

The practical theory of Ideas which we thus reach or, as Fries calls it, objective teleology, is obviously quite different in origin from the practical theory of nature or subjective teleology. The reason for giving it this name is that this theory sets out the laws of value simply as laws providing aims and tasks for our actions in nature. It is not concerned with the highest good in the world, but only with the highest good for us; not with the determination of human existence by reference to the goal of the world, but only with the aims which men as rational beings set before themselves for their own action. This is the business of ethics in the general sense of the term. Ethics, then, is practical theory of nature, or subjective teleology. It remains distinct from all practical theory of Ideas, or objective teleology, that is from the philosophy of religion.

Ethical value-legislation applies to nature in two ways: first to the inner attitude of individuals, and then to the external form of their reciprocal activity or, in brief, to society. Consequently we have here a double task; to set up a force through which the intrinsically valid law is made to apply in nature, firstly and internally as the force of a good disposition, which is called virtue, and then externally as the force of legal coercion, which constitutes the nature of the State. So the principles of the Theory of Virtue and of the Theory of Rights part company at this point. The first provides the theme for the theory of morals, and the other that for political philosophy.

4

The System of Metaphysics

We now come to the real aim of all our enquiries, the setting up of metaphysics as a system.

What does it mean to set up this system? We must be clear about this, if we are not to misunderstand both as a whole and in detail the system which we shall now consider.

The principles of metaphysics which have been deduced are not axioms from which a system of metaphysics can be worked out, as a body of higher or absolute knowledge of the Being of things, going beyond experience. They are not constitutive principles of a metaphysical knowledge of the world, which would as such be superior to our empirical knowledge; they are only criteria for possible judgments to be carried out in accordance with experience. The rule that all metaphysical knowledge is formal in character means that it is not possible by any logic however sophisticated to extract from the pure metaphysical forms a body of knowledge which would outbid empirical knowledge and which, if such a thing were possible, would really suppress and replace it—a claim which has always accompanied thoroughgoing attempts at Rationalism in metaphysics. The principles of metaphysics are in fact purely regulative principles underlying the empirical use of our knowledge and serving as guiding maxims in the various fields of experience. The system of pure metaphysics—which is our sole present concern—has no other purpose than to organize systematically the general metaphysical criteria for the various possible fields of empirical judgment, and to show the significance of these criteria as guiding maxims.

Once we take up the execution of this task a further limitation immediately applies. Even if the restriction just mentioned is accepted, it remains impossible to work this purely formal metaphysical knowledge into a strict system, i.e. a logically closed and unified whole.

In the centre of Fries' metaphysics there stands, even more definitely than in Kant's, the theory of Transcendental Idealism, which teaches that we have no positive knowledge of things-as-they-really-are. According to the tenets of the Critique of Reason with which we are now familiar, not only is our knowledge limited in general, so that it must be contrasted with a knowledge of the true Being of things-as-they-really-are, but even for this limited knowledge, and within it, there is a plurality of separate phenomenal forms of the true Being of things. There is no single closed system in which the totality of our knowledge could be combined. Our knowledge has several distinct and separate entrances. Nothing, therefore, is so important for the understanding of critical metaphysics as an insight into the principle, enunciated by Fries, that truth splits up into different world-views.

In establishing this principle Fries went beyond all his predecessors in metaphysics. It was this that gave a special impress to his construction of this science. All philosophers before Fries (with the exception of Kant) adhered to the preconception that our entire knowledge must admit of amalgamation into a single system. They all pursued this phantom of systematic form.

Fries showed why all their labours were in vain. He attacked this error at its root by destroying the preconception of the systematic unity of human knowledge. As the discussion in his Critique of Reason shows, the various modes of judging the existence of things go their separate ways for our knowledge; so much so, that in their principles they must always remain separate—they cannot be logically reconciled in some higher principle yet to be discovered. For this reason there are various world-views which are independent of each other, as they cannot be theoretically combined under common principles.

Fries' metaphysics therefore sets out to show the relative rights of these individual world-views; to justify the rights of each of them as against the claims of the others and thereby to limit the claims of each against the others. Fries thus succeeds in settling the various and apparently endless metaphysical disputes which run through the whole history of philosophy.

The first and most basic distinction, which is decisive for this splitting up of the world-views, depends on the difference between the concept of nature and Ideas. We have a natural and an ideal world-view. The natural world-view is that set up on the basis of the mathematically schematized Categories, and the ideal world-view is that developed on the foundation of Ideas.

In addition to this first division there is a further one within the natural world-view. Here the material and spiritual views separate, following the division between outer and inner sense. For outer sense our world-view is one of a spatial world, as all objects of external perception are conceived as being 'in space'; but for inner sense the world-view is one of a spiritual world without spatial relationships, as the unity of phenomena of inner sense can be achieved only in the form of pure self-conciousness.

The spatial view of the world, or of material nature, divides once more into two fundamentally distinct perspectives, which Fries contrasts as *morphological* and *hylological* using the Greek terms μορφή (form) and ὕλη (mass). The morphological view keeps simply to sense-perception of the corporeal world. It regards the shapes of perceived objects as the real Beings, and their sensibly perceived qualities as the properties of these Beings. For the hylological view we have to leave the ground of sense-perception, keeping hold of the guideline of pure intuition and following the mathematical Schematism of the Categories. What we call a 'thing' is on the hylological view, which could also be called the physicalist view, no longer something that comes under the senses and so can be sensibly perceived, but a dynamic unity conceivable only in thought. On this view the permanent mass constitutes the Being of things and the moving force their property.

We have similarly to distinguish between various spiritual world-views. We come to know spirit directly only in the form of self-consciousness, as the object of inner experience, and with the aid of this inner experience we can investigate its activities according to natural laws. But we also know ourselves to be members of a spiritual community. Here again the action and reaction of particular spirits on each other can be known through concepts of nature; for the spiritual community depends in nature on corporeal mediation and so can be judged theoretically according to laws of nature. But this world-view also provides the transition to the ideal world-view; for we must also judge the spiritual community which we find in nature according to Ideas, by the practical Ideas of ethics: the Ideas of purpose and value in human action.

By this division Fries distinguishes the psychological-anthropological world-view (for short, the psychological) from the ethical and political world-view. In the ethico-political world-view we come to know men as natural beings, as active in space and time, and yet judge them by Ideas; we judge their society by the ethical Idea of a realm of ends. Our intention here is not simply to explain human actions by natural laws, but also to judge their value in accordance with Ideas. So this perspective also is open to scientific development.

It is the perspective on which the historical sciences are based. (We see here that the separation of the psychological from the historical viewpoint—which certain philosophers have introduced with much ceremony as a new discovery—was already made quite clearly by Fries. The only difference is that Fries avoids the various metaphysical errors to which this distinction led those philosophers.)

Lastly, and above all these viewpoints, there arises the religio-aesthetic world-view. Its conceptually determinable bases are the Ideas of faith. These, however, are of negative origin, and cannot be worked out scientifically; they can only be subsumed in the ineffable feelings of intimation. This world-view therefore escapes all scientific formulation and exists only in the aesthetic-religious emotional moods.

(XIII) Classification of World-Views

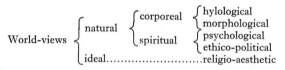

From these various perspectives there arise, by disregard of the limits of human knowledge, the various world-views familiar to us in the history of philosophy, where they engage in perpetual conflict. In each case the metaphysical Idea of the objective unity of the world is confused with a supposedly logical postulate for the systematic unity of our knowledge. This is the really decisive and damaging fundamental mistake in all dogmatic metaphysics. It leads to that confused notion nowadays called Monism, which is opposed by a Pluralism equally justified or unjustified because of the same confusion. For the error responsible for the search for an alleged systematic unity in our knowledge is also responsible for the misinterpretation of the splitting up of truth, which makes people think that because of this splitting up they must also abandon the objective unity of the world and assume a plurality of worlds, a corporeal world and a spiritual one, a world of the senses and a supersensible world. The world is one in fact, as the Idea of absolute synthetic unity requires; but our knowledge of the world is split up into a plurality of different and mutually independent world-views. It is vain to hope to reunite these theoretically under a single principle and thus to overcome that division.

Monism can take various forms, as many different forms as we have world-views, depending on which of these world-views it makes absolute. Thus Materialism is simply the hylological world-view claiming absolute and so exclusive validity. Spiritualism is simply the psychological world-view, again with the claim to absolute and therefore exclusive validity. More generally, Naturalism is simply the natural world-view claiming exclusiveness, and Supernaturalism is the ideal world-view with the claim to an absolute knowledge open to scientific development.

The dispute between all these world-views is settled by the theory of Transcendental Idealism. This teaches that in none of these various world-views do we have a positive knowledge of the Absolute, but that each offers us just a different subjectively limited view of the single true Being of things which cannot be positively known by us.

THE HYLOLOGICAL WORLD-VIEW

We now turn to consider in detail the hylological world-view. This is a metaphysic of external nature. It was worked out systematically in one of Fries' most profound works, a book which got buried under the rubbish of the so-called speculative philosophy of nature of the school of Schelling and Hegel. It was called 'Mathematical Philosophy of Nature'.

In this book Fries widens significantly the field of this science, in particular by extending its scope to include the problems of chemistry and biology, an extension which Kant had held to be impossible. Along with this, he also establishes the claims of Naturalism in every respect and defends them against all improper admixture of ideal or mental forms of explanation. He shows that in the field of external nature an unlimited naturalism holds sway. This is the most important thing about this world-view: it justifies Naturalism in a more consistent, firm, and unimpeachable manner than had previously been achieved even by Kant. In particular we find here a final and ruthless exclusion from natural science of all teleological explanation. Anticipating the advance later made in physiological chemistry and in the biological theory of evolution, Fries shows that the problems of these sciences are not beyond the scope of physical theory. In particular he provides a clear refutation of all vitalist hypotheses. Fries shows up the mistake on which all such hypotheses are based; that they wrongly introduce spiritual explanations into the realm of physics. Fries also shows that the attraction of this ever-recurring attempt is due to the fact that an intrinsically correct and fruitful thought is here misinterpreted. For this attempt is really based on a reversal of the causal relationship, a reversal undertaken as a thought-experiment when we try to investigate the causes, as yet unknown, of certain phenomena. We take the effect as given and ask what means would be required to produce that effect as an end. But this reversal of the causal series is only an heuristic principle. It does not provide any basis for explaining things. For the so-called drive towards organization or structure which underlies organic phenomena is not a drive in the psychological sense of the word. It is not a soul of the organism or a vital force innate in it from the beginning, but is itself a problem for explanatory science. This problem is soluble only by construction of an appropriate process of nature. The peculiar character of the organism arises from a closed system of actions and reactions working in such a way that the system as a whole tends to maintain itself. Once this concept is grasped in its strict universality, to the exclusion of all spiritual concepts of *the soul* or of *vital force*, it becomes clear that this problem is not really beyond the competence of physical theory. For in this general sense a structure, such as for example the system of our planets, comes under the concept of *organism*. This instance shows that the problem does not in essence go beyond the explanatory scope of theoretical physics. Normally of course we apply this concept in a narrower field, where the process is one of formation, which does demand construction in physical terms. But the decisive point of method, which is the mark of problems in this area, is the same in both cases.

Fries goes even further, holding that for the hylological world-view the principles of Naturalism are those of Mechanism. For he shows that the only fully scientific knowledge is that of a world of movements. Movement is the only natural phenomenon that can be constructed mathematically. But openness to mathematical construction is the condition for complete explanation in an area of natural phenomena. This is only a consistent development of a principle of method introduced by Kant into metaphysics of nature, the principle of the mathematical Schematism of the Categories. The final result of this principle is that mechanics is the basic science for all theoretical physics. This is the most important element in the systematic development by which Fries supplements Kant's metaphysics of external nature. He here shows that in addition to the general and purely intuitive Schematism, which Kant had shown to be the principle for construction of the general metaphysical principles of natural science, a particular and spatial Schematism is required in the application of Categories to external nature. This enables the general principles of pure natural science to take on their special form as metaphysical principles of the pure theory of motion.

This shows clearly why classical mechanics had for philosophers such an exceptional position among the natural sciences.

This reference to the role of classical mechanics may seem anachronistic today when this science has fallen on less happy times, and the hope once placed on the general postulate of mechanics seems to have come to final ruin. But our reference to mechanics does involve an idea which philosophically, at least, is highly significant. Who knows what fruits it may yet bear for physics, once the tyranny of empiricist dogma has been broken in this field?

For the present it does seem as though natural philosophy and empirical physics will have to go their separate ways, perhaps for quite some time, so we must not draw hasty metaphysical conclusions from the present unclear state of physics. Any attempt at such a metaphysical interpretation is quite inappropriate to the current position in physics, for it involves attributing to physical theory claims which it never makes and cannot make, for the simple reason that in physics one has at present much more elementary difficulties to contend with than the carrying out of some metaphysical postulates or other. While we have yet to satisfy, and indeed are not even in sight of satisfying the logical requirement of non-contradiction, it is quite inappropriate to make still more far-reaching metaphysical claims. The renunciation of such metaphysical claims and the adoption of the self-denying stance of Conventionalism, on which physical theory is of purely heuristic significance, seem in this situation fully justified. Indeed, paradoxical though this may sound, it appears to be the only stance that can really be reconciled with a critical philosophy of nature.

Let us, however, leave this point and take modern physical theory, with its revolutionary consequences for classical mechanics, as at least in intention final and definitive. The logically compelling character of those consequences, if closely examined, may then serve to set the principles of critical philosophy of nature in an even clearer light.

Of the many examples available let us take one which has the most radical effect on the foundation of the critical philosophy of nature, and which is in any case the most startling paradox in modern physics. This is Einstein's Theory of Relativity, which says that the concept of *objective simultaneity* cannot hold for events at different places, thus conflicting with the ideas of space and time which perception forces directly upon us. As this conclusion, so revolutionary for the previous spatio-temporal conception, was in fact occasioned by an experiment, the famous interference experiment of Michelson, people feel justified in inferring that here is an experimental refutation of the theory of critical philosophy about pure intuition. It is indeed true that in the modern Theory of Relativity the concept of *simultaneity*, in the objective meaning which it certainly has on the theory of critical philosophy, loses all application in physics. It is moreover quite consistent of physicists to infer from the fact that the concept is fundamentally inapplicable in physics that this concept has no reality at all within their science. In drawing this inference modern physics agrees entirely with critical metaphysics, which includes among the principles of modality in philosophy of nature Kant's 'postulates of empirical thought in general', one of which says that the criterion of existence consists of the possibility of experience: that which cannot be experienced has no claim to physical existence. This leads logically to Einstein's critique of the concept of *simultaneity* and of the principles of classical kinetics and mechanics, which are connected with this concept. So far, the line of thought taken in this theory agrees entirely with the criteria for philosophy of nature found in critical metaphysics.

But what about the first step, the physical assumptions whose application in the interpretation of the experimental findings involved such a revolutionary inference? Only when we look into this question can we see the real reason for the dispute between modern Theory of Relativity and critical philosophy of nature. The real reason for rejecting the concept of *objective simultaneity* is not the experiment mentioned. That experiment only provided the original and more or less contingent occasion for the relativistic critique of the old spatio-temporal conception. This critique could have been undertaken earlier, indeed it is quite remarkable that it took place so late, seeing that the general direction of thought on which it is based had for so long been the ruling force in physics. For it is really due to a postulate derived from Cartesian metaphysics—which lost ground, though only for a time, with the victory of the Newtonian theory of gravitation, and which since Faraday's intervention had been more generally rehabilitated. This postulate requires that all natural phenomena be reduced to forces of contact by trying to eliminate from physics all explanations which refer to unmediated action at a distance. Now if one follows out the consequences of this general postulate, one is forced to accept conclusions similar to those which were actually drawn under the impulse of Michelson's experiment.

Let us remember the metaphysical principles of Relation, Kants' 'analogies of experience'. Here we have in the third place the Category of reciprocal action, with the corresponding schema of simultaneity.

Simultaneity is the mathematical schema and so is the condition on which the metaphysical concept of reciprocal action can be applied. The principle which results from combining these two concepts could be formulated, in Kant's terms, like this: all phenomena in space, if they occur at the same time, act and react on each other. This principle is directly equivalent to the assumption of action at a distance; for only by action at a distance could simultaneous phenomena in different places act and react on each other. One has only to get a clear grasp of this single principle to see that the critique just mentioned of the concept of *simultaneity*, and the resultant relativizing of time, are logically necessary and obvious consequences of abolishing the third principle of Relation. For this principle sets out the condition on which experience of events at different places as simultaneous is possible. The relativist result of removing this principle, which brought modern physics into conflict with critical philosophy of nature, is thus in agreement, from the point of view of logical consistency, with the basic conception of that critical philosophy. If we are concerned only with non-contradiction, it is an entirely arbitrary matter which way we resolve this conflict, for neither standpoint is logically superior to the other in any way. One could equally well start by affirming the third analogy of experience and then, by assuming action at a distance, obtain a criterion for objective simultaneity.

That modern physics, if interpreted metaphysically, involves a reversion to Cartesianism is in any case clear in other ways, apart from its tendency to reduce all natural phenomena to forces of contact. By making space substantial, which is the essential point in the modern concept of a field, it revives yet another ancient legacy from Cartesian metaphysics.

If one takes these conceptual constructions and tendencies of modern physics in a metaphysical sense, one is bound to see in them a reversion to Cartesian metaphysics—which explains the contradiction between their consequences and critical philosophy of nature. Only, as we said, this contradiction does not have the metaphysical significance which people attribute to it. It arises through an interpretation which inserts into modern physical theory claims which, rightly understood, it cannot raise. The conventionalist conception of this theory is, I repeat, to this extent much nearer to the truth, for it regards that theory simply as an attempt to combine the experimental data mathematically for the sake of working out a consistent theory. In this situation all one can at present require, as I said before, is that researches in the fields of philosophy of nature and of experimental physics should go their separate ways, leaving it to the future to determine how far they can once more be combined. And when that future generation does try to build a bridge, it must infallibly revert to some form or other of the postulate of Mechanism. This results directly from the fact that metaphysics of nature, which sets the questions for physics, proceeds from the spatial Schematism of the Categories, which in its turn leads directly to the postulate of the mathematical construction of all natural processes, the postulate of Mechanism. For motion is the only natural phenomenon that admits of mathematical construction without remainder.

From this discussion we can now understand quite clearly the role played within Fries' mathematical philosophy of nature by the general principles of mechanics, to which the spatial Schematism of the Categories leads. For natural science in general these principles function as criteria, just as metaphysical principles in general are simply criteria for judgments made in accordance with experience. It is not the case that physical theory can itself be worked out from these principles as from premises. They are not constitutive principles for these theories, but only guiding maxims for those inductions by which alone we can discover the constitutive principles of theoretical physics. We must first bring under them the whole wealth of experimental physics, so that they can bear fruit in knowledge of nature. Which particular laws of nature actually hold in a given field of phenomena can never be learnt from mathematical philosophy of nature, which only works out the general criteria to which we must betake ourselves so as by rational induction to discover these particular laws of nature. But mathematical philosophy of nature can set out what forms of such laws are possible *a priori* and work out their consequences, so as to offer them as hypotheses to empirical scientific research. It is then for empirical research to make a suitable choice between the hypotheses permitted by natural philosophy, i.e. to single out one or another by experimental results as the law which actually holds good in nature. This idea enabled Fries to widen considerably the scope of philosophy of nature. This science becomes, as he puts it, 'an arsenal of hypotheses', for it has to erect hypothetically the laws of nature which are possible *a priori* and, using these as constitutive principles, to work out the corresponding theories purely mathematically.

THE MORPHOLOGICAL WORLD-VIEW

What about the morphological world-view? How far can it claim a place alongside the hylological view?

The morphological world-view involves a theory of nature which is simply descriptive and classificatory, in contrast with the explanatory theories of theoretical physics. In the hylological world-view of physics, permanent mass constitutes the Being of things, and moving forces constitute their properties. We therefore abandon the field of sensible perception completely and rely on the guidance of the mathematical Schematism. Here, however, we rest content with the sensibly perceived phenomenon and take the shape (which for sense-perception is the only permanent element) as the Being of things and the sensibly perceived qualities as their properties. This distinction between the hylological and the morphological view of external nature must not be misinterpreted as a dualism within nature, as if the morphological view had a different and supposedly autonomous set of objects and organic life were a distinct realm with its own rules, apart from the natural phenomena which physics has to explain. No such dualism is involved. Both views comprehend the whole of external nature.

There are two distinct ways of looking at one and the same external nature, not two realms of objects within external nature itself. An organism is subject to physics, just as inorganic nature is open to the morphological approach. What are usually considered inorganic phenomena, such as clouds, mountains and rivers, are in the morphological view regarded as individuals just as much as plants, animals and men. Neither sort, however, are substantial unities when regarded physically. For the physical approach, both merely constitute problems. For we find in them a merely perceptual unity of form, and even this is only of relative permanence. The self-preservation of an object is here treated simply as that of a system of reciprocal actions between continuously changing substances in accordance with the law of the interchange of matter; so destructive influences can at any time destroy the equilibrium of the system, thus annihilating the individuality of the object.

The boundaries of physics therefore are not set by some peculiarity in certain objects of external nature which precludes their explanation in terms of theoretical physics. The boundaries of physics are not due to the problem of formation. This is a question for physics, just as much as the inorganic processes of nature are. All the same, there is a boundary to the physical world-view and to the theoretical explanations it can provide. But we must not try to draw that boundary by delimiting a particular area of natural phenomena. The boundary lies elsewhere. It is set, first of all, by what Fries calls the law of the original contingency of mathematical combination.

This original contingency in the combination of phenomena in space and time can never be overcome, however far physics may be developed. This is evident from a fact very familiar to physicists, namely that in the differential equations of physics the constants of integration are arbitrary, i.e. they cannot be determined from these equations but must be derived from observation. Here the facts of observation appear as something additional which cannot be deduced from the law. But in addition to this basic contingency in the mathematical combination of phenomena, which remains indeducible for physical theory, there is a similar contingency in the qualities of sense-perception, though it was only by observing these that we made a start on physics. They cannot be understood by derivation from mechanical processes. They are not open to any sort of mathematical construction. From the perspective of the hylological world-view they remain unintelligible.

It is at this point that we move over, quite rightly, to the morphological world-view. Yet this in its turn cannot be built up as a complete scientific system. Its real significance for the world-view as a whole is that it provides a bridge from the corporeal view to the spiritual. The qualities of sense-perception are not determinations of external objects of a sort, determinable by their reciprocal relationship (which is the sole basis of explanation in all physical theory), but indicate the presence of bodies only by appearing to the mind.

The transition to the spiritual view of the world brings us to the absolutely irresoluable qualities of sense-perception. For the inner qualities (those presented by inner sense) do not admit even such resolution as physics provides for external qualities by tracing them back to motion.

The Psychological World-View

The metaphysical principles on which the psychological view of the world is based form a scientific system which is a discipline of its own with authority equal to that of the metaphysics of external nature. This 'Metaphysic of Inner Nature' was set out in classic form in a book of that name by Fries' disciple, Heinrich Schmid. This science shows us the criteria on which inner experience is based. For these principles also do not allow of direct theoretical application, but serve only as criteria, as guiding maxims for any rational induction in the field of psychology. But in the absence of any mathematical construction, there is only a limited application for these metaphysical principles. Psychic phenomena cannot be measured, so theoretical explanation of them is possible only in a limited degree. But that is not to say that they cannot be theoretically explained at all, for they can, within the limits set by the impossibility of measurement. Such explanation is based on the fact that the law of continuity holds good for psychic phenomena. Comparison of size can be made in this field in terms of degrees, by the metaphysical law of Quality that every sensibly perceived quality has an intensive magnitude which can increase or decrease continuously.

Following the rule that truth is split up into the internal and external views of nature, Fries in his metaphysics of inner nature holds strictly to the separation between psychological theories and all physiological and physical theories. Psychic phenomena cannot be explained physiologically. Conversely, we may also say that physical phenomena cannot be explained psychologically. What is psychic and what is physical cannot be combined in a single theory. There is no metaphysical principle for deciding the relations between psychic and physical which could serve as regulative for a rational induction. All we can do in this case is to ascertain the temporal relationship between one phenomenon and the other by empirical induction. Fries himself remarked that there is such a thing as 'comparative anthropology', i.e. an enquiry into the correspondence between psychic and physical phenomena. This is now called 'physiological psychology' or, in an even more unhappy term coined by Fechner, 'psychophysics'. But this enquiry is inevitably limited to pointing out the parallelism between the psychical and physical causal series as a fact of experience; it cannot give any further explanation of it. This parallelism provides no metaphysical explanation and can never enable us to combine the psychological and physiological approaches theoretically; which undermines all metaphysical hypotheses about the relationship between body and soul.

The concept of *life* has its proper place in the psychological world-view. It is not here used by analogy, as it is in organic theory. Life is simply inner activity, contrasted with all external activity. Life does not here mean simply the result of external actions and reactions, a result that might be traced back to other and more elementary phenomena. It cannot be resolved into external relationships. The living is what is active from within. This is not, however, given to us in perception as an object of inner nature, but has through pure self-consciousness to be added in thought to the phenomena of inner sense, as the identical subject of all the living activities perceived by inner sense. It is the sole basis for the unity of inner experience: we call it the *I*. This *I*, however, can only be known in the various determinate forms

S

it assumes in inner sense. The only scientific knowledge of spirit open to us is that bounded by inner perception.

We can thus reject Materialism, on the one hand, i.e. all attempts at explaining spiritual life on physical grounds; but at the same time we must also reject Spiritualism because it transgresses the boundaries of scientific knowledge of spirit. By Spiritualism I mean the theory that the mind is a simple, permanent, and self-existent being. This theory has no place in scientific knowledge of the mind, but belongs to a merely ideal approach. In experience the mental always appears as something not self-sufficient; further enquiry into it remains entirely dependent on external experience, which alone makes possible a precise determination of time. For if we were to limit ourselves to inner experience, we should not even be able to measure time. If we follow experience, our best comparison for the mind is with organism, as the form of only relatively permanent, changing substances. The *I* is in fact given to us only as the identical subject of possible determinations of inner sense; apart from this relation to the phenomena of inner sense we have no way whatsoever of determining the object of inner experience. So we cannot pronounce scientifically on the nature of the *I*, apart from what inner sense shows us of it, we cannot say whether it has any permanent or essential nature on its own. We therefore ought not to apply the concept of *substance* here, in the strict sense. For the same reason the *I* should not, as matter may, have forces ascribed to it in the strict sense, but only faculties. The *I* is not in itself active absolutely and originally, but only stimulable to activity; it requires some stimulus to set it in action in the first place. This stimulus itself, however, does not come within inner experience, but has to be added in thought to the phenomena of inner sense, following the metaphysical assumption that every change in inner activity requires some cause. Now this cause, which originally arouses the *I* to activity, is not itself to be found in inner experience; it does not consist in any activity proper to the *I*. So we cannot ascribe activity to the *I* absolutely, as its property, but only a capacity for activity which has to be externally stimulated in order to show itself.

The activity itself comes under the law of continuity mentioned earlier, whereby every activity has a particular degree of strength, which can increase or decrease continuously and whereby the activities, once aroused externally, can strengthen or weaken each other reciprocally. The unity of different activities in the *I* can thus be thought of only as an intensive unity; for in the absence of the perceptual form of a Being internally various yet all existing together at a given moment, no external combination of several activities in the unity of the *I* is possible. There is then an intensive unity in the living activity of the *I*, which at any moment has a particular finite degree and in which the various separate activities present at that moment must take part, as determined in detail by the laws of association. The various activities of the *I* can in consequence only be combined dynamically, without any perceptual form of coexistence alongside each other, and so without it being at all possible to construct them into a mathematical system. That is why the qualities of inner sense cannot be resolved.

A further point must be noted here. The activities of the *I* have originally to be aroused from outside, yet are themselves inner activities, i.e. genuine activities of the *I*, which must here be presupposed as an active subject. For we can think of any change only as proceeding by the law of cause and effect. But for inner experience there is only the *I* as internal cause, and nothing to appear as an effect distinct from the activity of the *I* and produced by that activity. The effect is simply the activity itself, not something further effected by that activity. One must not be misled here by false analogies from the external view of nature. For example, having ideas is one activity of the *I*. But it is not the case that anything is effected by this activity, any object of the idea apart from the idea itself. Rather, to have an idea is *ipso facto* to have an idea *of an object*, but this does not mean that the object is in inner experience distinguishable from the idea or in any way additional to it.

The activities of the *I* must be traced back to its faculties. The concept of *a faculty* is still hotly disputed in psychology. Fries points out in detail the mistakes which have led people to take exception to the introduction of this concept. It is in fact an indispensable concept for psychology. Admittedly a faculty is not something that we can observe through inner sense or perceive within ourselves. But that does not make it an occult quality alongside observable qualities, but only an expression for the regularity of the psychic process, which we are bound to presuppose as a condition for the possibility of inner experience, since without it there would be no unity of inner nature and even the simplest inference in this field would be impossible. So this is not a mystical assumption, just a formal metaphysical principle for the possibility of inner experience. If we are not to rest content with mere observations of inner sense but want to rise by means of inference to inner experience, or even to a psychological theory, we must employ this concept. This situation may be concealed, but it cannot be altered. If we claim the right to proceed by inference beyond the observed fact and to make one observed fact the basis for expecting another fact to occur, then we are really employing—whether we are clear about it or not—the concept of *a faculty*. For if we take for granted a rule by which a mental activity comes into action on certain conditions, we are ascribing to the mind a faculty for this activity. To do this is only to say, in other terms, that we do assume such a rule. So if in psychology we wish to avoid not merely the word 'faculty', but also the concept, we shall have to abandon inference in this field altogether and to give up all hope of a science of psychology. The concept of *faculty* is not eliminated from science by replacing this word by another, by using terms like 'tendency', 'disposition', 'determination', 'susceptibility', 'capacity', and other artificial expressions which simply reintroduce in a concealed form the concept of *faculty* which had been tabooed. That is just translating the word into another language.

We must, however, realize that to introduce this concept into psychology is in the first instance only to pose a problem. The rule in question has still to be discovered and can be determined only through experience. It is not enough to adopt verbal definitions of particular faculties and to assume a separate faculty of each particular circle of activities that may in a descriptive account appear as distinct from other activities, as people speak of a faculty of having ideas as different from that of knowing, or of a faculty of feeling as distinct from a faculty of desire, or of the understanding, the reason and the judgment as distinct faculties of knowledge, or of sense and imagination. In addition to the verbal definition there must also be a proper proof of existence if one is to assert the occurrence of a distinct faculty, and this proof of existence can be undertaken only by the aid of facts of inner experience.

The distinction between sensibility and pure reason is quite different from that between different faculties. For each of the basic faculties—the faculty of knowing something, the faculty of interesting oneself, and the faculty of willing—there holds good in equal measure the further distinction due to there being laws both of sensibility and of pure reason. It is not the case that sensibility and pure reason are proper basic faculties of the mind, for they concern only the distinction between the stimulability of a particular faculty and the form of stimulability by which its activities can be expressed. The distinction between sensibility and pure reason thus applies to each of the basic faculties, for its sole concern is to distinguish between what for each faculty is determined by sensible stimulation and what by pure self-activity.

Finally we must be careful not to confuse the distinction between different faculties with the distinction between the grades of development to be made out in the formation of each faculty. For each faculty can only be developed step by step. The rule is that each faculty is built up in stages, first sensible stimulation, then habitual continuance, and finally self-development at will through rational self-control. So we must also distinguish between the faculties themselves and the steps by which they are built up. We could call these the steps of sense, habit and understanding—a division which once more applies to all faculties equally.

If these various distinctions are all carefully observed psychology can and will develop as a science. We shall thus construct a theory of the faculties of the human mind, tracing its various activities back to the basic faculties, and shall also compile a history of its development, setting out the stages of development discernible for each faculty.

THE ETHICO-POLITICAL WORLD-VIEW

The distinctive feature of the ethico-political, as against the psychological world-view, is that the mind is here considered not in its inner, but in its outer relationships. These all depend on the effect of the mind on the corporeal world, or on the converse effect of the corporeal world on the inner world of the mind. It is clear that this relationship is not open to theoretical explanation, since there is no definite principle of connection by which we could unite the mental and the corporeal in a single theory.

This world-view can therefore be built up only by empirical inductions. These are principally concerned with the reciprocal relationship between mind and body. We can enquire how the individual mind (i.e. the individual man) acts for his own ends and influences the corporeal world, and also how this reacts upon his mind. Such an enquiry is concerned with how bodies are used as things, that is as means for the ends of the mind. A theory of prudence (*Klugheitslehre*) could be built up, showing the laws of the effects of things with respect to the ends of the mind; in short, a theory of the usefulness of things.

This would, however, bring us only to an economic and technical view, to what Fries called a 'pragmatic' world-view, not to an ethico-political one. We can reach the latter only when in addition to the concepts of *means* and *ends* we accept the necessary determinations of ends by practical metaphysics. This means that we are no longer engaged simply in determining what use of things is appropriate as means to any aim we like, but that the theory of prudence is brought under a theory of wisdom, a theory of the ends themselves, as given in the laws of practical metaphysics. The theory of prudence contains only hypothetical prescriptions of what it is good to do if this or that aim is chosen, but we now have categorical prescriptions by which one aim can be judged as intrinsically preferable to another. Here the application of practical metaphysics is combined with the theoretical view of nature, and this combination yields the ethico-political world-view. It is only at this stage that we gain entrance to the true world of the spirit, the world of spiritual community and not just the inner world of the isolated individual mind.

This community can only be established by means of bodies in nature, and a closer enquiry into this corporeal element depends on empirical inductions. The contribution which the ethico-political world-view does make, by way of metaphysical content, derives from practical metaphysics, the practical theory of nature. This brings us to the theme of Kant's *Metaphysics of Morals*. As a practical theory of nature, this, like the theoretical theory of nature, includes two parts, an inner and an outer, following the division made in the Critique of Reason. For we here apply the principles of practical metaphysics first to the inner aspect of the individual mind, and then also to the external relationship of individual minds, and so to society. In the first case we have the Theory of Virtue, in the second the Theory of Rights.

The Theory of Virtue

In the Theory of Virtue (or ethics in the narrower sense of the word) it is once more essential to distinguish, as Kant did, between the morality and the legality of an action. The metaphysical Theory of Virtue contains rules for judging the morality or, more generally, the disposition of the actor. But it also goes on to work out definite pre-scriptions for the man of good disposition, i.e. one who is prepared to subject himself in his actions to the laws of the good, and who therefore needs telling what it is good to do. The Theory of Virtue therefore divides into two parts, which Fries contrasts as ascetic and didactic. The theme of the first is the training of character, that of the second is the cultivation of moral insight. This distinction is of very considerable importance if ethics in general is to be soundly developed. Ascetics concerns only the virtue of one who is true to his moral convictions, so the content of his moral convictions makes no difference to his morality. This virtue is simply purity of character, and any question about the particular content of commands is irrelevant here. Fries was the first moralist bold and consistent enough to make this point quite seriously.

The requirements of character, which are the theme of ascetics, can be easily worked out. First of all, character requires prudence, which is simply intelligence in decision. This consists in the control of the will over motives which work impulsively, the affections as well as the passions. An affection is a transitory wave of instinct, a passion is its habitual engagement. Control of the will over the affections is strength of character; control of the will over the power of habit is vigour of character. Strength and vigour of character thus together make up prudence, and are the necessary conditions for morality of character. But this also requires, in addition to the mere form of intelligence in action, purity of character, i.e. superiority of the moral motive over all competing motives. This depends on a decision to follow the moral motive in all circumstances, even if it conflicts with other motives however strong. Man as a natural being can never rise above this command of character. There is for him no ideal of 'beauty of soul'; he cannot even think of attaining a state in which all battles between duty and inclination have died down and one need no longer overcome self in order to remain true to the good. For it is in nature a contingent matter how far requirements of duty will coincide with inclinations. The moral man must therefore always be ready to take up the battle with inclination in order to follow the command of duty.

Going beyond this theory of character, didactics provides a theory of the particular duties of virtue, as Fries calls the requirements of legality, in contrast to the single virtue of remaining true to one's convictions, or of character. This theory of the particular duties of virtue helps in the cultivation of moral insight and so applies only to one who has already decided to bring his action under the control of duty.

We can now see from a new angle how fruitful are the discoveries which Fries made in the theory of practical reason.

The principle from which didactics as a theory of duties begins, is the objective principle of duty, the law of right. All duties of virtue must therefore be traceable to the duty set by this law, the duty of respect for human dignity. Fries shows in his *Ethics* how the separate duties of virtue derive from this law.

It is characteristic of this law that it leads directly only to negative commands. In itself it commands only omissions, the omission of actions which offend against human dignity. It is not at all suited for positive legislation on human action.

From this there follows an important and indeed revolutionary consequence for ethics as previouly taught. It is that the positive requirements of ethics are all independent of morality proper and fall right outside the theory of duty.

It is not, however, the case, as even Kant had assumed, that apart from duty there are only the claims of inclination, i.e. the sensible drive towards happiness, for between the claims of duty and those of happiness there are the claims of perfection. Between respect and inclination there stands pure love. It is the claims of love that enable us to work out positive rules of value for human actions. The principle for such laws of value is provided by the ideal of perfection or of spiritual beauty. These laws concern, firstly, the particular life of individuals, setting before them the ideal of cultural development, and then the community of individuals in which the ideals of community take on their various forms of love, friendship, and communal spirit in public life.

By making the concept of *spiritual beauty* the focal point in ethics Fries revived the basic idea of Greek ethics, the idea of καλοκαγαθία, that the good and the beautiful are one in human action. For if we ask what it is that we really value in beauty we see that we are prizing what is good in itself, i.e. what is prizeworthy not just comparatively —for some end—but intrinsically and without any such comparison. But this, judged ethically, as an end for our action, is the perfect. Beauty and perfection are thus objectively one and are distinguished only by the point of view from which they are considered, i.e. by whether in prizing them we are prizing the existence of something (this prizing results from a mere feeling), or whether we conceive it as the object of some motive (here the rule of the motive is open to conceptual determination). Ethics, then, as the theory of what is intrinsically good in human life, is simply a theory of the beauty of human life, so far as this theory is open to conceptual formulation. It emerges, then, that a theory of this sort can be conceptually formulated, according to definite rules, just so far as it is the beauty of human action that is under discussion; or, to put it another way, just to the extent that the intrinsically good is practically significant for us. If we enquire into the intrinsically good for men, ethics answers in accordance with definite concepts. But we must not try to work out this answer from a theory of what is intrinsically good absolutely, of the highest good in the world. No theory can be objectively formulated about the highest good in the world; with this concept we once and for all desert the firm ground of a scientific world-view. But if we enquire into the highest good for men, science gives us a perfectly clear answer. At this point, then, aesthetics is united with ethics.

The Theory of Rights

In addition to the Theory of Virtue, as the practical theory of inner nature, there is also the practical theory of external nature, whose metaphysical basis is to be found in the philosophical Theory of Rights.

'Philosophical Theory of Rights' was the title of a work published by Fries in 1803, at the age of thirty. Fries wrote many works full of ingenious thoughts and discoveries, but this more than any other—any of his systematic works, at least—bears the stamp of genius.

The principle of this philosophical Theory of Rights is determined by the law of rights and so by the moral law itself. Fries shows that the law of rights provides the content of the moral law; a fundamental discovery which laid the foundations for the construction of the scientific philosophy of rights. In previous attempts at such construction, in the school of so-called natural law, the principle of the science had been looked for in the concept of *freedom*. This is a mistake which Kant also shared and which brought his metaphysic of rights to grief; indeed the philosophy of rights inherited this mistake from Kant and still retains the legacy today. Fries shows with great clarity and rigour that this concept cannot be used to determine the principle of the Theory of Rights. As he shows, it gives us no criterion of right at all, and if we try to use it for this purpose it turns out to be an unsocial principle, which he jokingly calls the 'principle of intellectual unsociability', because it would really abolish society, instead of providing it with a law. The point where Theory of Rights must be seen to apply is the point where men depend on each other, where they live in society. They act on each other, and so one is dependent on another, for the results of the efforts of one depend on the contribution of another. A reciprocal limitation of freedom is here unavoidable. The only question is by what rule this reciprocal limitation of the freedom of both is to take place. The first principle in the Theory of Rights is not, therefore, freedom, but rather the rule for this practically necessary limitation on freedom. This rule is given by the law of equality of persons. Not freedom, but equality, is the right. If right consisted in freedom then, as Fries pertinently remarks, the Theory of Rights would not be a theory of rights, but a theory of the limitation of rights, which is absurd. Combined with this advance towards the correct determination of the philosophical principle of the Theory of Rights is another which seems at first sight to conflict with it, that is the abrogation of natural right. The school of natural rights had tried to solve the problem of the philosophy of rights by proposing to work out from pure reason a code of rights. This attempt came to nothing, and Fries' theory shows why it was fundamentally impracticable. For the principle of equality of persons, which is the only one we can apply here, is not a constitutive principle of a system of rights, not, that is to say, a principle from which by a process of progressive proof a code of statements of rights could logically be developed; it is simply a regulative principle for experience. It merely helps in criticizing an ordinance of justice given on other grounds and positively determinate. There is no such thing as natural right; every determinate right requires positive legislation, 'positive' in the sense that it is determined not merely by insight but by arbitrary decree. So the principle of equality of persons is simply a criterion by which to judge positive legislation. It shows us how to develop any historically given legislation in accordance with the idea of right.

Fries thus overcomes at one and the same time both the opposed errors contending for hegemony in the philosophy of rights; the error of the school of natural rights and that of the historical school of rights. For while the school of natural rights looks for a code of rights derived from pure reason, the historical school of rights turns every right into a mere product of historical development, thus denying that there can be any genuine philosophy of right at all. This makes it appear as though rejection of natural rights would compel us to adopt the position of the historical school of rights, and conversely. This view, and the resulting conflict between the two schools, is unavoidable so long as one takes the philosophical principle of rights to be constitutive, disregarding its formal and limiting character.

Now it might seem that the purely philosophical content of the Theory of Rights is exhausted by the establishment of the basic rule of equality of persons. That is not so; and the reason, as Fries shows, is that for the law of right to be applicable in nature certain general conditions are presupposed, which must be fulfilled before the idea of rights can be applied to nature—conditions which can be worked out *a priori*, as conditions for the applicability of concepts of right in nature. For the law of right can be applied in nature only if one presupposes a community of rational beings. It does not require that rational beings live together in a community and so that they must found a society, but it does require that if they wish to live in a community they should treat each other according to the law of equality of persons. In nature, however, there is no direct community of minds, all community depending instead on physical mediation. So it is only by means of the physical conditions under which rational community can occur in nature that the law of right can find application. These conditions are contained in what Fries calls the formulae of subsumption of the philosophical Theory of Rights. We can discover them simply by analysing the concept of *a rational community whose interaction is physical in character*. We are not here concerned with the conditions for applying the law of right to a particular historically given situation—conditions which of course could only be determined empirically; we are concerned with conditions without which the law of right could not be thought of as applying in nature at all. These conditions therefore belong to the pure philosophical Theory of Rights, and the law of right confers practical necessity on them as conditions for its own applicability.

We obtain the particular laws of the pure Theory of Rights, what Fries calls 'general legislation', when we subsume under the basic rule of equality of persons these general conditions on which that rule can be applied.

In order for rational action and reaction, physically mediated, to be possible it is first of all required that thoughts should be communicated by means of language. For it is only by the use of a particular language, by the unambiguous coordination of external signs and thoughts, that rational beings in nature can recognize each other as such. As moreover every action by rational beings in nature consists of influencing external objects at will, rational action and reaction can occur only on the condition that things are used. And as the use of a thing at will by one person excludes the use of the same thing by another, the distribution into mine and thine, i.e. exclusiveness in the use of things on the part of one person or another, forms the second condition for a rational community in nature. The first condition implies the necessity of contracts; the second, that these contracts should concern the distribution of property.

These two conditions are not, however sufficient for justice to apply in nature, for rightness of conduct depends on the understanding of what is right and on the good will of the agent. If insight into right is lacking, which in nature is always possible, this leads to error and so to disputes about the right; if good will is lacking, this leads to deliberate trespassing on rights and so to crime. The settlement of disputes about rights requires a declaration of law independent of the contingent insight of individuals, in short, an external law and a verdict corresponding to it; and similarly the right settling of accounts with crime involves a diminution of rights corresponding to the deliberate offence against rights, in brief the combination of that external law with an appropriate law of punishment.

We thus obtain the four basic laws of the pure philosophical

Theory of Rights, deriving from the formulae of subsumption as conditions of the applicability of the law of rights in nature: the validity of contract, the distribution of property according to the basic law of equality of persons, legal decision of disputes about right in accordance with a positive law, and just punishment of crime.

These results of Fries' theory give him two particular advantages over his predecessors with their theory of natural rights. First there is the statement, of decisive importance in application of the theory, that the law of the State is no concern of the philosophical Theory of Rights, but only of the theory of political prudence, so that the labours of the school of natural rights, and even of Kant, to discover a principle for a just constitution of the State were due to a mistaken conception of the task. It also becomes quite clear that there is no principle for a natural law of property, and in particular that no such principle can be based, as intended by the school of natural rights and once more by Kant, on an alleged right of prime possession or of labour at a thing. All law of property depends in the first place on agreement, and is therefore positive in origin, and all the law of right can demand of this agreement is that the distribution of property should follow the principle of the equality of persons.

Politics

That is as far as the results of the pure philosophical Theory of Rights go. They only propound a task, describe an aim, which should be realized in human society. To realize it is the business of politics— and is additional to the pure Theory of Rights just as the task of seeing that the moral law is recognized is a task for education, additional to the Theory of Virtue. There the need is, following an imperative of virtue additional to the moral law, to set up an independent force to ensure that moral requirements are recognized in nature, and here the need is to set up such a force to ensure that the law of right is recognized in nature. The force here is the external one of State compulsion.

In developing this theory of politics great importance attaches to the statement just mentioned; that there is no principle for a just constitution of the State, so that judging between possible constitutions is always a matter for the theory of political prudence. This assertion leads to a destructive critique of all the theories of the State based on natural rights, which led to so many attempts at determining the so-called rights of the ruler and rights of the people and their reciprocal limitations, with the intention of devising a constitution which would provide a political guarantee for a just relation between people and ruler. This is a pseudo-problem. The business of politics, on the theory of rights, is not to deal with the relations between people and ruler, but with the proper relations between individual members of the people. It is the task of establishing some power for the external protection of the proper relationship between individuals. This is called the power of the government. The relationship between people and ruler is therefore based on the addition of a power to a relationship of right which is separate and independent of it. It is contradictory to try by means of the constitution to give a political guarantee to the relationship of right between ruler and people.

This also settles the old dispute about the right to revolt. The proposition that there can be no right to revolt is correct in itself; but in the form in which we find it in the natural-right theory of Absolutism, and also in Kant, it served simply as support for the reactionary inference that revolution must be prohibited or that the ruler has a right against revolution. On the other hand it has been quite rightly disputed whether there is any original right to rule, and so great efforts have been made to defend the right to revolt in the name of the sovereignty of the people—a view which if followed to its logical conclusion leads to complete rejection of the State, i.e. to anarchism. Fries' discovery shows that there is neither a right to revolt nor a right against revolt. So when Fries repeats Kant's asssertion that 'the people has no right to revolt', he adds 'and the ruler has no right against it'. This single statement destroys at one stroke that whole grand series of constitutions based on natural rights, which one and all—autocratic as well as democratic, absolutist as well as anarchist— take the same pseudo-problem as their starting-point.

Having once got rid of this pseudo-science of natural rights, which survives even today in constitutional law, the way is open for us to tackle without prejudice the only task that is appropriate at this point. If the relationship between people and government must not be decided on legal but only on political grounds, by its suitability for the purpose of guaranteeing rights, and if in particular there are no political institutions to compel the ruler to respect the rights of the people—since otherwise there would have to be set over him some higher power to limit him, which would contradict the concept of *a ruler*—if therefore the use of government power depends in any case on the ruler's insight and intention at a given time, then the only way to get a government which will guarantee right is to make those with sufficient insight and character into rulers—a proposition which takes us straight back to Plato's ideal that rulers should be chosen neither by birth nor by election but by an education appropriate to their calling.

In working out his political philosophy Fries gives a clear and forthright statement of the consequences of applying to human society criteria derived from the philosophy of right. He thus comes to what he calls the critique of all positive legislation. Political philosophy here acquires a genuine content. Unlike the critique of constitutional philosophy which, in opposing the dogmatic theory of natural rights, had of necessity been polemical, the basic ideas in this critique of all positive legislation can be worked out *a priori*. The principle most fruitful here is the law that property should be distributed in accordance with the basic rule of equality of persons. This is the necessary limitation imposed by right on all positive ordinances.

Dominant in this field at that time was the well-known theory of the older Liberalism, such as we find in the writing of Wilhelm von Humboldt, who tried to define the limits of the activity of the state. This theory rejects any intervention by the state in the free play of forces as an unjustified limitation of freedom. It is, in effect, just a consistent application to the field of political economy of the principle of freedom derived from 'natural rights'. This theory, which had achieved unlimited dominance, is sharply and decisively attacked by Fries. He sees clearly the anti-social consequences which the application of this principle of economic freedom is bound to bring about.

His contribution is all the more valuable in this respect as he is very far from falling into the opposite error, easily committed, of dogmatically denying all economic freedom and so all private property —a mistake in which most of the later pioneers of Socialism were involved. Instead he remains entirely loyal to the view that the law of equality of persons is only of regulative significance. He shows that individual equality, correctly understood, does not require equality of possessions, but only equal opportunity for a decent standard of living, i.e. that it should be equally open to everyone by his own labour to satisfy his needs. Now these needs are different in degree and kind for different individuals; indeed, as we develop culturally, work itself —and not just work in general, but a particular sort of work—may become more and more of a need, so that a uniform distribution of possessions would be even more unjustified the more these needs come to differ in the course of development. But the decision exactly how far the limitation of individual freedom must go in a given case, if we are to come as near as may be to condition of individual equality, this decision must be left to experience. It cannot be settled in general on philosophical principles, but only in each given case by reference to the circumstances of that case.

Fries' battle in the economic field against the dogmatic theory of freedom marks an advance which raises him, as a pioneer of modern social politics, far above the limitations of his age. It is even more remarkable how boldly he wages the same war in the field of cultural policy. For he shows that the slogan of Liberalism, the dogma of tolerance, is of no more use as a guide here than in economics. For mere neutrality on the part of the State cannot guarantee individual freedom here either; freedom from State control does even less here than in economic matters to prevent the oppression of one person by another in the State. Indeed it is only to the State that the person oppressed can in either case look for help against his oppressor, and find it. The principle of tolerance would merely support spiritual tyranny and priestly despotism. It is precisely in the defence of individuals against spiritual slavery that state intervention becomes essential.

Fries is not, however, content to apply his principles of right simply to politics; he extends their application to the whole of human society, and also to the interrelationships of States. In this field Kant had anticipated him. But what appears in Kant more as a happy lapse from logic is derived by Fries as a necessary consequence from the principle of the Theory of Rights. He provides a justification for international law sufficient for all modern requirements and for the foundation of a world federation of States.

Moreover while Kant had restricted the State to a purely legal function, Fries goes further, taking political philosophy beyond the sphere of the Theory of Rights to a philosophy of human history. He makes it a theory of the goals of social life in general. Following his theory of the three types of impulse he divides the political task in this sense into the special tasks set by the three goals: popular welfare, educational development, and justice. The purely philosophical part of politics is identical with the application of the Theory of Rights. For only the realizing of right is practically necessary; all other social aims, popular welfare as well as educational development, are conditional upon the claims of right being first fulfilled.

I think I should make special mention here of the important consequences for Fries of his introduction of the impulse towards perfection and of the ideal of intellectual development. This ideal requires us to make the development of culture independent of contingent private interests and to treat it as a public concern. This is a very important idea, especially in considering the relation between State and Church. Fries shows that as only the law of right can hold good as a public law, since it alone concerns the external aspect of society, the Church should not be looked on (as even Kant proposed) as an institution for moral education coming under public laws of virtue. The concept of a public law of virtue is intrinsically contradictory. The Church can only be a public institution for the cultivation of religion. But we must make a further distinction here. Religion, as a mere feeling of devotion, is a purely personal affair and cannot be public. But there is public worship, which is a properly public matter. Here it is the business of the State, by maintaining an independent teaching body, to promote the general scientific and aesthetic education of the people and to combat any hierarchical thirst for power.

Fries thus combines political philosophy, in its deepest sense, with ethics into a theory of the art of ennobling mankind. Its general concern is with the tasks which men set themselves in history, and which they should discharge there by their own efforts—tasks, to use Fries' own words, of 'self education of the human race, the greatest achievement of which would be to bequeath the truth and virtue that has been acquired and to destroy superstition and prejudice'.

THE DISTINCT TASKS OF PHILOSOPHY OF HISTORY AND PHILOSOPHY OF RELIGION

The construction of the ethico-political world-view can only be completed by distinguishing it clearly from the religious world-view. Everything here depends on our understanding the discovery of Fries that, as he put it, the historico-philosophical task is distinct from the religio-philosophical. By philosophy of history Fries means the theory of the tasks for human life in society. He shows that these all come within the field of ethics in the wider sense, understood as practical theory of nature, and that the subject matter of the philosophy of history is therefore quite distinct from that of philosophy of religion. We thus eliminate a very old mistake, which had always been one of the greatest hindrances to the construction of a science of ethics; a mistake responsible also for the miscarriage of Kantian ethics and which involved the most famous philosophers in the history of philosophy after Kant in another mystical adventure. The elimination of this mistake was not only a great contribution to the philosophy of religion, but also cleared the decks for unprejudiced empirical historical research freed from all the mists of metaphysics.

THE SYSTEM OF METAPHYSICS

Fries distinguishes sharply between subjective and objective tele-ology, i.e. between an account of the purposes of human action and one of the purposes for which things exist at all, the goals of the world. This distinction between subjective and objective teleology co-incides with that between the practical theory of nature and the practical theory of Ideas. The practical theory of nature concerns the purposes of things in so far as these can be experienced, while the practical theory of Ideas concerns the purposes of things so far as these lie beyond possible experience. All scientific knowledge, how-ever, is limited to the field of possible experience. The practical theory of Ideas cannot therefore be a science. So a philosophy of history, if it is to be a science, must consist of a practical theory of nature. It is concerned only with the aims which men do, or at least ought to, set before themselves in their communal life. These must not be confused with the objective purposes for which things exist at all, or even with the objective purpose of human history in particular.

The theory of the highest good is thus excluded from ethics alto-gether. The highest good is the object only of religion, not of ethics. It is an unworthy notion that Providence in realizing the highest good in the world depends on the support of men. The aim of mankind is not the aim of God. We are not responsible for the course of the world—but it is up to us to remain loyal in our acts and omissions to the aims which we set ourselves as rational beings. Our destiny can be known to us just as far as is practically necessary, as far, that is, as we strive to know what we ourselves ought to do. But if we go on to ask about the meaning of our life or the destiny of our existence in the world as a whole, our ideas get lost in ineffable feelings. Here, as Fries remarks, 'all human wisdom falls silent, and only the chatter of fools is left'.

The attempt to construct a scientific theory of the purposes of nature had after a long and hard battle been excluded to an increasing extent from the field of external science of nature. But people were all the keener to flirt with this will-o'-the-wisp in the field of history, and the search for an objective teleology was here all the more obstinately entrenched. This took the form of attempting by means of philo-sophical speculation to riddle out the meaning or goal of world history. The most important task to confront Fries here was the expulsion of these speculative will-o'-the-wisps from their final hiding-place; or, to put it another way, the vindication of Naturalism in the historical or ethico-political world-view as well.

Kant's teleology was the breach through which mystical specula-tions were once again able to gain entry to philosophy. This mistake

T

comes out very clearly when Kant reverts to confusing the ethical with the religious world-view, and clearest of all when he confuses the highest good in the world with the highest good for men. The result of this mistake, as can clearly be seen in Kant, is that the subjective problem of getting from the natural view of human history to the ideal view of the eternal Being of things is changed into a supposedly objective problem of getting from the imperfection of the limited and finite human condition to the perfection of divine existence. Hence the supposed task of the philosophy of history of portraying God's coming-to-be as a gradual development in human history, a task which absorbed the energies of the philosophers of the system of identity, who never noticed how foolhardy it was. So once more we have the crazy attempt to develop a theory from Ideas. Fries showed that the apparent fertility of this notion is due simply to the illusions of logical Mysticism and so can be traced back to yet another misuse of that Amphiboly of Concepts of Reflection whose discovery we owe to Kant.

This mistake leads in the philosophy of history to an idealizing and optimistic view of history, confident of unravelling the deeper meaning of history by following out that idea of God coming-to-be: to which can be opposed with equal justification a pessimistic view of history, appealing to the teachings of experience which do not fit in with optimism at all. But owing to the equally mistaken amalgamation of the two world-views, once optimism is abandoned all religious faith in the goodness of the world is also lost, faith which otherwise could have been ranked above that hopeless view of finite being; so that all metaphysics here ends in a pessimistic despair, as can be seen in detail in the history of philosophy in the nineteenth century.

The kernel of truth in this pessimistic view of history, as in every dogmatic metaphysics, is to be found in the negative starting point by which it faces the opposed dogmatism. For there is something unsatisfactory in our view of history, something we could not overcome if we were compelled to consider it the ultimate and final truth of our world-view. This view of history, being open to scientific construction only by the aid of experience, leads to no conclusion about the ultimate aim of history. It shows us only the flourishing and decay of individual peoples and their cultures. Indeed we must regard it as fortunate if anything that one age achieves is bequeathed to another. We have therefore even less reason to expect continuous progress through time. Indeed, we can foresee a predetermined destruction for the whole of developing mankind, following the laws which govern the conditions of organic life on the surface of the earth and which set an end to the continuance of life on the ageing earth. And even if we disregard this limit, which lies outside history, still the general picture is unsatisfying. For the progress still possible within this limit relates only to the impersonal whole. The fact that some final goal can be achieved—if it is a fact—is of no benefit to any one generation: they have all been used simply as a means to an end for this impersonal whole.

This brings out very clearly how unsatisfactory this historical world-view is if we allow it to stand as our final and conclusive world-view. We are led on beyond it solely by recognizing that all human knowledge is limited, so that the religious world-view ranks above all natural views—including the historical.

THE RELIGIO-AESTHETIC WORLD-VIEW

Turning now to the metaphysic of the religious world-view, we require, following the conclusions reached in the Critique of Reason, to consider first its speculative basis and then, with the aid of the practical Schematism of the Ideas, to derive from it the proper principles of the philosophy of religion. Finally, we must deal with the field of intimation, as the proper content of the religio-aesthetic world-view.

The Speculative Basis

The speculative basis for the religious world-view consists in the Idea of the Absolute. This, according to the ideal Schematism of the Categories, is formed by the idea of negating the bounds of the nature-form of our knowledge and thus also those of the basic form of all the world-views considered so far.

We thus obtain a theory very different from that of Kant. Kant had rightly seen that the basic concepts of the philosophy of religion consist in the Ideas of *God, freedom* and *immortality*. But he could not discover the correct justification for the reality of these Ideas, owing to his false theory of transcendental illusion and the resulting view of Ideas as regulative principles for natural science and as postulates of practical reason. Fries shows that these concepts, correctly understood, are simply Ideas of the Absolute which result from schematizing the Categories belonging to the moment of Relation—Being, Cause and Community—by the Idea of negating the bounds to the nature-form of our knowledge.

There is in fact only one way of viewing our knowledge from the perspective of the Absolute, and that is to regard as deleted everything that conflicts with the requirements of that Idea. What remains after this abstraction has been made does permit of an absolutist interpretation. For here the statement holds good—in flat contradiction to Kant's theory of transcendental illusion—that it is not so much the assertion as the denial of transcendental truth for some item of knowledge that requires justification. Wherever in the field of our knowledge no ground can be found for thus denying transcendental truth, the assertion of this transcendental truth must stand, for on the principle of the self-reliance of our reason it is true immediately. According to this principle we must admit as transcendental truth whatever in our knowledge does not conflict with the highest law of our reason, i.e. with absolute synthetic unity and necessity.

Let us then see what is left in our knowledge after performing the required abstraction. Just so much, clearly, and no more, as is still preserved in the pure-intuitive basic form of our knowledge once its continuity and incompletability have been removed. For this continuity and incompletability are limits which, on the Idea of the Absolute, we have to deny.

Let us therefore think of continuity and incompletability as eliminated from the pure-intuitive basic form of our knowledge. We come then to the qualities of sense-perception, which do not conflict with that idea. But we are not able, at least as far as the qualities of outer sense are concerned, to separate these from the pure-intuitive form in which alone we can conceive them intuitively or perceptually. Matter also is not possible without space, which includes it conceptually and in which it is infinitely divisible—and so matter cannot be thought of as something intrinsically existent. So the corporeal view of the world disappears altogether when the required abstraction is made. Nothing positive is left of it at all to stand firm before the Idea.

The situation in the spiritual view of the world is quite different. Here an interpretation based on Ideas is still possible to some extent. The object of this world-view, the mind, which as the *I* is added in thought by pure self-consciousness to the phenomena of inner sense, does not itself come into the forms of pure intuition. And even its qualities, in which it appears to inner sense, namely knowledge, interest, will, are indeed conceived by us in a definite temporal sequence, but do not disappear altogether when we abstract from the form of time. So an interpretation by Ideas is still feasible in this case, though the positive concepts with which to frame it into a proper theory are simply not available. Something real is left, a genuine object, which in itself, i.e. apart from the laws of nature, to which its appearances are subject, does not conflict with the criterion of the ideal Schematism, so that to this extent the Idea of absolute Being can be applied to it, although this object cannot be known from the Idea. Our knowledge of spirit remains bound to the form of nature just as our knowledge of the corporeal world; but the object of this knowledge, the mind itself, does not disappear when we think away the form of nature. So the Idea of absolute Being becomes for us the Idea of the autonomy of the mind, or in brief, the Idea of the soul.

It is only by analogy with the spiritual that we are able to give any sense to the absolute existence of things at all. Consequently we can think of absolute Causality only as action, i.e. as activity of the mind, in accordance with the Idea of the freedom of the will, i.e. its independence of laws of nature.

It is, however, only by the Idea of absolute Community that we come to the ultimate concept of the complete unity of everything that is really real in the dynamic unity of the world. We can think of this absolute Community only through the common dependence of every conditional reality, not on some abstract law, which would possess no essential reality and would disappear once the form of nature was removed, but on a single absolute Cause, which in its turn can be thought of only as the action of an absolute Being—thus bringing us to the Idea of divinity. These are the fundamental thoughts in the profound deduction by which Fries was able to fill the most important gaps left by Kant in his justification of speculative metaphysics and so to resolve the problem of the philosophy of religion.

Fries is very careful to ward off the illusion that this derivation of Ideas would add yet another to the attempts at proving rationalist metaphysics. For from the fact that we are able to think the relationships only in the manner here specified, no inference can be drawn about the Being of things themselves. Nothing is further from Fries' intention in his deduction than a revival of such a psychological fallacy.

A deduction is, however, provided here for the speculative Ideas and so a complete justification for them. For according to the principle of the self-reliance of our reason such a justification requires only that the Ideas be shown to coincide with the immediate knowledge of reason, and this is what is here achieved. As Fries says, there is indeed a science *of* Ideas, yet the critical theorem still holds good that there is no science *from* Ideas.

The Practical Schematism of the Speculative Ideas and the Principles of the Philosophy of Religion

We have now noted the speculative foundation of the philosophy of religion. According to the theory of the Critique of Reason, we shall obtain the proper principles of the philosophy of religion itself only when we combine these speculative foundations with the practical Ideas of absolute worth. This combination is achieved by the principle of the practical Schematism of Ideas. Following this we combine the Idea that absolute worth is practically necessary with the speculative foundation just obtained, and thus obtain the three principles of the philosophy of religion.

Firstly, schematizing the speculative Idea of the soul by the practical Idea of absolute worth we are led to the religious principle of the worth of the independent spirit. The spirit, which was there thought of speculatively as independent, is here thought of practically as an end in itself.

This principle is the one most closely connected with finite phenomena, i.e. in ethics. But the connection is negative. It can be applied only as a prohibition, to the effect that a person must not be used as a mere means for our ends. It is not for us to decide to give positive worth to a person. We can only recognize that worth, and this recognition belongs not to knowledge but to faith.

As an article of faith this principle yields an Idea which cannot be more precisely conceptualized and so admits of no theoretical development, the Idea of the eternal destiny of man. This Idea signifies an insoluble mystery for our knowledge. The eternal destiny of man is not open to investigation. It is an object which we can acknowledge only in faith.

Secondly, by combining the practical Idea of what is of value absolutely with the speculative Idea of freedom of the will we are led to the religious Ideas of good and evil, or to what Fries called the principle of religious accountability.

It is important to get a clear idea of the relation of this religious accountability to the practical view of nature. For the practical view of nature the Idea of the good only sets a goal, that of becoming good, a task dischargeable by the formation of virtue, the gradual strengthening of character. Education can make men better; this possibility exists for them according to laws of nature. The judgment of religion, however, turns out to be quite different. It knows of no getting better, only of being good; and whatever is not completely good is rejected completely, by the religious judgment, as radically evil. What is absolutely good cannot appear in nature; for that would require an infinite force of virtue, the holiness of our will, contrary to the laws of nature, by which every force in nature is finite and can be overcome by a stronger opposing force. The mere fact that the human will is able to appear in nature is therefore something for which the human will must religiously hold itself accountable. If it were not wicked, it would be a holy will, and so could not appear in nature at all. It must therefore hold itself accountable for the fact that it does so, and for all the resulting phenomenal shortcomings, in the form of guilt. It must not seek the reason for this outside itself. That is what the religious principle of accountability asserts.

The religious Idea of the sanctification of our will does not, then, name for us some task of developing our being in nature. It must not be understood as a conversion, completed in time, of the individual or of the human race as a whole; nor as a gradual and progressive process of purification in a future life, for even in this process we should still be subject to the form of nature. It signifies for us a quite insoluble mystery, which can only be acknowledged in faith and is not open to any sort of scientific enquiry.

In the third place, we must combine the Idea of divinity with the Idea of absolute good. Along with the speculative concept of world-unity we have here the practical concept of a world-goal, and the religious principle consists in asserting that the two are identical: that the world can be thought of by us as one only by thinking that it has a single goal, that the ground of Being is conceivable only through the Idea of being-good. The goal of the world must therefore be thought of, in accordance with the Idea of divine holiness, as that which determines the existence of the world. We can think of divinity only as the holy cause of everything that is intrinsically real. This is the principle of religious optimism, in which the Idea of the highest good first reaches complete expression, free of any phenomenal relationship, as the Idea of eternal goodness.

As far as knowledge goes, however, this is yet another insoluble mystery. Fries calls it the mystery of the governance of the world. We can go no further than to state that the governance of the world is the world-rule of the good; and this we can acknowledge only in faith, without being able to work the Idea out scientifically at all. Every attempt to do so involves us in insoluble antinomies. This is one of the enigmas for the mind of every man, to which the differences in intellectual development between men can never make any differ-ence—nor can one man rather than another ever be initiated into this enigma by receiving news of some secret doctrine or by the gift of a higher inspiration imparted to him as a chosen one. Every science of the super-sensible that men may dream up, whether theosophy or Gnosis or any other mystical secret doctrine, even if it really succeeded in extending the bounds of our natural knowledge beyond this earthly life, would still be without any religious interest, for it would still adhere to the finitude of time and so would remain bound to nature. The bounds of the natural form of our knowledge would have to be overcome to achieve a solution of those enigmas. Just as one can say *a priori* with apodeictic certainty that no man will ever succeed in breaking the bounds set to the nature-form of his knowledge, so one can assert with the same apodeictic certainty that every claim to have achieved this always betrays the claimer as a self-exposed philosophical ignoramus, if nothing worse.

Natural Religion and the Principle of Aesthetic Realism

Thus far the theory of faith takes us, i.e. to recognition of the necessary bounds of all human knowledge. It is the foundation of natural religion. Through it we acquire the certainty that there is such a religion, independent of all revelation, of all historic or superstitious beliefs, and to which every man can gain entry by virtue of his rationality. But this is just the abstract foundation of religion. Religion itself is not a matter of concepts, nor even of belief, but of life. The positive moment which needs to be added to those negative Ideas of faith, if we are to go beyond mere beliefs and achieve religion, is not contrary to natural religion. It would involve such an opposition only if this positive element is misinterpreted as a positive truth of faith, in short as a dogma. The significance of that Idea of the denial of limitations is precisely this: it makes clear that what is positive in religion is not to be sought in a dogma, in any truth of faith, since this is merely negative in origin. The positive content of religion is exclusively aesthetic in origin. There are, moreover, two elements which need to be distinguished here.

Positive religion is not confined to the emotional life. For this is a property possessed privately by each individual and cannot be shared. The element additional to feeling which makes religion something shareable consists in the symbols, i.e. in the pictorial means of expression by which the Idea of faith is set out positively. Only poetry can create these religious symbols. So no science can pass judgment on questions of precedence in such a symbolism, nor can any dogma decide these matters. Good taste is here the sole and final judge, since if we understand the matter right the question here is not one of scientific truth but only of the beauty of the picture.

In this field therefore philosophy has no direct claim; it can only reject the encroachments of a false and misleading philosophy. The situation is rather different as concerns the emotional element in religious life. Here certain basic forms of religious life can be outlined philosophically. For there is here a natural division of the emotional moods, which can be shown with the aid of the table of the Ideas of faith. For these emotional moods are simply the means for subsuming perceptual phenomena under religious Ideas. This subsumption cannot be performed by means of any inference. No mediating concept is available with which to perform such an inference, but in place of this mediating concept there appear what we call the religious emotional moods. The judgment in which we subsume the perceived phenomena under the Ideas of faith is not theoretical but aesthetic. The object of aesthetic judgment is what we called an aesthetic Idea, i.e. a form of intuitive unity which escapes all conceptual determination and which is for that very reason appropriate for subsumption under the Idea of the Absolute. This subsumption is accomplished in the religious feeling which Fries calls the feeling of intimation.

Now clearly a classification can be made by associating with the three Ideas of faith set out in the moment of Relation an aesthetic Idea in the feeling of intimation. By this division we obtain three possible basic moods of the religious feeling of intimation, namely inspiration, resignation, and devotion. Inspiration is the mood of feeling by which an aesthetic Idea is related to the religious Idea of the soul. It consists in the self-reliance of the mind on its eternal destiny. Resignation is the mood of feeling by which an aesthetic Idea is related to the religious Idea of freedom; it consists in humbly subjecting oneself to fate, conscious of one's own guilt. Devotion is the mood by which an aesthetic Idea is related to the religious Idea of divinity; it consists in the trust that the world is ruled by eternal goodness.

Corresponding to this classification there are the three basic forms of the aesthetic Ideas themselves which, following Fries, we could call the epic, dramatic, and lyrical aesthetic Ideas. (See Table XIV.)

Connected with this classification of the aesthetic Ideas according to the three forms of Relation is another depending on whether the Idea to which they are referred is speculative-religious or practical-religious, the Idea of absolute unity in the Being of things or the Idea of the absolute purpose of their existence. To this corresponds the distinction between the speculative and teleological forms of aesthetic

(XIV) The Aesthetic Ideas Classified by the three Forms of Relation

| | Ideas | | Moods | Aesthetic |
Categories	Speculative	Practical	of feeling	Ideas
Substance	Soul	Worth	Inspiration	Epic
Cause	Freedom	Guilt	Resignation	Dramatic
Community	Divinity	Holiness	Devotion	Lyrical

Ideas. Hence the contrast between so-called beauty of form and beauty of expression. Beauty of form—beauty of figure for example, or of performance—involves an aesthetic Idea in so far as it is related to the Idea of absolute unity. Beauty of expression involves an aesthetic Idea in so far as it is applied not so much to the Idea of unity but to the Idea of an absolute purpose. This distinction coincides with one made in more recent aesthetics between the spirit of Greek and of Gothic art—which is indeed a very fruitful division for aesthetics. The discovery of this distinction was, however, already clearly made in Fries' separation of the speculative from the teleological form of aesthetic Ideas.

This shows that a genuine aesthetic cannot be constructed independently of religious philosophy, and that the traditional way of thinking which separates aesthetic from religious philosophy leads to an artificial severance and to the exclusion from aesthetics of what is real. It is only in relation to the religious Ideas that the aesthetic Ideas acquire their deeper interest and obtain their proper significance. If we abstract from this relation, all the serious and important background of aesthetic judgments disappears, leaving us merely with a play of amusement for our imagination, following the idea, central to Kant's aesthetics, of a subjective pleasure in beholding the beautiful as the supposed basis for aesthetic judgments. The true nature of aesthetic appreciation consists rather in what Kant called the intellectual interest in the beautiful, which should not, however, be taken in a moral sense, but is identical with the religious interest in the beautiful. We are thus brought not to aesthetic Idealism, which in Kant is simply the final result of his mistaken Formal Idealism, but to aesthetic Realism, which claims for aesthetic judgment the full seriousness of truth, a truth to be found in that of the religious world-view. It is in this theory of the truth of beauty that the significance for the world-view of the self-reliance of our reason finds its most profound and conclusive expression. Absolute truth, if human knowledge can attain to it at all, is the property of the religio-aesthetic world-view, and for the very same reason which requires us to deny it to the other world-views. This brings out the profound meaning of that remark of Fries' about the truth of beauty, which is 'the truest truth of our mind'. Science itself, realizing its own limitations, subjects itself to the higher truth of this religio-aesthetic world-view.

Postscript*

Schiller, with the grandness, precision, and fearlessness of judgment which are characteristic of him, writes to Goethe about the work of Kant:

'It does not shock me to think that the law of change, from which no work of man or even of God is exempt, will destroy the form of this as of every philosophy. Yet its foundations will remain; for in every age of the human race, while Reason existed, people have implicitly recognised those foundations and have acted more or less in accordance with them. The philosophy of our friend Fichte may not be in this position' (28th October, 1794).

Nelson's *Progress and Regress in Philosophy* is in fundamental agreement with this judgment of Schiller's (Nelson ranked Schiller above Goethe as a thinker, and made a systematic study of his ethical works). This is clear from three far-reaching assertions of Nelson's:

1. that there are unshakable foundations for philosophy;
2. that the work of Kant and of his true successor Fries in laying these foundations was epoch-making;
3. that for Fichte, Schelling and Hegel to claim succession to Kant is a usurpation.

To these must be added a fourth main theme of *Progress and Regress:* that Empiricism is no more adequate than idealistic speculation as a scientific philosophy.

Schiller's assessment is pertinent and profound, but lacks further justification. In Nelson it is justified with great precision and applied in detail. It can be said without exaggeration that the development and presentation of this body of thought in Nelson is unusually transparent. A particular clarity in the sequence of thought and in expression was already evident in Nelson's earliest works. It was also a typical and impressive characteristic of his activity as a teacher, from which resulted among other things his *Progress and Regress in Philosophy*.

* This postscript by the late Julius Kraft refers to Volumes I and II which, in the German edition, were published in one volume.

The aim of the present posthumous edition was to select the fullest versions, and those most mature in presentation, from the lectures on 'Progress and Regress in Metaphysics' (1919–1926). Some abbreviations and changes were unavoidable, but these have been kept to the minimum in order to preserve Nelson's individual style of presentation.

The link between book and lecture gives the work a liveliness which—combined with its transparence—makes it a *gradus ad Parnassum* of philosophizing. An unbiased and attentive reader is thus afforded an unusual opportunity of taking part as one competent to pass independent judgment—under the guidance of a mind of remarkable penetration and constructive power—in one of the most significant intellectual developments of recent times.

This is indeed an unusual privilege, for few philosophers of importance have dealt with the history of philosophy. Among them Aristotle was the first, and Russell one of the last. To them we may add Nelson—in direct line of succession to Fries' classic, *The History of Philosophy and the Stages of its Scientific Development* (1837, 1840). Fries' name also stands for the sytematic approach on which Nelson's work is ultimately based. It is Kant's approach, purified by provision of a consistently constructed psychological starting-point for the Critique of Reason, and by an equally consistent construction of a non-agnostic world-view. This critical world-view provides the background to Nelson's work; though the principle which really animates the argument is not this so much as elementary logical and psychological considerations which at the same time lead to that philosophical world-view.

2

The title of Nelson's lectures, 'Progress and Regress in Metaphysics' was replaced in the book by *Progress and Regress in Philosophy*. The title Nelson gave to his lectures marked them off explicitly from a history of logic. For good reasons of his own he devotes most of his exposition to a discussion of the critical enquiry preliminary to metaphysics and puts much less emphasis on the construction of the corresponding metaphysical systems. This procedure would not meet the expectations of most readers of a book on the history of metaphysics, and for this reason alone an alteration in the title seemed appropriate.

On considering the work as a whole certain differences can be made out in the character of its main parts.

In his discussion of Hume and Kant Nelson appears mainly

as a profound logical and psychological analyst who exposes the structure of a major body of theory so as to identify and eliminate any parts that are structurally unsound. Anyone who works through this analysis carefully, without losing sight of the overall major connections, will gain much greater clarity and freedom in approaching the work of Hume and Kant.

In his discussion of the post-Kantian *Regress* Nelson's critical and polemical powers really celebrate their triumph. Anyone who is open to logical reasoning can here persuade himself that the post-Kantian development in the nineteenth century went astray, how far it went astray, and why the mistakes were made—mistakes which the twentieth century has continued in other forms.

The section on Fries is the first systematic discussion of his work as a whole and is therefore of the greatest scientific interest. Had Nelson been granted longer life, he would certainly have completed this exposition by providing a critique—for which he had laid the basis in his earlier works.

This systematic approach is not the only remarkable feature of the work as a whole. What strikes the reader is the way it is sustained by Nelson's well-founded conviction of its significance and general cultural value, described by Nelson himself in this way:

'In general: to go into detail only where this is necessary to correct the work of others; not to recapitulate their work. Others can do the rest. They can't do this. But to give special attention to points not found in previous critical expositions or not made sufficiently clear there. What I am giving is a revision of the philosophical and cultural tradition of the nineteenth century. And to expound also my conception of the significance of critical, i.e. Friesian philosophy for the history of culture in general and for the history of philosophy in particular.'

The assurance expressed in this written monologue also comes out in another document containing Nelson's preparatory notes for the bold and heretical position which he took up in the philosophical interpretation of modern physics, some hints of which he developed in his chapter on Fries entitled 'The Hylological World-view'. An understanding and interested reader will appreciate the relevant passage from Nelson's notes, which brings out his intensive and disciplined mode of work and is also a measure of the concentration needed in order to penetrate into Nelson's *Progress and Regress in Philosophy:*

'Let us rather put the question the other way: mystical tendencies in contemporary physics? Criticism is needed for instance of the modern field-concept: Cartesian substantializing of space. (Pythagoreanism, not Neo-Platonism.) Faraday (Lines of Force), Maxwell (Period. Changes of

Condition), Lorenz (Ether), Hertz (rigid Combinations), Einstein-Minkowsky. Geometrizing of Physics. Influence—the Cartesian prejudice against *actio in distans* and against the concept of force in general. The dynamic approach losing ground. Restoration of Cartesianism as against the justification of dynamics in Newton-Kant-Fries.

Geometrizing of physics but at the same time empiricizing of geometry. Falling out with geometrical intuition. Replacement of Euclidean space and Newtonian time by Minkowski's space-time-schema. Minkowski's world the substantialized space-time-continuum. Physical Spinozism.

Exclusion of action at a distance (restriction to optical means of comparison of time) leads automatically in combination with the problem of measurement of time to the theory of relativity. This therefore: metaphysical reinterpretation of the subjective limitations on measurement of time: anthropomorphism, not recognized as such. Comes out in the theory itself by making absolute the speed of light, and length. (Radius of curvature of space as straight line.)

Difficulties of even requiring absence of contradiction in phys. theory involves necessity perhaps for lengthy periods to dispense with more far-reaching requirements of rational induction (synthetic criteria).

Pragmatic interpretation justified and important, as expression of this renunciation (forgoing the claim to truth), but ridiculous as a final aim.

Important: as warning against hypostatizing the world of Minkowski.

In general: Nominalism *and* Realism in modern physics

Conventionalism, as result of Empiricism

as *mathemat.* Mysticism. (Pythagoreanism.) see above but also *logical*: e.g. Energy as substance.'

Nelson's analytic and critical treatment of the history of philosophy contrasts sharply both with the historicism of the older histories of the subject and with the modern hermeneutic approach. Its business is not to assemble and compare scraps of philosophical thought, nor is it engaged, on the pretext of interpreting facts from philosophical history, in turning them into their opposite—as Jaspers, for example, in *The Great Philosophers*, first quotes the clear and important statement of Kant's:

'It was my serious endeavour to prove statements or disprove them, not for the sake of proving a sceptical theory, but because I suspected an illusion of the understanding, and wished to discover in what it consists',

and later states as a general principle for interpreting philosophical ideas, including those of Kant, that

'Circles, tautologies and contradictions cannot be avoided when philosophising.'

In contrast to such arbitrary interpretation, Nelson's method in the history of philosophy is to apply precise philosophical and psychological abstractions analytically and critically to carefully sifted sources: not with the philological and historical aim of reproducing as many details as possible of a philosophical idea, but rather in order to illuminate systematically its typical features.

There are various possible approaches to such an elucidation. For instance, Nelson's epistemological approach in discussing Kant and his successors could be fruitfully complemented by a treatment mainly concerned with the world-views of the philosophers in question. This would make it clear that the various elements of dogmatic metaphysics in Kant lend further support (apart from the dogma of epistemology) to the speculations of the school of Fichte, Schelling and Hegel, and so also to the materialist and positivist reactions against those speculations.

A combination of the metaphysical approach with that of the Theory of Reason would also make it possible—and absolutely necessary—to carry these analytic and critical soundings right on into the twentieth century. Only then would a well-balanced and profound assessment become possible of that motley and changing philosophical development which begins with Schopenhauer, Nietzsche, Positivism and Pragmatism, and continues with Existentialist Irrationalism and Linguistic Philosophy, these public declarations of bankruptcy of philosophical knowledge.

Beyond this there is a still more comprehensive aim, that of applying the idea of 'progress and regress' to the whole history of philosophy. That is a task for more than one generation of competent minds capable of profound penetration into the object of their study.

4

Nelson's *Progress and Regress in Philosophy* raises even more profound questions concerning the development of philosophy itself. Here there is wide scope for the Critique of Reason and for systematic philosophy. In both these fields there are fundamental problems still unsolved which require to be tackled. Let me name a few of them:

1. It can be shown that even sophisticated formulations of the Critique of Reason are not free of logical difficulties (particularly those of circularity). The problem therefore arises of so limiting the scope of this critique that these difficulties disappear.

2. The analysis given here of all the elements of knowledge, from perception to ideas, cannot be regarded as definitive. In each of these areas some problems remain open, for example the problem of the necessity of completing the pure intuition of Space and Time by a pure intuition of non-spatial and non-temporal mathematical givenness.

3. Modern developments in cultural life have produced a series of notions and forms new in type, whose correct location needs to be determined philosophically.

These forms stretch from symbolic logic, abstract mathematics and the sciences of experience with their various degrees of precision to modern art and to religious, social and political life.

For lack of proper philosophical classification these modern phenomena give occasion for a general attack on reason in the name of modernity.

Philosophy must reject such pseudo-revolutionary claims and at the same time garner the philosophical fruits of these modern cultural developments.

4. Systematic philosophy awaits a thorough-going re-working of all its disciplines, from logic to the philosophy of religion. The results of the enquiries postulated under 2 and 3 would be indispensable aids here. Elementary questions, such as the question whether certain fields, ethics for example, can be treated purely *a priori* at all, must be discussed afresh. Subtle analyses, such as that of the character of a transcendent object, must be carried out.

This survey gives some idea of the range and depth of the systematic enquiries opened up by Nelson's *Progress and Regress in Philosophy*. Nelson has cleared the way for new constructive work. On this basis the task can more easily be undertaken of adding further advances to the great steps forward made in philosophy since Hume and Kant.

Frankfurt-on-Main, 1960   Julius Kraft

U

BIBLIOGRAPHICAL NOTE

on foreign titles englished in the text

[*ET* = English translation]

164 J. F. Fries, *Reinhold, Fichte und Schelling* (1803; reprinting in *Sämtliche Schriften*, 24)

267 J. F. Fries, *Philosophische Rechtslehre und Kritik aller positiven Gesetzgebung* ... (1803; reprinted in *Sämtliche Schriften*, 9, 1970)

251 J. F. Fries, *Die Mathematische Naturphilosophie nach philosophischer Methode bearbeitet. Ein Versuch* (1822; reprinting in *Sämtliche Schriften*, 13)

248 J. F. Fries, *Neue Kritik der Vernunft* (1807); 2nd ed. Anthropologische Kritik der Vernunft (3 vols., 1828–31); reprinted in *Sämtliche Schriften*, 4–6, 1969)

168 J. F. Fries, *System der Logik* (3rd ed., 1837; reprinted in *Sämtliche Schriften*, 7, 1971)

190 J. F. Fries, *Die Geschichte der Philosophie, dargestellt nach den Fortschritten ihrer wissenschaftlichen Entwickelung* (1837–40; reprinted in *Sämtliche Schriften*, 18–19, 1969)

265 J. F. Fries, *Handbuch der praktischen Philosophie oder der philosophischen Zwecklehre*, Teil I. *Ethik oder die Lehren der Lebensweisheit* (1818; reprinted in *Sämtliche Schriften*, 10)

76 G. W. F. Hegel, *Enzyklopädie der philosophischen Wissenschaften im Grundrisse. Zum Gebrauch seiner Vorlesungen;* I *Die Logik*, II *Die Naturphilosophie*, III *Die Philosophie des Geistes* (1817; 2nd ed., 1827; 3rd ed., 1830) [*ET* of I from edition of 1843, W. Wallace, *The Logic of Hegel* (1873)]. The notes or additions (*Zusätze*) were compiled by the original editors from notes taken at successive lecture-courses: cf. W. Kaufmann, *Hegel* (1966), p. 228.

98 G. W. F. Hegel, *Naturrecht und Staatswissenschaft im Grundrisse. Zum Gebrauch für seine Vorlesungen. Grundlinien zur Philosophie des Rechts* (1821) [*ET* T. M. Knox, *Hegel's Philosophy of Right* (1942)]

27 F. H. Jacobi, *David Hume über den Glauben, oder Realismus und Idealismus. Ein Gespräch* (1787)

165 I. Kant, 'Untersuchung über die Deutlichkeit der Grundsätze der natürlichen Theologie und der Moral' in *Dissertation qui a remporté le prix proposé par l'Académie Royale ... avec les pièces qui ont concouru* (Berlin, 1764) [*ET* in G. B. Kerferd and D. E. Walford, *Kant Selected Pre-critical Writings* ... (1968)]

3 I. Kant, *Critik der reinen Vernunft* (1781) [*ET* N. K. Smith, *Immanuel Kant's Critique of Pure Reason* (1929), with paging of editions of 1781 (A) and 1787 (B)]

264 I. Kant, *Die Metaphysik der Sitten* (1796–97); see also *Grundlegung zur Metaphysik der Sitten* (1783) [*ET* H. J. Paton, *The Moral Law* (1948)]

73 I. Kant, *Metaphysische Anfangsgründe der Naturwissenschaft* (1786)

30 S. Maimon, *Versuch über die Transcendentalphilosophie, mit einem Anhang über die symbolische Erkenntnis und Anmerkungen* (1790; reprinted in *Aetas Kantiana*, 1970)

30 S. Maimon, *Versuch einer neuen Logik oder Theorie des Denkens* (1794: 2nd ed., 1798, reprinted in *Aetas Kantiana*)

30 S. Maimon, *Kritische Untersuchungen über den menschlichen Geist, oder das höhere Erkenntniss- und Willensvermögen* (1797; reprinted in *Aetas Kantiana*, Brussels, 1969)

103 K. Marx, *Das Kapital* [*ET Capital*, trs. Eden and Cedar Paul, 1933]

107 K. Marx, *Der Bürgerkrieg in Frankreich* (1871) [*ET* anon. *The Civil War in France* (London, 1933)]

25 G. S. A. Mellin, *Enzyklopädisches Wörterbuch der kritischen Philosophie, oder Versuch einer fasslichen und vollständigen Erklärung der in Kant's kritischen und dogmatischen Schriften enthaltenen Begriffe und Sätze; mit Nachrichten, Erläuterungen und Vergleichungen aus der Geschichte der Philosophie begleitet und alphabetisch geordnet* (6 vols., 1797–1804; reprinted in *Aetas Kantiana* Brussels, 1969)

38 C. L. Reinhold, *Briefe über die Kantische Philosophie* (2 vols., 1790–92)

38 C. L. Reinhold, *Versuch einer neuen Theorie des menschlichen Vorstellungsvermögens . . .* (1789)

38 C. L. Reinhold, *Beyträge zur Berichtigung bisheriger Misverständnisse der Philosophen* (2 vols., 1790–94)

38 C. L. Reinhold, *Über das Fundament des philosophischen Wissens* (1791)

90 M. J. Schleiden, *Schellings und Hegels Verhältnis zur Naturwissenschaft (als Antwort auf die Angriffe des Herrn Nees von Esenbeck . . .)* (1844)

164 M. J. Schleiden, 'Jakob Friedrich Fries, der Philosoph der Naturforscher', in *Westermanns Monatshefte* (1857)

76 O. Schloemilch, 'Philosophische Aphorismen eines Mathematikers', in *Zeitschrift für Philosophie und philosophische Kritik*, 70.1 (1877)

258 Heinrich Schmid (Professor of Philosophy at Heidelberg), *Versuch einer Metaphysik der inneren Natur* (1834)

52 [G. E. Schulze], published anonymously *Aenesidemus; oder, über das Fundament der von Herrn Professor Reinhold in Jena gelieferten Elementarphilosophie, nebst einer Verteidigung des Skepticismus gegen die Anmassungen der Vernunftkritik* (1792; reprinted in *Aetas Kantiana* Brussels, 1969)

25 Johann Schultz, or Schulze, *Erläuterungen über des Herrn Professor Kant Critik der reinen Vernunft* . . . (1784; 2nd ed., 1791, reprinted in *Aetas Kantiana* Brussels, 1969)

25 Johann Schulze, *Prüfung der Kantischen Critik der reinen Vernunft* (2 vols., 1789–92; reprinted in *Aetas Kantiana* Brussels, 1969)

NOTE ON FRIES

None of Fries' writings has yet been translated into English. For a short list of his writings, and a note of some German books about him, see the entries in Baldwin's *Dictionary of Philosophy* and in the *Encyclopaedia Britannica* (11th edition; later editions give shorter versions of the same entry). Both mention E. L. Th. Henke, *Jakob Friedrich Fries aus seinem handschriftlichen Nachlass dargestellt* (1867). Henke's book is a comprehensive biography of Fries, but gives no introduction into his philosophy. A concise and very apt exposition of the main lines of that philosophy is contained in a contribution by Alexander Mourelatos to *The Encyclopaedia of Philosophy*, ed. Edwards (1967). Mourelatos stresses both the close connection of Fries' philosophical thinking with Kant's Critique of Reason and the critical development of Kant's Critique by Fries. The only book in English, apart from the present volume, is Rudolph Otto, *The Philosophy of Religion based on Kant and Fries* (1909; trs. E. B. Dicker, 1931). This gives a substantial and competent exposition of Fries' revision of Kant's theory of knowledge and of morality, and then applies this to theology.

The rare and brief references to Fries by English writers on the history of philosophy appear to be traditional formulae handed down from his Hegelian opponents. In the German-speaking countries, too, the consideration given to Fries' writings is rather superficial—a phenomenon analysed by Nelson in this present volume (p. 161f).

Nelson considered Fries the only one who really developed Kantian philosophy in the nineteenth century. Two works translated from the German provide some useful summaries: H. Höffding, trs. B. E. Meyer, *A History of Modern Philosophy* (Macmillan, 1900, republished Dover 1955), Book VIII, C—vol. II, pp. 241-8; and J. E. Erdmann, trs. W. S. Hough, *A History of Philosophy* (1890, frp, 3rd edition, 1877), vol. II, pp. 453-7 = S 305.4-6. A short note on Fries and Nelson appears in J. Passmore, *A Hundred Years of Philosophy* (Penguin, 1966, pp. 556-7).

In 1847, Ernst Friedrich Apelt, a pupil of Fries and his successor at Jena University, together with three other friends and followers of Fries, established *Abhandlungen der Fries'schen Schule*. But after publication of the second volume in 1848 this group broke up because of differences in political views. Apelt himself wrote a textbook of Friesian philosophy entitled *Metaphysik* (1857, republished by R. Otto, 1910).

Nelson re-started the *Abhandlungen* in 1904. The first volume of the new series contained his own dissertation *Jakob Friedrich Fries und seine jüngsten Kritiker*. This discussed in particular the relation between psychology and philosophy in Fries' work, thus defending it against the reproach of psychologism. This series continued until 1937. In an issue of that year there is a list of all Fries' writings. In 1958 one of Nelson's pupils, Julius Kraft, started the English and German periodical *Ratio* to continue in a new form the philosophical aims pursued in *Abhandlungen der Fries'schen Schule*.

INDEX